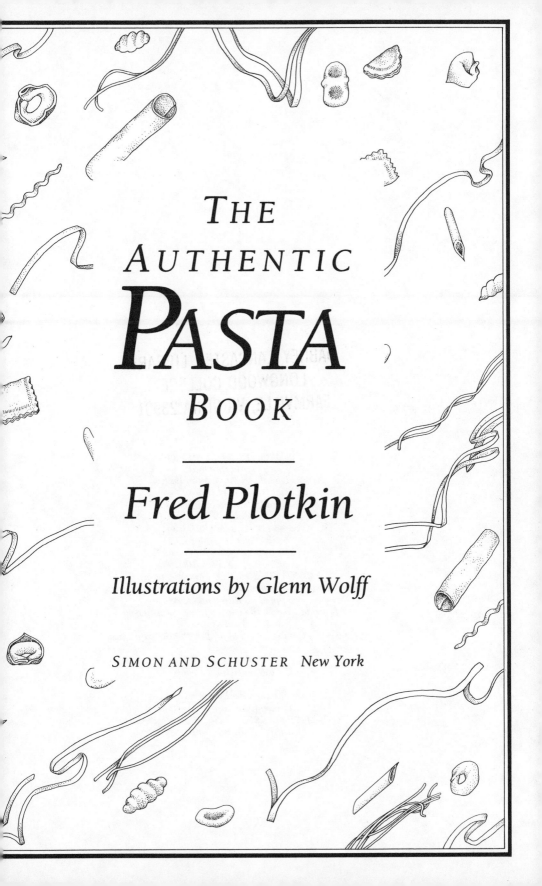

THE
AUTHENTIC
PASTA
BOOK

Fred Plotkin

Illustrations by Glenn Wolff

SIMON AND SCHUSTER   New York

Published by Simon and Schuster
A Division of Simon & Schuster, Inc.
Simon & Schuster Building
Rockefeller Center
1230 Avenue of the Americas
New York, New York 10020
SIMON AND SCHUSTER and colophon
are registered trademarks of Simon & Schuster, Inc.
Designed by Karolina Harris
Manufactured in the United States of America
3 5 7 9 10 8 6 4 2
Library of Congress Cataloging in Publication Data

Plotkin, Fred.
The authentic pasta book.

Includes index.
1. Cookery (Macaroni)   I. Title.
TX809.M17P56   1985   641.8'22   85-2417
ISBN: 0-671-50909-8

Acknowledgments

It is a task almost as difficult as writing a good book to thank all the people who help an author bring a book to life. The insights of friends and relations subtly shape one's ideas. In my case, the kindness of all those who shared their recipes with me made this book possible in a real sense.

Yet there are some people I would like to single out whose contributions proved particularly significant. My editor, Carole Lalli, is endowed not only with great warmth and wit but with the ability to strike chords in people that bring out their best. She has my greatest admiration. There is also Jo Stewart, my wise and gracious agent. And my parents, Bernice Price and Edward Plotkin, whose love I cherish and whose patience I admire—they were able to go for weeks without asking, "How *is* your book going?" Six friends were especially helpful to me in the course of writing the book: Mai Browne, J. B. Gallegos, Ethell Geller, Gail Milgram, Andrea Visconti and, in particular, Stephanie Rosenberg, who typed a large part of the manuscript. Finally, special thanks to Marion Zola, whose infectious optimism, faith, and encouragement gave me the context in which to dream that I could ever write this book.

TO ALL OF THE WONDERFUL ITALIANS WHO
BROUGHT ME INTO THEIR KITCHENS AND THEIR LIVES.
THEIR GENEROSITY, HUMANITY, AND SPIRIT
ARE THE INSPIRATION FOR THIS BOOK.

Contents

Introduction

Pasta, an ancient staple in the Italian diet, is uniquely suited to what cooks and eaters want today: economy, nutrition, elegance, and adaptability to individual taste. It appeals to those aware of health because of its low fat and high protein content. Pasta is inexpensive and nutritious—one pound feeds twice as many people as a pound of lean meat and has only half the calories. The quick preparation of most pasta dishes means that active, busy people can make and eat a good meal in a short period of time. In entertaining, few repasts are as elegant, inexpensive, and pleasing as an imaginative pasta dish. For the creative cook, pasta is a food suited for improvisation. Finally, in a time when more people eat many meals alone, few foods rival pasta as the center of a lunch or dinner for one.

Back in Greek and Roman times there surely was food made of flour and water that resembled pasta. Many scholars speculate that the dish the Romans called *lagana* was the forerunner of what is now known as lasagne. *Pasta* in Italian means paste or dough. This dough was cut into dumplings *(gnocchi)* or rolled out and cut into noodles such as spaghetti or tagliatelle. "Noodle" comes from the Latin *nodellus* (little knot), suggesting the way some pasta gets twisted into a series of knots in a bowl.

In ancient times comparable foods were eaten in China, Japan, India, Thrace, and in the Arab world. If Marco Polo brought Chinese noodles back to Venice in 1279, it was probably to compare them with the pasta already made on the Italian peninsula. Spaghetti, it seems, first appeared in Sicily, though the date is uncertain.

Pasta was first made commercially in small shops. It was sold in the seaport of Amalfi around the year 1000. Centuries later, pasta factories appeared in Sicily, Campania, the Abruzzi, Latium, Sardinia, and Liguria. In his travels Goethe slept in a pasta factory in Sicily.

Clever factory owners created and manufactured metal forms to turn pasta into the many shapes we know today. In Liguria they modeled *corzetti* (page 167) after a coin used in the Republic of Genoa. These different shapes are very important. The same sauce put on two types of pasta will result in two different dishes. Obviously, the appearance changes, yet so does the taste—2 types of pasta have 2 different textures, each producing particular sensations in the mouth.

Until 1919, factory-made pasta was dried in the sun. In that year a device was invented in Torre Annunziata (near Naples) to dry pasta by blowing hot air on it. This meant that pasta could be mass-produced in Italy and exported to the large Italian immigrant populations in the United States, Canada, Argentina, and other parts of the world.

The 3 nations just mentioned have acquired a great appreciation for pasta (especially the products of Naples) thanks to the presence of so many Italian immigrants. According to some estimates, Buenos Aires is 35 percent Italian. There is the old story of 2 men from Buenos Aires who went to Rome and, when they looked in the telephone directory, were surprised how many Argentines there were in Italy's capital.

Yet the exportation of pasta is not new. Thomas Jefferson brought pasta-making equipment home to Virginia after an ambassadorial journey to Europe. Yankee Doodle knew about pasta when he stuck that feather in his cap. Gioacchino Rossini (1792–1868), the great Italian composer and gourmet, lived the last 39 years of his life in Paris. During all of that time the only pasta he would eat had to be from Italy.

You may note an operatic streak throughout this book. During its writing I worked as the Performance Manager of the Metropolitan Opera in New York. The Italian virtues of fantasy, passion, drama, creativity, color, and perspective have informed both the cuisine and the arts of that nation. Some recipes were kindly given to me by

Italy's finest opera singers. However, this is not a celebrity book; these Italians are serious about food and have provided me with classic, authentic preparations from their native regions.

Though Italo-American versions of pasta were familiar to me as a child growing up in New York City, I did not discover the glories of pasta until I visited Italy before entering college. I spent a summer in San Vincenzo, a small coastal town in Tuscany. I returned to Italy again during college and remained for a few years, traveling throughout the country and collecting many of the recipes you will find here. They come from the parents of friends, from small restaurants and *trattorie,* and from what I was able to learn by watching Italians at work in their kitchens.

Much of my time was spent in Bologna, universally acknowledged as the capital of Italian gastronomy. Its specialty is pasta, and the city is the birthplace of many major types, including tagliatelle and tortellini. While in Bologna, where I studied theater and opera and also attended the university, I learned the local cuisine at the elbows of many fine cooks. This information forms the core of this book.

Pasta has always pleased both rich and poor. Yet now there are some wealthy, image-conscious people in Italy who disdain pasta as fattening and not chic. I could say their loss is our gain, but that would suggest I agree with the claim that pasta makes you fat. It is relatively nonfattening and contains only essential nutrients. There is no reason why one must always drench pasta in butter, cream, rich cheeses, and so on. There are many sauces based on vegetables, fish, lean meats, and herbs that require little or no cooking fat and only a judicious addition of cheese. A bowl of pasta and a glass of wine, followed by a salad, make a balanced and healthy meal.

You will notice that many recipes are given with ingredient amounts suitable for 1 or 2 persons. I have tried wherever possible to do this, since one of pasta's great virtues is that it can be prepared in individual portions. Most of these recipes may be made for more people simply by multiplying the ingredient amounts listed by the number of eaters. You might have to alter the recipes a bit as you enlarge them, so rely on your eyes, nose, and mouth to tell you.

Before you start using the recipes in this book, take time to read the following chapters. The first is a short introduction to Italy, a country two-thirds the size of California yet so intensely regional that it has many more local cuisines than the entire United States. To understand the roots of many recipes you should know something about the regions they come from. Then read about what pasta is; how to make it, cook it, sauce it, and eat it; and what ingredients and equipment to use.

I hope you enjoy discovering the magnificence of Italy and its national dish as much as I have.

Buon appetito.

Fred Plotkin
New York City
July 1984

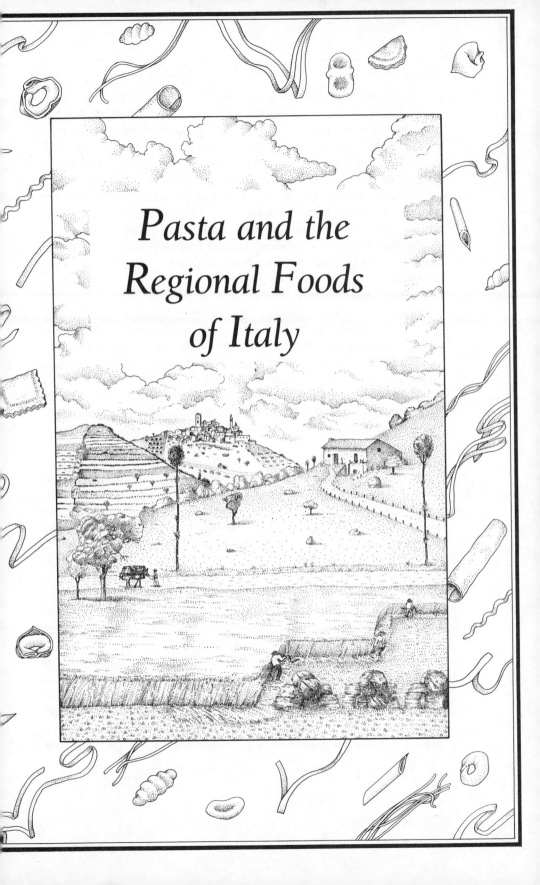

Pasta and the Regional Foods of Italy

Though pasta and noodles are indigenous to many nations, I think few people would strenuously disagree with my assertion that it is found at its most glorious in Italy. When I was growing up in a typical Asian-Hispanic-Jewish-Black-Italian-Irish-etcetera neighborhood in New York, the Italians I knew were mostly immigrants from Naples and Sicily and their American-born children. Their kitchens smelled of tomatoes and garlic, and it seemed as though a big pot of water was always boiling on the stove. This, I later learned, was for spaghetti. Many of these Italians were somewhat religious and tied to traditions I knew nothing about. In their homes, certain foods always seemed to appear at the same time each week or each year. Their lives had what seemed to be a prescribed order, one that most of them accepted, believed in, and often cherished. This, I think, was their main link to the Old Country. For these Italians living in America, the rhythms of their daily lives were the vestiges of older, more basic rhythms that existed in Italy even.before there was a Rome.

The Etruscans and the other early peoples who lived on the Italian peninsula flourished because they understood both the resources and the limitations presented to them. Roads were built through mountain passes and across plains to transport materials and facilitate communication. Food was largely derived from available crops: wheat, olives, grapes, and so forth. Wine was made and stored in vases similar in shape to those used today to bottle wines such as Verdicchio. When the Romans created their civilization, their awareness of weather and seasons was acute. Festivals and traditions arose to coincide with the annual arrival and departure of particular foods and events. Food and the calendar are still closely connected for most Romans. Much of the salt the ancient Romans needed to preserve their food came from areas across the peninsula on the Adriatic Sea. The trade route that developed was called the Via Salaria, the Road of Salt. This route is still an important one, it still goes from the Adriatic to downtown Rome, and it is still called the Via Salaria. Many scholars and historians view the Via Salaria as the line that divides northern and southern Italy.

This designation—and the many distinctions it implies—goes back thousands of years. The south was the domain of the Greeks, Saracens, and Holy Roman Empire, and it later endured centuries of occupation by foreign powers, mostly Spanish and French. The north was the land of Etruscans, Goths, Celts, Veneti, and Longobards, and it later became a region of glorious, prosperous, and often combative duchies and city-states. In the last century the north fought to free itself from French and Austrian domination and then led the fight for Italian national unity. Rome is a special case. It straddles the line between the north and south, and draws from both. Its citizens are exceedingly conscious that they are descendants of a great civilization. The city is also the home of Roman Catholicism, an institution that many Romans cherish and others despise, but which nonetheless imposes itself on the life of the city.

The division of north and south in Italy is one whose implications are much older, and in many cases deeper, than the factors that separated blue and gray during the American Civil War. The north views itself as richer (it is), more cultured, more socially responsible, and more European than the south. Many southerners refer to northern Italians as Germans. The south considers itself genuinely Italian, more devoted to the Church and in every sense more adherent to tradition as they believe it should be. Many northerners refer to southern Italians as Africans.

But these are generalizations that should be viewed as just that and taken with a large grain of salt (purchased, perhaps, on the Via Salaria?). In fact, Italy is far more regional than a simple north-south division would imply. Since it is composed of 20 regions (we might say "provinces") containing 95 provinces (we might say "counties"), attitudes and identities are even more decentralized. And it was only as recently as the 1860s that these regions were finally united to become the country of Italy.

So regional is Italy that the Sienese and the Florentines, Tuscans all and separated by a mere 53 miles, still differ over which city's dialect gave Italy its language. In the 9 provinces of Lombardy, the people of Bergamo, with their lilting accent, are still regarded as rustic, slightly foolish bumpkins. Indeed, the Bergamasque characters of the *commedia dell'arte* were usually oddballs; Bergamo today is one of the few places where that marvelous type of theater is still studied and appreciated. Throughout Italy there are so many local dialects that it is not an exaggeration to say that citizens of towns 20 miles apart often cannot understand one another. Television, introduced in the 1950s, has been a great linguistic unifier, though recently there has been a revival of interest in regional dialects and local customs. A debate is raging among Italian educators over the pros and cons of bilingual instruction in schools. By bilingual I do not mean Italian-English or Italian-Russian but Italian-Neapolitan or

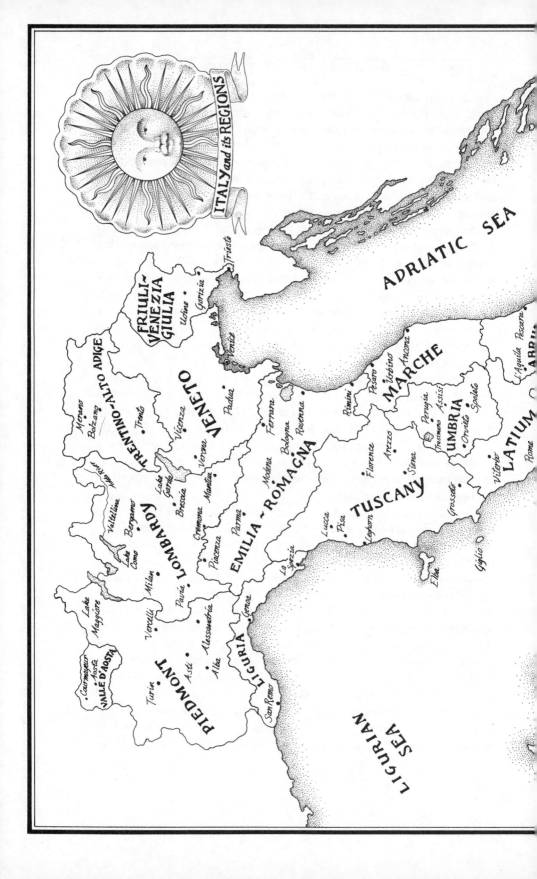

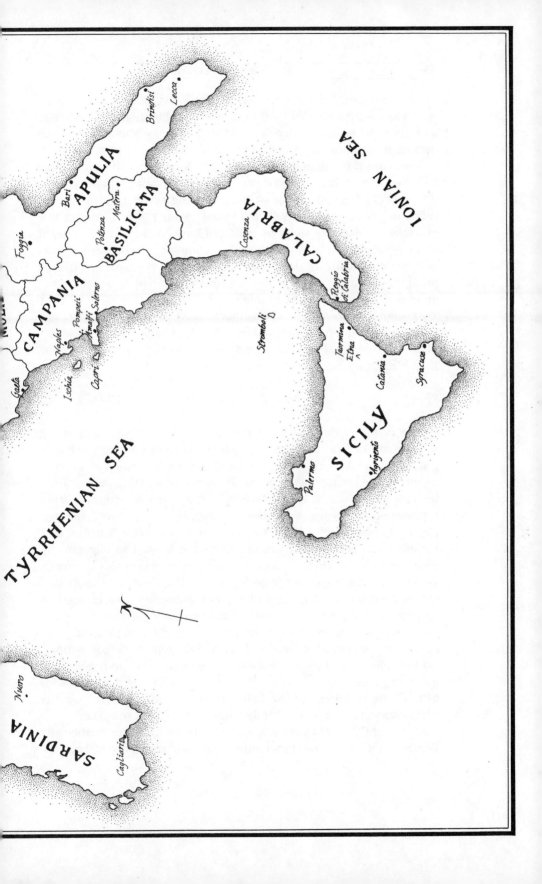

Italian-Venetian. Needless to say, almost every little province like-wise has its own special food or way of combining foods, and that, as relates to pasta, is largely what this book is about. But let us discuss more about Italy before we get to the subject of pasta.

It was not the Italian families I knew in New York which led to my fascination with Italy. I was 8 years old when I first heard of Venice, a city of 118 islands, without cars, floating serenely in a lagoon, reflecting in its glory. The Grand Canal seemed to me a street like no other. Venice was a city of artists, of merchants, of publishing, of an elaborate governmental system, of stunning architecture, of the-ater matched only by Paris and London, of pragmatic people, of passion, of danger and intrigue, an exotic city whose peculiar geo-graphic composition heavily influenced its development. Only New York seems to possess nearly as much as what Venice had, and as a passionate and proud native New Yorker, I suspect that this ex-plains my abiding love and admiration for Venice, the Most Serene Republic.

The Veneto

Venice is one of the few major Italian cities that was not significant in Etruscan or Roman times. The islands in the lagoon at the north-ern end of the Adriatic were populated by poor fishermen and served as refuge for mainlanders fleeing the constant tribal invasions from the east, north, and west. In the fifth century, regional councils were established to govern the lagoon. As the population grew, commer-cial traditions developed that brought immense wealth to the city. Venetian traders imported riches from the East. The city govern-ment, run by the Doge and the councils, oversaw Venice's growth. Venetians were no longer poor fishermen; they became expert sail-ors, navigators, soldiers, crusaders, and statesmen who created an empire covering what is now northeastern Italy (source of the Re-public's food staples and market for its imports), Yugoslavia, parts of Greece, and much of the Middle East. Salt, pepper, ginger, nutmeg, saffron, cloves and tarragon flavored Venetian food and supported much of its commerce. Marco Polo is said to have brought noodles from China to Venice in the 1270s, though many scholars now say that pasta existed in central Italy before then. I tend to agree.

As one of the world's great seafaring nations, Italy—and especially Venice—not only spread its culture and institutions throughout the world but often served as Europe's testing ground for ideas, materials, foods, and spices brought from faraway lands. In the regatta held each year in Venice, boats from Italy's four great old maritime republics—Amalfi, Genoa, Pisa, and Venice—race through the city's canals while marchers dressed in glorious red, green, gold, and white Renaissance costumes parade through St. Mark's Square.

Only Venice remained free of domination by popes, powerful ducal families from the mainland, emperors from the north, and other outside rulers, from its beginnings until Napoleon moved into the city in 1797. Venice governed itself through barbarian times, through the Middle Ages, the Renaissance, the Enlightenment, and practically into the nineteenth century. Following the French, the Austrians ruled Venice and in 1846 built the first bridge from the city to the mainland. After that, Venice was not the same. The bridge created a sense of dependence and a decline in Venice's self-image. Heavy industry developed on the mainland at the turn of the century, the lagoon became polluted, and the sinking of the city began to accelerate. What the future holds for Venice, we do not know.

Not surprisingly, Venetian cooking is based largely on the great variety of Adriatic fish. But Venice is only the capital of a diverse region with beautiful towns, stunning countryside, and many terrains that produce an abundance of good food. The Veneto, as the overall area is known, is divided into three smaller regions: Venezia Euganea, Friuli-Venezia Giulia, and the Trentino-Alto Adige.

Venezia Euganea, which includes the cities of Venice, Verona, Vicenza, and Padua, arcs around the Adriatic in its lower section, rises to the Euganean hills, home of many thermal baths, and then continues farther upward to the Dolomite mountains and the Austrian border. To the west and south are Lombardy and Emilia-Romagna. The lowlands provide fish and rice. The central section of the region is the most classically Venetian. Verona, near Lake Garda, is the stunning town of Romeo and Juliet. Shakespeare described Verona so well that it is hard to believe he never saw it. I love Verona too for its wonderful Roman arena (A.D. 100) where legendary opera productions are given each summer. The elaborate *Aida* mounted there is a must for anyone with even a passing interest in opera. I even heard Sarah Vaughan in concert there once.

Near Verona is an agricultural region producing famous apples, pears, peaches and, especially, grapes that are turned into Soave, Bardolino, and Valpolicella wines. Vicenza is a noble town filled with the classic theaters, houses and villas of Palladio; they provided the real-life sets for the film version of *Don Giovanni*. Padua contains Italy's oldest café, a great university, and the Scrovegni chapel with frescoes by Giotto, the first great Renaissance artist. It has been a major center of activity for the Red Brigades, which is notable particularly because the Veneto is probably the most conservative region in northern Italy. In the Dolomites one finds Cadore, birthplace of Titian, and Cortina d'Ampezzo, site of the 1956 winter Olympics. This area has been a favorite vacation spot for many Europeans, among them Sir Rudolf Bing who summered there during his years as General Manager of the Metropolitan Opera. Sir Rudolf probably returned for the fresh air, the hearty mountain cooking, the alpine flowers, the stillness and the tranquility after a year of dealing with divas, nervous tenors, and prima donnas. The mountain people of the Dolomites, and the citizens of Veneto in general, are more religious than other natives of northern Italy. The Veneto is also somewhat poorer than mighty Lombardy, Emilia-Romagna, and Piedmont to the west.

Friuli-Venezia Giulia, or simply the Friuli, is sandwiched between Yugoslavia and the rest of the Veneto. Its principal cities are Trieste, Udine, and Gorizia; the last two were devastated by a massive earthquake in May 1976 that was felt from Naples to Moscow. Rebuilding is going well, but many lives and many architectural treasures were lost. The feeling of the region is as much mittel-Europa as it is Italian. Its famous foods are the superlative San Daniele ham and several excellent wines.

The Trentino-Alto Adige is a blend of Italy and Germany. At its northern end is the Brenner Pass that leads from northern Europe to Rome (to which, of course, all roads have led for centuries). The region enjoys a certain amount of autonomy in terms of self-government and is fully bilingual, though you tend to hear more Italian in the cities and more German in the countryside. Its own political entity, the *Volkspartei*, regularly sends representatives to the Chamber of Deputies in Rome. The major cities are Trent (site of the Council of Trent in 1555), Merano, and Bolzano. The terrain is a combination of valleys and alps, and the cuisine is quite Teutonic. German-type white wines prevail, as do barley and oats. The grapes of Merano are supposed to have miraculous properties, and visitors to the city eat them by the bunch. Though I am skeptical about any special properties the grapes might have, they are delicious. Merano is a popular spa and vacation spot where Freud spent some time with his sister-in-law Minna. If any miracles happened, Freud didn't mention them in his writings.

One more food note before leaving the Veneto: This is *polenta* (cornmeal) country. Often prepared in rustic inns, using large wooden sticks, giant cauldrons, and an incredible amount of the cook's energy, polenta supplants pasta as the favorite staple of the Veneto. Everything from meat sauce to sparrows goes on top of polenta. When it hardens it is covered with sugar and eaten for dessert. Though you can find polenta in other places in Italy, this example of a strictly regional dish will bring to mind the Veneto whenever it is discussed. It is also the only use of corn that I know of in Italian cooking. People in the pig-breeding region of Emilia-Romagna will tell you that corn is for pigs and not for humans. Most Italians look at bright yellow corn with a jaundiced eye, except in the Veneto.

Lombardy

Let us move west to Lombardy, one of the regions Italians from elsewhere love to hate. I unabashedly love it, and most Italians ascribe this to my being a New Yorker who feels at home in urban Milan, Lombardy's capital. True, Milan is the financial, industrial, editorial, sartorial, and operatic capital of Italy, but as I have stated, my New York feelings are evoked more by Venice. To me, Milan is modern Italy, a summation of economic, social, and cultural factors brought to their highest state by an industrious and fair-minded people. Socially, I think Milan is far ahead of the rest of the country: Women seem freer and in many ways have anticipated the feminist movement that has flowered widely in Italy only in recent years. The Milanese appreciate hard work, tell you proudly that they pay a disproportionate share of Italy's taxes, and are in the forefront of political and social movements.

The city brims with cultural activity—artists, writers, and journalists abound. Giorgio Strehler is the director of the Piccolo Teatro, Italy's finest theater. Dario Fo is one of Europe's greatest actors, directors, and playwrights. I once saw two productions of one of his works while it was playing simultaneously in East and West Berlin. Fo's lack of recognition in America is largely due to his leftist politics; he was denied entry to the country several times before November 1984, when he was permitted to come to New York for the opening of his play, *Accidental Death of an Anarchist.* His role in Italy's—and especially Milan's—cultural life is enormous. Most of Italy's great publishing houses, newspapers, and magazines are based in Milan. Alessandro Manzoni, a Milanese, wrote *I Promessi Sposi* (The Betrothed), the novel held above all others in Italian literature. Verdi's *Requiem* was written in honor of Manzoni, though it was later played to honor Rossini as well.

Then there is La Scala. One day I will write a book about La Scala, Italy's greatest opera house, so I will be brief here. Suffice it to say that as Moslems go to Mecca and gastronomes go to Bologna (more of that later), opera lovers go to La Scala. Some people will tell you that Verdi helped lead the fight for national unification from the stage of La Scala with his nationalistic operas.

It is said that for every church in Rome, Milan has a bank. Perhaps. It is also Europe's fashion center. Milan is a victim of crime and terrorism, but its citizens view this injustice with indignation and humor rather than resignation. As in other major Italian cities, what gives Milan greatness is its people.

The fairness and understated friendliness of the *milanesi* is characteristic of Lombards in general. Their region extends from the valley of the great Po River to the peaks at the Swiss border. Though upper Lombardy is heavily industrial, there is a good deal of agriculture too, especially in the Valtellina, whose red wine (Valtellina) is my *vino da tavola.* Around the beautiful lakes of Maggiore, Como, and Garda, all hemmed in by Swiss or Italian Alps, one smells the fragrances of bougainvillea, almonds, pomegranates, oranges, and lemons, which grow in abundance even though the area is on the same latitude as Montreal.

Lower Lombardy is one of the most agricultural regions in Italy. Cattle are plentiful, so it should not surprise you that as beef eaters Lombards are rivalled only by the Tuscans. This is also dairy country, and the cream used in Lombard and Emilian cuisine comes from here, as does butter, the basic cooking fat in the Lombard kitchen. This is also a prodigious cheese-producing area, with Gorgonzola, grana padano (grana of the Po), mascarpone, and Bel Paese leading the way. The scene is especially impressive around Cremona, where modern Lombard agricultural methods draw greater yields from the land than anywhere else in Italy. Lest you think Cremona is just another cowtown, you should know that it also gave us Stradivari and his violins, and Monteverdi, father of Italian opera. Near Cremona is elegant, austere Mantua, site of *Rigoletto* and home of the illustrious Gonzaga family. One room in their castle was painted by Mantegna, by itself one of the artistic high points of the Italian Renaissance.

The last word in Lombard cooking: rice. What polenta is to the Venetians, rice is to the Lombards. The abundant rice fields in southwest Lombardy, near Pavia, are flooded each year, and the air is thick with mosquitoes. I did graduate work in Pavia, and I always hoped that in one of the rice fields I would encounter Silvana Mangano, whom I have dreamt of since seeing Visconti's *Bitter Rice.* No luck. Lombards almost always choose risotto, their rice dish, instead of pasta, so this book will contain relatively few recipes from this part of Italy.

Lombardy's history is a bloody one, from tribal invasions after the fall of Rome to the very heavy destruction during World War II. It was here that Mussolini was captured and executed by Resistance fighters. At different times Milan and Pavia were capitals of the Italian peninsula. Pavia claims the longest reign—several hundred years during the first millennium A.D. Milan was a splendid and powerful duchy under the Visconti (1277–1447) and the Sforza (1450–1535) families. I think Milan's greatest contribution during that time was providing a home for Leonardo da Vinci, who worked and created there for many years. If he had done nothing else in Milan, Leonardo's *Last Supper* in the Church of Santa Maria delle Grazie is worth every lira his patrons spent to maintain him.

Before leaving Milan let us not forget the Duomo, the great Gothic cathedral (1396) in the city's very center. Atop the church sits the *madonnina*, the little gold-colored madonna. On a clear day you can see her from the Alps 50 miles north. She is one of Milan's many symbols, and a city ordinance dictates that no structure may rise as high as the *madonnina.* So if it seems to you that all of Milan's skyscrapers end abruptly, you know the reason why.

Piedmont

Now we move further west to Piedmont, the third in the trio of great regions in the Italian north. Piedmont (*piemonte* means at the foot of the mountains) is actually a combination of plains to the south, hills in the center, and mountains in the north. In some ways Piedmont is similar to Lombardy. The French sound of some Lombard and Piedmontese dialects can be attributed to France's possession of the area during and after Napoleon's reign. The capital of Piedmont, Turin, once the most Italian city in France, is now the most French city in Italy, largely because of its proximity to the French border. Gastronomically, and especially enologically, Piedmont shares much with the regions of France.

Lombardy and Piedmont are also alike in that they are agriculturally important though they are at the same time the most heavily industrialized regions in Italy. Much rice is grown in western Lombardy, but production does not match the Piedmontese regions of Novara and Vercelli, Europe's largest rice-producing areas. Piedmont grows barley, apples, cherries, peaches, chestnuts, and grapes of high quality. The grapes produce what most wine experts consider Italy's finest wines. Most wine production occurs around Alba and Asti, the town that gave the world sparkling *spumante*. Alba is famous throughout Italy for its truffles, whose fragrance and delicate taste transform many dishes—including pasta—from delicious to memorable. Piedmont, and especially Turin, is responsible for most of Italy's production of vermouth and *grissini* (bread sticks).

Throughout Piedmont, small and large companies provide employment for many Italian workers; among the most notable are the Olivetti office machine company in Ivrea and Borsalino, the hat maker, in Alessandria. Industry in Turin means automobiles. What Detroit is to America and Stuttgart is to Germany, Turin is to Italy. Turin is filled with poor workers from elsewhere in Italy who came north and west to jobs in Fiat's plants. But unlike Detroit, whose name now is synonymous with urban decay (and whose new Renaissance Center was inspired by, of course, Italy), Turin, with more than one million people, does not look like a heavily industrial city. As in the case of Milan and other European industrial centers, Turin's factories are located outside of town.

Urban planning in Europe takes an approach opposite to ours. Suburban living tends to be for workers, while the wealthy aspire to live in the city center. Turin displays its wealth in elegant stores on long French-style boulevards. The *torinesi* live well, though not ostentatiously. The industrial suburbs are filled with high-rise housing for workers. An apartment tower called luxurious by a New Yorker would be considered alienating by an Italian forced to live in a unit that has hundreds like it. This has led to the sort of Industrial Age problems that have not yet affected Italy beyond parts of the north. As a result, the labor movement is big in Turin. On this subject, I recommend three very different and illuminating films: Francesco Rosi's *Three Brothers*, Lina Wertmüller's *The Seduction of Mimi*, which you should try to see in its uncut version, and Vittorio de Sica's last picture, *A Brief Vacation*. The first two films deal with Turin, the third concerns Milan.

Culturally, Piedmont gave Italy Cesare Pavese, one of its finest twentieth-century writers. Turin's opera house was the site of the world premiere of *La Bohème*, which was, incidentally, a resounding flop. Only later productions in Milan and elsewhere brought the opera the esteem it now holds. This is also where Maria Callas took her first crack at operatic direction, and her debut was not much better received than *La Bohème*.

Piedmont has distinguished itself the most in politics. Cavour, Piedmont's prime minister in the 1860s, led the movement for Italian unification, along with Garibaldi and Mazzini. The first king of united Italy was Vittorio Emanuele II, of Piedmont's 800-year-old House of Savoy. This brings us back again to Giuseppe Verdi. When he wrote operas such as *Nabucco* and *I Vespri Siciliani*, he used thinly veiled plots about oppressed people overcoming the tyranny of foreign rulers. Italians responded to Verdi's call, and *viva Verdi* became a rallying cry of the unification movement. But *viva Verdi* had two meanings: It praised the composer, but it also implied *viva V.E.R.D.I.* (Vittorio Emanuele, Re d'Italia). In other words, "Long live Vittorio Emanuele, King of Italy."

North of Piedmont is a small, semi-autonomous region known as the Valle d'Aosta (Valley of Aosta). Its tiny capital, Aosta, is of Roman origin, and some impressive ruins remain. The Valle d'Aosta is the rooftop of Europe, and the continent's highest mountain, Mont Blanc, sits above Courmayeur on the French border. The region is pastoral and idyllic, and except for the iron industry at Cogne, is largely devoted to agriculture and tourism.

The Valle d'Aosta is bilingual, French being the other language. The region's cuisine draws from France and Switzerland as well as Piedmont. Game and dairy products are outstanding, and the great Fontina cheese comes from here. The cheese is used locally for fondue, but its wonderful melting properties make it ideally suited for use with pasta. When cooking with Fontina, accept no substitute from Scandinavia, whose Fontina is a pallid imitation of the Italian article.

Liguria

Let us now travel south, through Piedmont, to Liguria, the crescent-shaped region extending from the French border to La Spezia, near Tuscany. You might know Liguria by another name: the Italian Riviera. In Italy I find that my sense of sight is most stimulated by Venice, my hearing by Rome, my taste buds by Bologna, and my sense of smell by Liguria. Flowers for export and for perfume cover the region, especially near San Remo which has a wonderful flower market. Rosemary, marjoram, oregano, sage, mint, parsley, pinoli, olives, and walnuts all grow in Liguria and lend their distinctive flavors to the local cuisine. It is the scent of basil, however, that tells you this is Liguria. This herb is found in countless local dishes, but nowhere does it achieve greater glory than in the classic *pesto*, which many people consider the finest pasta sauce of all. Another favorite dish of mine is fresh tomatoes, sliced saltless mozzarella cheese, and basil leaves tossed with a few drops of virgin olive oil. (You may have noticed that until now I have not mentioned the tomato. Most Americans view the tomato as the basis of Italian cooking, yet Lombardy, the Veneto, Piedmont, and the Valle d'Aosta do not rely heavily on this food, and Ligurians most often eat it in the manner I've described above. However, we shall see more of the tomato as we head south.

Genoa, one of Italy's largest cities, is the capital of Liguria. This is the largest port in the Mediterranean, and the town has some of the roughness of Marseilles, Barcelona, and Piraeus. The Genoese have been navigators and shipbuilders for centuries and were rivalled only by the Venetians. They are also considered by most Italians to be incredibly parsimonious. In Bologna I was taught that "the Bolognese eats more in a day than a Roman eats in a week and a Genoese eats in a month." Whether this is meant to honor the gluttony of the Bolognese or the stinginess of the Genoese, I do not know, but it does reveal an attitude that is held throughout Italy.

It is often said that Ligurians are a breed apart. Most of them consider the Celts their ancestors, which certainly would make Ligurians ethnically different from other Italians. Through the centuries, though, there has been so much mixing with fair-haired northerners and the classically Mediterranean people further south that most Ligurians now resemble their compatriots from other regions.

Genoa's most famous citizen is Christopher Columbus, whose house you can visit. But Columbus was not the only Ligurian to play a major role in American history. Many Genoese headed to California in the gold rush of 1849. When things didn't pan out near the Barbary Coast, the resourceful _genovesi_ went into other lines of work. Many of them planted grapevines and launched the California wine industry, which is the reason for the large number of modern American wine producers with Italian surnames. Many of the Genoese sailors who landed in San Francisco had little more than the shirts on their backs and the pants on their bottoms. These trousers were made of a material Ligurians called _blu genova_, which we know as denim. _Blu genova_ became our blue jeans, and Levi Strauss of San Francisco was one of the first to recognize its value. Think of America without blue jeans!

A modern Ligurian who figures prominently is Italy's octogenarian president, Sandro Pertini. The Honorable Signor Pertini is one of the few politicians Italians consider honorable. Indeed, he is a highly principled, compassionate, and moral man who gives great distinction to his largely ceremonial office at an age when his colleagues are quietly collecting their pensions.

Liguria's economy is based not only on Genoa's harbor but on a reasonable amount of industry and a large chunk of Italy's tourism. The towns of Bordighera (whose palm fronds are imported by the Vatican every Easter), San Remo, Portofino, and Santa Margherita are sunny and welcoming to hordes of German, French, British, Swiss, Milanese, and Turinese visitors. Liguria has more sunshine than almost anywhere in Italy, along with a rocky landscape that plunges dramatically into deep blue Mediterranean water.

Many tourists visit the pasta museum at Pontedassio, in a building that used to be a spaghetti factory. Much of the research for this book was collected in that museum. Though Liguria's mussels are famous (see the recipe for Spaghetti con le Cozze), its cuisine uses less fish and seafood than you would expect in a coastal region, perhaps because the local waters have been heavily fished and are quite depleted. Most Ligurian meals rely on the foods mentioned earlier, plus stuffed vegetables and fresh fruit. Genoa's great contribuiton to this book are _ravioli_ (this is plural), which are popular with sailors. The region's dominant cooking fat is its excellent olive oil. Before you leave the Genoese kitchen, try some cake: Ligurians are among Italy's finest bakers.

Emilia-Romagna

East of Liguria and south of Lombardy and the Veneto lies Emilia-Romagna, one of Italy's most intriguing and underrated regions. This is the heartland of fresh pasta cookery and the area that gives this book many of its great recipes. I have a special feeling for Emilia-Romagna because I lived, studied, and ate with great pleasure in Bologna, its capital. On my travels, when people asked where I lived, their comment when I responded was, *"Ah, Bologna! Si mangia bene!"* ("Oh, Bologna! One eats so well there!") Men would often add a comment about another of life's great pleasures: Italians say the women of Bologna know more about the ways of love than do any others throughout the passionate peninsula. I have learned from Italians who know about such things that Bolognese prostitutes in brothels all over Italy charge more than their co-workers, and no one finds this objectionable.

In fact, what makes the women (and the men, for that matter) of Bologna so special is that their lovingness extends far beyond the domain of sex. They are genuinely warm, caring people who passionately engage in politics, commerce, and culture and enjoy seeking and sharing the pleasures of both bed and board. Bologna embraced me as it embraces almost everyone. It is not surprising that even in an intensely regional country such as Italy, few people speak badly of Bologna. To me the prototype of the Bolognese is Rossini. Though born in the Marches, he studied and lived in Bologna for many years; a square in the city center has been named for him. Rossini's infectious good humor, his love of food and good company, and his special feeling for the human spirit are all classic Bolognese traits.

Bologna is an old and historic town. As Felsina, it was one of the 12 original Etruscan towns, and the streets are still laid out as the Etruscans planned them. The Romans named it Bononia and made it the hub of many trade routes, one of them being the Via Emilia, about which I will tell you more soon. Bologna developed its unique architectural style in the Middle Ages when it became a city of towers and porticos, all done in red clay. The wealthy built towers for protection from rival families. Most of these towers are gone, but the famous *due torri* (2 towers) remain in the town center. Both towers, one of the Garisenda family and the other of the Asinelli family, lean more precipitously than their famous cousin in Pisa. In fact, the Garisenda was trimmed down for fear of its toppling over.

The porticos were built for 2 reasons. First, they provide shade during the hot summers and protection during the wet winters. Second, homeowners added spare rooms on top of the porticos when Bologna was gripped by a sudden housing shortage around the year 1100. Why did this occur? The University of Bologna was incorporated in 1069, though its roots go clear back to 425. Students needed housing, and families built rooms to rent. The university also has the world's oldest medical school where many Americans are now enrolled. An old tradition dictates that any student who climbs the 447 steps of the 320-foot Asinelli tower before graduation will never complete his studies. For my entire stay in Bologna I yearned to climb that tower but resisted until the day of my departure.

In the center of town is the Piazza Maggiore, one of the most beautiful squares in Italy. The piazza contains fancy shops on one side, the unfinished but imposing church of San Petronio on another, and municipal buildings on the other sides. Bolognese men, in typical Emilian fashion, stand in large groups for hours, vigorously debating the relative merits of politicians or soccer teams. In an adjacent *piazzetta* stands Giambologna's virile statue of Neptune, one of Bologna's symbols. On a wall near Neptune is a listing of all the *bolognesi* who died in the Resistance. Though Bologna was originally one of the most loyally Fascist cities in Italy (Mussolini was from nearby Forlì), it became one of the leading centers of the Resistance. After the war Bologna elected a Communist mayor, and the city has remained Western Europe's most solidly Communist city. It is now known as the buckle of Italy's Red Belt, covering Emilia-Romagna, Liguria, Tuscany, and Umbria.

Around the Piazza Maggiore are the finest food markets I have ever seen, including the famous markets of Paris and Lyons. All of the products from the farms of Emilia-Romagna, Italy's richest agricultural region, are for sale. Especially abundant are tomatoes and products made from wheat, which Emilia produces more of than anywhere else in Italy. The region is third in rice and cattle production. Pork butchers display prosciutto, *zamponi* (pig's feet), *mortadella* (a princely version of what we call bologna), and sausages. Parmigiano-Reggiano, or Parmesan, is just one of many magnificent dairy products. The region's wheat is used to make Italy's finest fresh pasta. You can look into shop windows and watch women knead the dough and then cut it into tagliatelle, lasagne, and tagliolini, or fold it into tortellini and tortelloni. Fish, cake, wine, candy, and other edibles are displayed to make mouths water. The dazzling color and vitality of the markets, merchants, and shoppers represent, for me, the leading attraction for a visitor to Bologna.

Emilia-Romagna is slightly larger than Massachusetts. Its soil is as fertile as Iowa's. Six of the region's 8 provincial capitals—Piacenza, Parma, Reggio Emilia, Modena, Bologna, and Forlì—are connected by Via Emilia, which runs from the border of Lombardy in the north-west to Rimini on the shores of the Adriatic. Only Ferrara and Ravenna are not on that important route. Via Emilia was built by Marcus Aemilius Lepidus, a Roman who oversaw its construction in A.D. 187. We can loosely say that Emilia (named for Lepidus) extends northwest from Bologna to Piacenza. Romagna was Roman and later papal territory for centuries. As ancient Rome declined, the emperors moved to Ravenna, which now has some of the finest churches and Byzantine mosaics in the world. While Romagna remained intact, Emilian cities were separate duchies governed by influential families. Modena and Ferrara were ruled by the brilliant and enlightened Este family, though Alfonso d'Este might have erred somewhat in marrying Lucrezia Borgia.

Each Emilian city has a very rich history which I encourage you to study on your own since they cannot be discussed in great detail here. I must mention Parma, which inspired Stendhal only slightly less than Milan did. Parma has given us beautiful violets, luscious cheese and ham, tomato paste, Correggio, Giuseppe Verdi, and Arturo Toscanini. The audience at Parma's opera house is the most demanding in Italy.

Modena is where I learned to use nutmeg in pasta cookery. Modena is, per capita, the richest city in Italy, thanks to the income derived from sales of its agricultural products and its Lamberghini and Alfa-Romeo sports cars. Its most famous son is Luciano Pavarotti. Finally, there is Rimini on the Adriatic. The city is the chief town in a series of coastal resorts that make up Italy's version of Miami Beach. Thousands of tourists from all over Europe flock to its sandy beaches. The *riminesi* boast that their beaches are superior because the sand is more appealing than Liguria's rocks. I am especially fond of Rimini because it is the home of one of the loveliest women I have ever known and it is the birthplace of my favorite film director, Federico Fellini. Maestro Fellini perfectly captures the sights, sounds, and emotions of Romagna in his brilliant *Amarcord.*

The Marches and Umbria

As we head south from Rimini, down the Adriatic coast, we enter the small region of the Marches. Its people are known for their friendliness, and their livelihood is largely dependent upon agriculture in the hills and fishing. The region's capital is Ancona, a major seaport and the birthplace of tenor Franco Corelli. The Marches is most famous for its Verdicchio wine from the Jesi hills and for Rossini, a native of Pesaro, of whom I spoke earlier. Rossini probably feasted on the Marches' fish stews and *porchetta* (roast pig), variations of which are found throughout central Italy. The most interesting spot in the Marches is the hill town of Urbino, whose favorite son, Raffaello Sanzio, made a name for himself as a painter. We call him Raphael. The Renaissance court of Federigo da Montefeltro was one of the most enlightened in Italy, and its legacy is a magnificent art collection located in the ducal palace.

West of the Marches is Umbria, described as the "Green Heart of Italy." The region is a collection of quiet old hill towns sitting on a broad plain hemmed in at various points by the Apennine mountains. Its people are gentle and often pious, as personified by the most famous Umbrian of all, St. Francis of Assisi. Umbria's beautiful towns, such as Gubbio, Orvieto, Spello, Assisi, and Spoleto, look much as they did centuries ago.

The region moves at its own pace and has none of the animation one sees in Bologna, Rome, or Naples. The liveliest town is Perugia, Umbria's capital and the home of Buitoni pasta, Perugina chocolates, and the Università per Stranieri. This university attracts thousands of foreign students who come for intensive courses in Italian language, literature, and culture. For some reason I have not yet figured out, Perugia is also the jazz capital of Italy. Why this city of 100,000 should exceed Rome or Milan in this regard, I do not know. Perhaps it is the heavy presence of foreigners, though this is a condition not unique to Perugia. The town is of Etruscan origin, as is much of Umbria. The region's other main cultural center is Spoleto, where one of the world's great music, dance, and theater festivals is held each summer. Gian Carlo Menotti, who established the festival, recently created Spoleto USA in Charleston, South Carolina, which is already a significant event on the American cultural calendar.

Umbrian art reflects the gentle character and the limpid light of the region. Native painters include Perugino, Luca Signorelli, and Piero della Francesca. The region benefits from the presence of Lago di Trasimeno, the largest lake on the peninsula. It provides Umbria with fish and a calming effect on the climate. Cattle and pigs (for *porchetta*) are raised in Umbria, and the local wheat goes into Perugia's pasta production. The black truffles of Norcia are as famous as the white truffles of Piedmont. These fragrant tubers grow underground and are found in late autumn with the help of specially trained dogs and pigs. Finally, the straw-colored wine of Orvieto, home of a stunning cathedral, deserves its reputation as one of the great white wines of Italy.

Tuscany

North and west of Umbria is one of Italy's largest regions and the one most closely identified with what the world knows as Italian culture: Tuscany, the cradle of the Renaissance. It shares the Etruscan origin of its neighbors, Umbria and Emilia. The region is also bordered by Liguria on the Tyrrhenian coast and Latium, Rome's region, to the south.

When the Romans conquered the 12 great-Etruscan cities in 280 B.C., one of the towns they acquired was Fiesole. Though Fiesole did not grow under the Romans the way cities such as Bologna did, it managed to keep body and soul together for a few centuries until it gave birth to a city in the Arno valley below: Florence. As it grew, Florence was different from other Tuscan cities because it developed around a river, as did Rome, Paris, and London, rather than on top of a hill. The only other great Tuscan river town was Pisa, which reached its peak in the late Middle Ages and has declined, more or less gracefully, ever since. But, as we know, Pisa was a maritime power and depended more on the sea than on the Arno.

The glorious history of Florence is so well documented that I need not dwell on it here. Let us simply recall a few names to remind us of the city's contribution to our civilization: Giotto, Dante (who left Florence when times got rough and settled in Ravenna, where he was buried. Florence stole his body, but Ravenna stole him back; it is in Ravenna, we hope, where Dante rests), Leonardo da Vinci,

Michelangelo, Amerigo Vespucci (who gave his name to America), the Medici family, Machiavelli, Botticelli, and Leon Battista Alberti. You may not know Alberti, but he is worth discovering. Author, critic, artist, architect, city official, chronicler of his city and its people, and census taker (1427), Alberti quietly fulfilled the role of Renaissance man as few others did.

As far as we know, the word "snob" originated in Florence. As the merchant class burgeoned during the Renaissance, these nouveau riche Florentines sought recognition and acceptance in the upper strata of local society. In one census taken by the city in the fifteenth century, a notation was made to distinguish between the true nobility and the wealthy who aspired to nobility. Next to the names of this new class the census takers wrote *s.nob—senza nobiltà* (without nobility). I mention this simply to point out that the personality of the modern Florentine, according to other Italians, has very distinct roots.

Unlike the Bolognese, who are well liked throughout Italy, the Florentine is regarded with suspicion. Other Italians say that the Florentine is convinced his city, culture, and language are the best Italy has produced. It really is not fair to generalize, but while most Italians acknowledge Florence's great contributions and beauty, the city and its people are not held in great esteem in many parts of Italy. It is true that many Florentines are of regal bearing and seem somewhat aloof, yet we should note that the city has been crowded with curious visitors for hundreds of years, all trying to absorb its beauty and culture. As a result, Florentines are under greater scrutiny than most people, and they resent the intrusion. A friend of mine, a native of the city, once told me that he is asked 5 times a day on the average how to find Michelangelo's David. One gets the feeling it's an occupied city. The leaders of the onslaught have always been the British; and more recently, the Americans have joined them in great numbers. Most American visitors will tell you that Florence, not Rome or Venice, is their favorite Italian city.

It is an uncontested fact that the modern Italian language came from Tuscany, though the Florentines and the Sienese, who have always disagreed on practically everything, each claim the language came from their city. In fact, though the language is pure, the accent can be a bit confusing to an outsider. Many Tuscans replace the letter *c* with the sound of *h*, which does not exist elsewhere in Italy. So in Tuscany you don't drink cappuccino, but happuhino. I got a real shock the first time a Florentine served me a Coca-Cola and called it hohahola.

But Tuscans don't bother much with soft drinks because this is the region of noble Chianti wine. As a young table wine it is luscious and eminently drinkable. In its classic mature state, the great Chiantis rival Bordeaux. With their Chianti, Tuscans eat *bistecca* (steak) from their prized local cattle. The favorite vegetable is the bean, with spinach a close second. In fact, Tuscany is a veritable garden, and the array of vegetables in the Tuscan kitchen is dazzling. The region's food is usually prepared simply, using excellent ingredients and treating them carefully. Meat is grilled and vegetables are lightly cooked and then eaten with olive oil and lemon juice. Sauces are not nearly as important here as they are in Emilia.

I cannot let the reference to olive oil go by. Lucca, a beautiful walled city northeast of Pisa, produces the finest oil in Italy, if not the world. Its flavor enhances everything. I have had many excellent lunches using only the following ingredients: a plate of green virgin olive oil, raw spinach or lettuce for dipping into the oil, Tuscan bread for dipping, and a carafe of young Chianti. Puccini, a native of Lucca, once wrote to his mother from London saying that he was creatively blocked and very depressed. According to Puccini, the oil his mother sent him lifted his spirits and led him to write beautiful music.

Let me quickly list a few of the many other notable Tuscan towns. Montecatini, a spa famous for its water's healthful, curative properties—if you believe in that—is a chic resort. Marcello Mastroianni retreated there in Fellini's autobiographical *8½*. Massa-Carrara provided beautiful marble to generations of sculptors and architects. The great seaport of Livorno is the home of the region's best fish cookery. It was also the birthplace of the brilliant and tragic Amedeo Modigliani, my favorite modern artist. With its many medieval towers, San Gimignano is known as the "Manhattan of Italy." Volterra retains traces of its Etruscan past. Siena, Florence's rival, has a beautiful square that is the site of the *palio*, a horse race held every summer since the Renaissance. The city's palaces, churches, and museums contain many masterpieces of early Renaissance art. Since the Middle Ages, Siena's forte has been making *panforte*, a toothsome cake dense with dried fruits and nuts that is now known throughout the world.

Latium

Down we go on the *Autostrada del Sole* (Highway of the Sun), which begins in Milan, heads through Emilia to Bologna, then to Florence, through Tuscany and part of Umbria, to the city where all roads lead: Rome. The capital of the region of Latium is also the capital of Italy and of Christendom, and is the mother of cities throughout Europe. Rome is richer in the treasures of human history than any other city on earth. It is a place of superlatives, intensely alive and contemporary, yet always aware of its glorious past. Walk down a Roman street and you will pass an ancient column, a medieval church, a Renaissance palace, a baroque facade, a Fascist monument, and an ultramodern art gallery. Rome is filled at every turn with places that arouse the imagination of people the world over: the Coliseum, Pantheon, Vatican, Sistine Chapel, Via Veneto, and so on. How many times have I sat at an outdoor café and stared down a small street toward the Castel Sant'Angelo, imagining that I saw Tosca leap to her death!

The opening scene of my favorite film, Fellini's *La Dolce Vita*, neatly encapsulates much of what Rome is. We hear the sound of a helicopter, a modern machine (though Leonardo created designs for it 500 years ago). When it appears we see that attached to the helicopter is a rope carrying a statue of Christ, his arms spread wide. Jesus and the helicopter, followed by a second helicopter carrying journalists and photographers, fly past ancient Roman walls and aqueducts, over housing developments sprouting around the fringes of the city, toward the Vatican. At a certain point the journalists' helicopter flies over a roof filled with beautiful sunbathing Roman women. Despite the importance of their mission, the journalists spin around and descend to the roof in an attempt to get the women's telephone numbers. When their advances are turned down, they shrug, smile, wave good-bye, say *ciao*, and fly on to the Vatican, where Jesus will be delivered to a cheering throng. *La Dolce Vita* is a marvelous study of the beauty and brutality of Roman life.

Earlier I spoke of the ancient rhythms that still set the pace of Italian life; in Rome, one can know the time of year by the foods that appear. Romans traditionally start the year with *zamponi*, stuffed pig's trotters from Modena, which they eat with lentils. January 16 is the day of St. Honorious, and a delicious cake is named for him.

March 19 is St. Joseph's Day, and little sugared puff pastries appear in his honor. Easter means *abbacchio*, roasted young lamb with rosemary. (*Abbacchiato* is a local word used to describe someone sheepish.) The farms of Latium offer tender spring vegetables, especially asparagus, artichokes, peas, and zucchini. In early summer there are strawberries, cherries, then *anguria* (watermelon) and, in late August, rich, sweet *moscato* grapes from Frascati. Soon, autumn vegetables such as local broccoli appear. Almond pastries sweeten the sorrow of All Saints' Day, November 1. Roasted chestnuts and tortelli are eaten at Christmas time. *Porchetta* is for special events all year.

Certain foods and drinks come only at special times of the day or week: cappuccino in the morning, espresso during the rest of the day, *aperitivo* around 6 P.M. *Spaghetti alla carbonara* only in the very late evening, to absorb wine consumed earlier. Gnocchi on Thursday, cod and chick-peas on Friday, tripe on Saturday, fettuccine on Sunday. These are all ancient traditions, not intractable but certainly so comfortable and familiar that few people would think of changing them.

Rome is so outstanding that people often ignore the rest of Latium. The hills outside Rome are wonderful for cooling excursions from the city. Little towns such as Frascati and Marino produce the famous local wine, and Castel Gandolfo has the summer residence of the Pope. The Ciociaria, an agricultural center, is famous for its excellent pasta and the beauty of its women, among them Gina Lollobrigida. On the Tyrrhenian coast we find ancient Tarquinia, the port of Civitavecchia (mentioned in *Tosca*), the old seaport and the modern resort of Ostia, and the resorts of Nettuno and Anzio, site of very heavy fighting during World War II. Finally, near the border of Campania, is Gaeta, where justly famous olives are grown.

Campania

Beyond Gaeta, we leave Latium for Campania, a small region with the highest population density in Italy. Upon entering Campania there is no question that we are in southern Italy, the land of the Greeks. This region was part of Magna Graecia (Greater Greece) before becoming a playground for the Romans. Many Neapolitans (Campania's capital is Naples) are Greek descendants.

Much of the rich soil in Campania is of volcanic origin, and it yields fruit and vegetables of high quality. These foods, along with fish from the sea, go on or into the staple of the Campanian diet: pasta. The town of Gragnano, near Naples, is credited with devising the process of drying and storing pasta. Whereas pasta in Bologna is usually fresh, in Naples it is dry. The most popular type, of course, is spaghetti.

In his notes for the Metropolitan Opera production of *The Barber of Seville*, Herbert Kupferberg wrote: "One day in the late 1850s when Gioacchino Rossini, who by then was a Parisian social lion, wit, and gourmet, was out marketing, he rebuked a shopkeeper for trying to sell him Genoese pasta when he had asked for Neapolitan. Later, when the crestfallen merchant discovered who his customer had been, he said, 'Rossini? I don't know him, but if he knows his music as well as he knows his macaroni, he must write some beautiful stuff.' Rossini afterwards remarked that this was one of the greatest compliments he had ever received, and there is no reason to doubt that he meant it." Though Genoa is famous for its *pesto* and other sauces, it is true that the pasta itself in Naples is often of exceptional quality.

Campanian cuisine is a people's cuisine: poor people with limited resources developed dishes that were inexpensive, unsubtle but flavorful, and nutritious. Before the tomato was brought from Peru in the sixteenth century, what did Campanians put on their pasta or pizza (another Neapolitan invention)? It is hard to imagine. Yet whatever was available went on pasta, so this book contains many recipes from Campania. Another important food native to Campania is mozzarella cheese. The best mozzarella comes from the milk of water buffaloes, which is probably why pizza tastes better in Campania than anywhere else.

Although natives of Campania often seem animated and joyous, life is not easy for most of them. Frequent earthquakes, such as the one centered in the neighboring Abruzzi on November 23, 1980, do great damage here. Mount Vesuvius' eruptions, when they occur, are usually violent and destructive. We have only to think of what happened to Pompeii and Herculaneum in A.D. 79. Much of the region suffers from water shortages followed by heavy rains, soil erosion, and floods. Droughts and erosion, in fact, are problems that have always plagued all of southern Italy, Sicily, and Sardinia. In Campania, unemployment is chronically high, public services are often inadequate, and Naples has the highest infant mortality rate of any city in Europe. The Bay of Naples is polluted, and cholera epidemics are not uncommon. These harsh living conditions and the extreme density of the population have led many Campanians to seek a better life elsewhere. This is why so many Americans are of Neapolitan origin and why Italian-American cuisine is principally adapted from Neapolitan cooking.

Naples itself is the largest city in Italy after Rome and Milan. It is very crowded and poor. Life occurs not at home but in the streets, which are always filled with people talking, eating, yelling, cooking, screaming, washing clothing, arguing, praying, singing, selling something, or playing cards. Laundry flaps in the wind like flags on the mast of a ship. Excluding traffic, which adds noise to any city, Naples is probably the most clamorous town in Italy. Cooking smells are in the air. When Neapolitans are done eating, they drink their rich, dark espresso, Italy's best.

People in Naples are festive, capricious, yet often pensive, much like Fiordiligi and Dorabella, the Neapolitan women in Mozart's *Così Fan Tutte*. Two famous citizens of Naples are Sophia Loren (actually from nearby Pozzuoli) and Enrico Caruso, who sang at the Teatro San Carlo before achieving fame and fortune in America. The Teatro San Carlo opened in 1747, 31 years before La Scala, and is probably rivaled only by Venice's La Fenice as the second-best opera house in Italy. But opera is not the only music of the city. Neapolitan popular songs are often hauntingly beautiful, and many have become standards far beyond Campania.

Outside Naples are some of the most famous attractions in Italy —tourism is big business here. Pompeii and Herculaneum are known for much more than their erotic art; they are among the most perfectly preserved cities of the ancient world. The islands of Capri and Ischia, jewels in the Bay of Naples, were playgrounds for Tiberius and still cater to well-heeled visitors. Jack Lemmon and Juliet Mills went skinny-dipping off Ischia in Billy Wilder's *Avanti*. Near Vesuvius, back on the mainland, is Sorrento, where Britons traditionally spend a fortnight. It is the only town in Italy I can think of where all the bars start brewing tea every afternoon at 5 minutes to 4. South of Sorrento is the breathtakingly beautiful Amalfi Coast, including Positano, a favorite with writers, Amalfi, Ravello, and other pretty little villages. Further still is Salerno, site of the oldest medical school in Italy after Bologna's. The Allied forces landed in Salerno in September 1943 and fought there for 3 weeks before freeing Naples and moving north.

Then comes Paestum, home of 3 perfectly preserved Greek temples that we should all be glad survived not only centuries but also the intense battles in nearby Salerno. Paestum was the flourishing Greek city of Poseidonia, which also thrived in Roman times before much of its population succumbed to malaria in the early Middle Ages. Only the Parthenon, and possibly the temples in Agrigento, Sicily, are better specimens of Greek Doric architecture than Paestum's Temple of Neptune of the fifth century B.C.

The Abruzzi and Apulia

If we go northwest from Campania we reach the regions of Abruzzi and Molise, which are often lumped together and called the Abruzzi. Although you might think this area should be part of northern Italy since it borders mostly on Latium, Umbria, and the Marches, the Abruzzi's topography has made it exceptional. Although 75 percent of Italy is mountainous, no region we have visited thus far, except for a large part of the Veneto plus the Valle d'Aosta, has been so affected by its mountains. Italy's highest peaks south of Milan are found in the Abruzzi, including the Gran Sasso d'Italia (Great Rock of Italy), which soars over 9,500 feet. The Abruzzi has a long coastline on the Adriatic, and the mountains come almost all the way to the shore, so that those arriving at ports such as Pescara find it difficult to venture inland. As a result, the Abruzzi has been difficult to penetrate for centuries, and few people have tried to do so. With this forbidding geography, the area was cut off from many of the cultural and political upheavals—and advancements—in the regions surrounding it.

The people of the Abruzzi—not a heavily populated region— would be described by big-city Italians as coarse, unsophisticated, and bound by tradition. For the most part they are still cut off from the major currents of Italian society and continue to live by older rhythms created for them by the topography and the climate. A Piedmontese friend of mine who lived for many years in Pescara once observed that the sensation an Italian gets upon encountering natives of the higher reaches of the Abruzzi could only be compared to what a modern American would feel if he were transported back to one of the cowtowns of the Wild West. One of the most vivid images I retain of the 1980 earthquakes is that of families standing in front of the rubble that was their homes, refusing to relocate to shelters because they could not bring themselves to leave the land they knew. This powerful attachment to the land, especially the little parcel of land that is home, is a phenomenon of provincial parts of southern Italy that is very difficult for mobile Americans to comprehend.

The local animals, pigs, sheep, and goats provide the staples of the diet: ham, pork, lamb, goat meat, and goat cheese. These ingredients are often combined with the local *maccheroni*, which is nationally famous. In fact, much of the finest imported pasta we have in America comes from Chieti, one of the Abruzzi's provincial capitals. The region has a tradition of feasting, and the banquets are called *panarda*. The average *panarda* has about 30 courses, begins around noon, and goes on until late in the evening. The cuisine is much more refined than you might expect and uses not only the excellent mountain food but also the varied fish of the Adriatic. This is Italy's only saffron-growing region, though most of that spice is shipped to Lombardy, where it is highly prized for gilding *risotto* and other Milanese specialties.

The 2 most famous citizens of the Abruzzi were both poets. Ovid was born in Sulmona in 43 B.C., and the ruins of his villa can be found just outside the city. Sulmona is also rich in Renaissance architecture. Gabriele D'Annunzio, aside from his love affair with Eleonora Duse, his embracing of Fascism, and his wild life-style in his villa on Lake Garda in Lombardy, also produced some of the finest writing Italy has seen.

Finally, let me mention L'Aquila, the highest regional capital in the nation. It was established by Frederick II in 1240, making it a rather new city by Italian standards. L'Aquila (The Eagle) has a bird's-eye view of most of the region below it, and in one direction there is an awesome vista of the Gran Sasso. Most tourists stop in L'Aquila en route to ski resorts nearby.

Since the Abruzzi is hemmed in on the north by its mountains, it tended to look south for contact with the outside world. Directly south of the Abruzzi is Apulia (*Puglia* in Italian), whose name derives from the ancient Apuli tribe. Fresh Abruzzi mountain water has always been used to irrigate the parched Apulian plain. Apulia is long and narrow, extending from the calf to the heel of the Italian boot. It has over 400 miles of coastline, the longest of any Italian region. Fish and seafood, especially Taranto's oysters and mussels, are dietary staples. Apulia is one of the largest wheat-growing areas of Italy and regularly competes with Tuscany and the Veneto as the region that produces the most wine. The olive oil produced is also famous, as are the figs, nuts, almonds, and grapes. Much of the region's income derives from the export of its food products, especially the wine, which few people ever taste since it is shipped to Piedmont to be turned into vermouth. With all the wheat available in what is generally a poor region, it should not surprise you that Apulians eat more pasta per capita than anyone else in Italy.

The region was part of Magna Graecia and today seems much more Greek, for example, than Campania. Thousands of European tourists pass through Brindisi to catch ferries to and from Greece. Brindisi is the terminus of Rome's Appian Way, which, of course, still links this city with the capital. In Italian, *brindisi* means a toast (as in "to your health"), but according to Waverly Root the town got its name from the "Messapic language spoken in Apulia from 1000 B.C., when it was brought into the region by the Illyrians," and means "stag's head," which describes the shape of the harbor. Virgil died here in 19 B.C. after a trip to Greece.

Bari, a city of 500,000 people and dozens of pasta factories, has been the most important town in Apulia for 2,000 years. The Greeks conducted a large amount of business there, and it always has been a major commercial center, with the second largest trade fair in Italy after Milan's. Bari is one of the most politically conservative cities in all of Italy. Its politics are somewhat to the right of those of one of its sons, the late Aldo Moro, who was a Christian Democrat. Bari, and Foggia to the north and Taranto to the south, were major American bases during World War II.

Predating the Greeks and going back perhaps to the Bronze Age are the *trulli* of Alberobello: cone-shaped dwellings that resemble beehives. Even today when a citizen of Alberobello constructs a new house more often than not he will build a *trullo*. He will erect a square stone bottom, add a door and windows, and cover it with a conical sandstone roof. Some *trulli* are whitewashed, giving the area the look of certain Greek towns. Alberobello has hundreds of *trulli*, and the oldest ones have been designated as landmarks by the government.

Except for tourists passing through Brindisi and businessmen going to Bari, not many people visit Apulia. Parts of the region are desolate, and many people are quite poor. Its men leave the region to look for work in Turin, Milan, Switzerland, Germany, and Belgium. This is true of men from southern Italy, where the strongest social institution is the family (the Church is second). The rupturing of family life has had significant impact on life in the south and, consequently, on the nation as a whole. One *pugliese* who left the region to seek his fortune in America achieved fame but died very young: Rudolf Valentino.

Basilicata and Calabria

Traveling directly west from Apulia we reach the last 2 regions in the Italian peninsula. Since they have a great deal in common, we will discuss Basilicata and Calabria together.

Basilicata is a small and very mountainous region at the instep of the Italian boot. Because of their elevation, parts of the region are much colder than we would expect in the deep south. Basilicata is the poorest region in Italy; its soil is not very productive, and water is in short supply. The Roman name for the region is Lucania, and this brings us to Basilicata's most famous food. *Lucanica* (also called *luganega*) is a tasty and popular sausage that has always been held in great favor in Lombardy and the Veneto. Basilicata flavors its food with hot red pepper, which often finds its way to pasta along with *lucanica* and an occasional vegetable.

The two principal cities are small and poor. Potenza was almost completely destroyed by an earthquake in 1857, and few traces of its early history remain. The city's cold weather is partly due to its 2,700-foot elevation. Matera, the other important town, is much more picturesque than Potenza. Many of its residences are actually caves that were carved out of the soft rock on which Matera sits.

Calabria is Italy's toe. The region has one of the longest coastlines in the country, yet the interior is about 75 percent mountainous. Though the scenery is often spectacular, the variety of terrain tends to inhibit communication from one part of the region to another. The insularity of Calabria is reflected in the character of its people, most of whom seem rather solemn and brooding. Life is hard in Calabria. The land is not generous, droughts are common, unemployment is high, and the region is the poorest in Italy except for neighboring Basilicata. Little is left of the glorious period when this was part of

Magna Graecia because Calabria has been repeatedly struck by earthquakes.

There are 3 books—all classics in modern Italian literature—that will give you a better understanding of the problems suffered by all of southern Italy, but especially Basilicata and Calabria: *Christ Stopped at Eboli* by Carlo Levi, and *Bread and Wine* and *Fontamara* by Ignazio Silone.

Most of the towns in Calabria were built on hilltops to defend against invaders and to escape the malaria that attacked the low-lands. The coastal towns are older, often of Greek origin, and have gained popularity with tourists seeking unspoiled and underpopulated beaches. Only the southernmost part of Calabria is fertile, and this area grows eggplant, the region's favorite vegetable, as well as magnificent lemons, oranges, bergamot (that special smell in Earl Grey tea), and lavender, which is Italy's favorite perfume. Pasta is at the heart of Calabrese cuisine, as it is throughout the south. It is usually eaten with vegetables or fish, or simply with garlic and oil.

At the very tip of the region is Reggio di Calabria, and from here we get the steamer for the 4-mile crossing to Sicily, on the other side of the Strait of Messina.

The Islands: Sicily and Sardinia

Sicily is the largest island in the Mediterranean, and its natives echo Goethe's claim that if you haven't seen Sicily, you don't know Italy. The region is heavily populated and pulsates with life. In fact, civilization on this island goes back almost 3000 years. Ancient peoples —the Siculi, the Sicani, and the Elymi—who probably came from other parts of the Mediterranean, were living on the island when the Greeks arrived in the middle of the eighth century B.C. The first Greek town we know of was Naxos, which was destroyed by Syracuse a few centuries later. Richard Strauss's opera, *Ariadne auf Naxos*, though delightful, will not exactly give you an idea of life in old Magna Graecia.

Greek cities that have had more permanence include Syracuse (which was the island's most important center all the way up to the Middle Ages), Agrigento, Palermo, Catania, and Taormina. Sicily is studded with temples and amphitheaters from its Greek period that have fascinated tourists, writers, and scholars for years. The most stupendous collection of Doric temples, as I mentioned earlier, can be found at Agrigento, in the southern part of Sicily. The five temples overlook the Mediterranean nine hundred feet below. Almond blossoms add color and fragrance to the setting. Though many people now visit the site, such was not the case in Goethe's time. The poet could not even find a room for rent in town and had to sleep in a spaghetti factory.

After the Greeks, Sicily was ruled by the Romans for a few centuries, though Greek culture remained strong. The character of the island changed radically with the arrival of the Saracens soon after the year 800. Much of the Sicilian dialect is based on words of Greek and Arabic origin. Architecturally and gastronomically, Sicily also drew heavily from the Saracens. And it was under the Saracens, in 831, that Palermo replaced Syracuse as Sicily's major city.

Palermo is a large city, more or less equal in size to Genoa, and exceeded in Italy only by Rome, Milan, Naples, and Turin. It is the site of one of Verdi's more nationalistic operas, *I Vespri Siciliani* (The Sicilian Vespers), based on an uprising that occurred in 1282. The opera's famous bass aria, "Tu, Palermo," is a beloved paean to the city. Palermo also reflects five centuries of Spanish rule, and you can find traces of Norman civilization too. Sicilians say that the surprisingly high number of blonds is a legacy of Norman rule. Palermo today seems almost as animated as Naples, especially in the commercial and market districts. The city provides many of the civil servants who run the government in Rome, as well as many of the food canners and processers who handle the island's agricultural output. The citrus grown in the *conca d'oro* (golden shell) around Palermo are prized throughout Europe, especially the deep red "blood" orange that has a hint of raspberry in its juice. Much of the fish, in particular tuna, caught around Sicily is packed in Palermo.

All of coastal Sicily thrives on fish, and many of the local pasta dishes use seafood sauces. The island does not raise many animals that would provide meat. Goats, for example, are kept to give milk for making cheese. Sicily has an abundance of vegetables that form the nucleus of much local cooking. Eggplant is ubiquitous, and the delicious tomatoes are used for their flavor in countless sauces. These two vegetables are the base for *caponata*, the famous Sicilian vegetable combination that turns up everywhere. We must also note the purple cauliflower from the region north of Catania. Finally, Sicily has always been known for desserts such as *cassata* (ice cream with local candied fruit), cannoli, cheesecake, ices, and dozens of pastries, cookies, and tarts. The great wine of the island is Marsala, best known as an aperitif and for cooking.

Sicily is not only temples, foreign influence, and delicious food. Its people, like all the people I've mentioned in this chapter, are deeply affected by the land itself and the rhythms it sets for them. Rural Sicilians do not need clocks—they rise early, follow the schedule of the animals and the crops they raise, and then go to bed. There is a respect for the land and a fear of it too. Earthquakes, such as the one that killed eighty thousand people in Messina in 1908, are a threat. Mount Etna (10,749 feet) may erupt again at any moment. Sicilians cherish the familiar and distrust that which is out of the ordinary. The need to protect oneself has lead to extreme measures. For many people it is routine to carry guns. The Mafia's development was actually not an offensive but a defensive measure by people who wanted protection when they were threatened with loss of land, property, or social position.

If you are lucky enough to see a rare screening of Rossellini's *Stromboli*, with Ingrid Bergman, you will understand more about the tradition-bound aspect of Sicilian life that faces adversity with a combination of frustration, violence, and resignation. Stromboli is an island off Sicily; it is of volcanic origin and is inhabited mostly by fishermen. Many Sicilians have emigrated to America, Australia, Canada, Argentina, and elsewhere because life was hard and prospects few. Though conditions have improved significantly, life is still difficult for many Sicilians.

The intensity of experience in Sicilian life has influenced much of the culture the island has produced. Lampedusa's *The Leopard* is one of the most universally known and quoted books in Italy. Pirandello was one of the first dramatists to receive a Nobel Prize. Leaders in their fields were Giovanni Verga in poetry and Vincenzo Bellini in music, with Bellini a pioneer of the *bel canto* style of opera.

The other major Italian island in the Mediterranean is Sardinia. The Italian word for island is *isola*, so you can quickly deduce where we got the word "isolate." Indeed, isolation is the key word in a discussion of Sardinia. It is a 13-hour steamer trip from Palermo or Genoa. Contact with the mainland has always been spotty, and Sardinia remains more distant from the homogenization of Italian society than any other region. Furthermore, Sardinians have always isolated themselves from one another. You see none of the spirited interaction here that one finds on the mainland.

This is an island of shepherds, many of whom roam the countryside for months with their flocks and their sheep dogs searching for
suitable grazing land. Shepherds live on bread and the cheese they
produce—*pecorino*, one of Italy's greatest cheeses—and keep warm
with clothes made of wool. The bleakness of Sardinia's shepherd
existence was captured in the Oscar-nominated *Padre, Padrone* by
the Taviani brothers.

Sardinian women remain in their communities while the men are
gone. They devote themselves to weaving and to baking the large
loaves of bread called *chivarzu*. This bread is carried by the shepherds during their peregrinations, and it remains a powerful link to
home and family. The traditions of church and family are strong in
Sardinia, whose customs are that of an ancient society only beginning to encounter the twentieth century.

Life on Sardinia goes back to the Stone Age. Over 3,000 years ago
massive stone structures called *nuraghi* were built. They still provide shelter for those shepherds who don't carry their own makeshift
huts with them as they wander. Sardinia's largest city, and its only
provincial capital to be found on the coast, is Cagliari. The city was
founded in 814 B.C., 61 years before the birth of Rome. Though Sardinia was "visited" by invading Carthaginians, Greeks, Romans, Saracens, Genoese, Pisans, Catalans and, finally, nineteeth-century
Piedmontese, the island remains remarkably devoid of foreign influence and seems, rather, to be following a course set much longer
ago. Only a Latin-based dialect and Catholicism have penetrated
Sardinia in the past 2000 years.

Sardinians have largely avoided the sea, since it has traditionally
brought them nothing but trouble. At times the coastline was dotted
with areas of heavy malaria infestation. And, since foreign invaders
have always arrived by sea, Sardinians developed their life-style in
the barren interior of the island. Today malaria is no longer a problem, yet Sardinians remain inland. The seashore, especially the *costa
smeralda* (Emerald Coast), is one of the most fashionable holiday
destinations in all of Europe. The contrast between the "beautiful
people" from the Continent and the Sardinians is dramatic.

Since the natives of Sardinia have avoided the sea, fish, though
available, is not as important in local cuisine as you might expect.
Rather, Sardinians eat more meat than do most poor people. Sheep
are plentiful, and there is also a large population of pigs, goats, and
cattle. Sardinians eat most of this meat since it is too costly to

transport it to the mainland. Vegetables are not available the way they are on the Italian peninsula, so pasta is usually served with meat, cheese, or fish.

In addition to Cagliari (population 105,000), the other provincial capitals are Sassari (population 95,000) and Nuoro (population 35,000). The rest of the 1.5 million Sardinians live in tiny communities dotted around the island, or they live alone with their sheep. Sardinia's most famous citizen was probably Enrico Berlinguer of Sassari, secretary of Italy's Communist party, the largest and most powerful in Western Europe. Sardinia, in general, is more conservative than Berlinguer, who spent most of his time on the mainland until his death in 1984 at an election rally in Padua.

Now that we have visited all 20 regions of Italy, I hope you have discovered that Italy is much more varied than the Neapolitan and Sicilian cultures we have learned about here at home. Americans and Germans probably have more in common than the Milanese and the Sardinians. This is even more amazing if you consider the size of the country—the total area of Italy and its islands is 116,304 square miles, while New Mexico is 121,666 square miles and the United States is 3,548,974 square miles.

The meaning of all this information for those of us who use cookbooks of Italian food is that we must never refer to it simply as *Italian* food. It will be Modenese or Palermitano or Novarese, and so on. As you use this book, try to drink wines from the region that corresponds to each recipe. And if you keep in mind the history and culture that went into creating each dish, the experience of cooking and eating your pasta will be much richer.

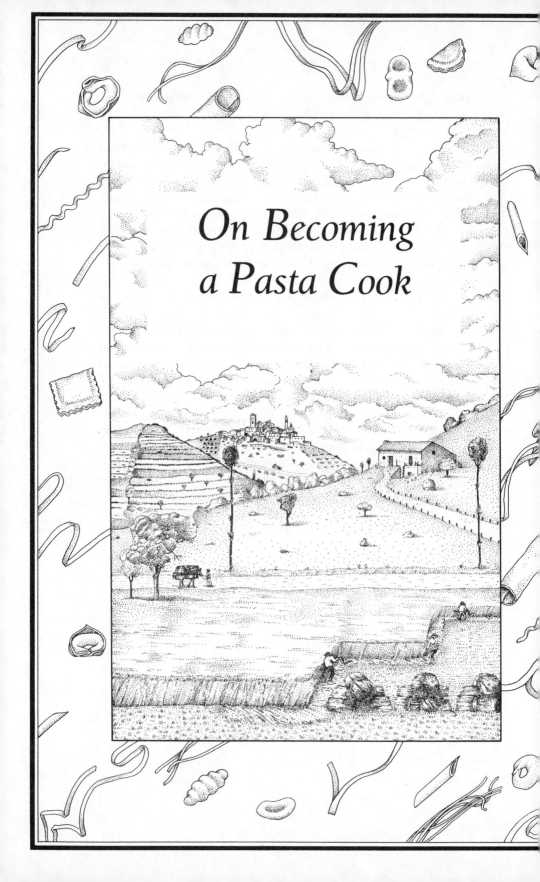

On Becoming
a Pasta Cook

The pleasures of cooking, saucing, and eating commercially produced dried pasta (*pastasciutta*) such as spaghetti and macaroni should be your first experiences as you develop your skills as a pasta cook. When you learn the proper state of doneness of a noodle, when you feel comfortable with saucing and, in general, when you think you have developed a confident feel for the rhythm and timing of making a bowl of *pastasciutta*, then, and only then, should you venture into the world of fresh, handmade pasta.

I do not say this to intimidate you. Think of a singer approaching a particular aria. Before she starts to sing, she must do warm-ups and scales. Then individual passages are learned, and eventually the notes are in the singer's head. But she must keep singing the aria, refining details and making choices as to what should be emphasized or understated. Suddenly she stops producing words and sound and starts making music. If she is talented and does her work carefully, the singer's performance will be confident and filled with the character that she alone can give it. With any luck, the aria will provide sheer joy and rapture to its audience.

You must also warm up, do your scales, learn the notes, and develop an instinct for deciding what works and what does not in cooking and saucing dried pasta. Soon you will be creating rapturous dishes of *pastasciutta* and will already have many of the skills necessary for working with fresh pasta. You will find that you will have fewer problems than you expected in cooking and saucing *pasta fresca*. Since it is now possible to purchase fresh pasta in many stores, your range of pasta cookery is that much broader.

Yet there is one more major hurdle to overcome before becoming a full-fledged pasta diva: You must learn to make fresh pasta by hand. *From scratch.* Let me warn you that your first few attempts will probably not prompt anyone to yell *bravo* or *encore*. Be prepared to devote some time to learning, making errors, and perhaps wasting a little flour and a few eggs. Pasta making is a skill, but not a hard one, so eventually you will be fully proficient at producing the most delicious *sfoglia* for tagliatelle, fettuccine, lasagne, cannelloni, ravioli, and tortellini. Before making *sfoglia*, you might want to play around with gnocchi (page 73) and corzetti (page 167) to get used to the feeling of dough in your hands. If you are a complete novice when it comes to pasta cookery, see the special note to you on page 93.

I was fortunate enough to learn to make *pasta all'uovo* (egg pasta) in Bologna, the heartland of fresh pasta cookery. Mothers and grandmothers of my schoolmates were pleased and a little startled that a young American was so eager to learn the craft that had been passed from generation to generation in their families. Some young Italians have not demonstrated an interest in these older, more careful and loving ways of making food.

In Bologna, the *sfogline* (pasta makers) work nimbly, quickly, and above all without pretense or unnecessary fuss. In a time when most supposedly fashionable food is burdened with stuffy, snobby pretensions, the appeal of *pasta all'uovo* is that it is sublime yet simple. Or, to speak in more American terms, *pasta all'uovo* is honest.

Making Fresh Pasta

An honest *sfoglina* needs very little to make her magic: a good working surface (*la spianatoia*), a rolling pin (*il matterello*), a good knife, perhaps a pasta-cutting wheel (*la rotellina tagliapasta*), flour, fresh eggs, strength, patience, and skill. These are the essentials. Of course, you may also add pasta machines, ravioli trays, fancy racks to dry noodles, and so forth, but you can produce any fresh pasta recipe in this book using only the essentials. Read more about equipment on page 299.

In Italy, fresh pasta is made with flour known as "tipo 00." The wheat used to make this flour is softer (contains less gluten) than that used to produce semolina, the essential flour for the orecchiette of Apulia and the commerically made spaghetti and maccheroni of Naples. Flour in North America is different from tipo 00 in that it contains more gluten, which means that you will have excellent pasta but will have to use a little more effort to roll it out. Do not be daunted. In addition, the eggs used in Italy are often a little smaller than ours.

What I am suggesting is that there are many factors involved in determining what the ideal flour-to-egg ratio is in making fresh pasta. In Italy, the rule of thumb is 100 grams of "tipo 00" flour to 1 egg. I can tell you that *my* ratio, using unbleached white flour from North America and large eggs (not medium, not extra large), is ⅝ cup of flour to 1 large egg. This ratio will produce 5–6 ounces of pasta, which is a generous portion for 1 person. Double the amount (1¼ cups of flour and 2 large eggs), and you will have enough pasta for 2 people as a main course or, depending upon the sauce, enough for a light first course for 3 people.

These measurements are not carved in marble. The flour you use and the size of the eggs you have at hand will make for small differences. Use this ratio as a point of departure as you experiment to find the ratio best suited to your ingredients. Your goal is to produce smooth, elastic dough that is neither too loose, in which case it cannot be rolled out, nor too dry, which would mean that the dough would fall apart.

The following directions for making fresh pasta assume that you are starting with 1¼ cups of flour and 2 large eggs. If you are using more, you should knead all of the ingredients at once and then, unless you are quite proficient at rolling, you should divide the dough into 2 or 3 parts, keeping covered the parts you are not rolling. Let's make *pasta all'uovo:*

(1) Place your flour in the center of a working surface made either of smooth wood or formica, at least 2 feet by 3 feet. Form what looks like a cross between Mount Etna and a lunar crater. This image should yield a little hill of flour with a large hollowed section in the center—Italians call this *la fontana*—into which you can break the eggs. Be sure you do not make the *fontana* so deep that the eggs can seep through to the working surface. Keep the sides of the "crater" high enough so that the eggs don't spill over.

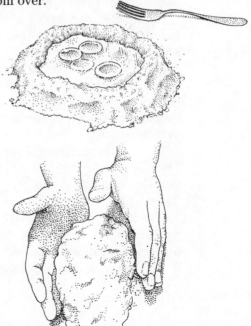

(2) Break the eggs into the *fontana.* If the recipe calls for salt, add it now. Beat the eggs with a fork for a minute or so. Some Italians beat the eggs in a separate bowl before adding them to the *fontana.* Do as you wish.

(3) After the eggs are beaten, push a little flour from the sides of the *fontana* into the eggs. Slowly incorporate more flour into the eggs, using the tips of your fingers, until the eggs are no longer runny. Now, with your hands, bring the outskirts of the crater into its hole, working the

ingredients into a soft, sticky ball. Take it into your hands, firm the ball a bit, and place it to one side.

(4) Scrape the extra flour to one side of the working surface, and if your hands are caked with flour, wash them in tepid water and dry them.

(5) Now start to knead the dough. You should begin by forcing the heel of your hand into the ball, pressing it down against the working surface. If you think the ball is too soft or sticky, dust it with a bit of flour from the side of the working surface. But be careful: If the pasta is too dry, it is useless. Knead the pasta for at least 10 minutes—more if you are using larger amounts of flour and eggs—folding the pasta in half, pressing it hard, turning it, extending it outward with your palm, folding it again, and so on.

(6) If, after 10 minutes of kneading, you poke your thumb in the ball and it comes out moist, or if the dough sticks to your hand, knead in a *little* more flour.

(7) When little bubbles start to form on the surface of the dough, form it into a ball, give it a light dusting of flour, cover it with a towel or cloth, or wrap it loosely in plastic wrap. Let it repose, as the Italians say, for 30–60 minutes in an area free of drafts or extremes in temperature.

We are now ready to roll out the dough, that is, to make *la sfoglia.* There are two roads you can take to roll out the *sfoglia* and cut it into the form you desire. One is to use a rolling pin and a knife or fluted wheel, the other is to use a manual pasta machine. Doing it by hand will not yield the uniformity of the machine's product, but you will be able, with skill, to beautifully roll the dough to the very thickness you desire and then to cut the pasta precisely as you want it. The machine makes rolling much easier, and it neatly cuts the dough into tagliatelle or tagliolini exactly alike. Is perfection based on beauty or uniformity? The choice is yours.

ROLLING OUT THE DOUGH BY HAND: As you have probably figured out, I prefer this method to using a machine. Although it is more work, I think the product is superior. The essential difference is that you are making the dough thinner by extending it rather than by compressing it.

It is necessary that you use the correct rolling pin. The American type, with two handles attached, is acceptable only if you absolutely cannot get your hands on something approximating an Italian rolling pin. The main problem with the American rolling pin is that it is too thick and usually not long enough to roll out the dough. My rolling pin, which I bought in a Bologna department store for about $1.50, is simply a cylinder made of smoothly sanded wood. It is 1½ inches in diameter and 22 inches long. Some Italian rolling pins are longer, but mine suits me fine. A *sfoglina* taught me that when your rolling pin is new, you should wash it in warm water and gentle soap, making sure to rinse it thoroughly. Wipe it with a clean towel and let it air-dry. Rub the pin very lightly with corn oil or some other neutral vegetable oil. Wait about 10 minutes and then lightly dust one hand with flour and "massage" the rolling pin gently. You should give your pin this treatment about once a month if you use it with any regularity. If you cannot buy an Italian-type rolling pin, see if you can have one made at a lumber yard.

(1) Uncover the dough, place it on the working surface, and knead it briefly with lightly floured hands. Then give the dough a couple of good open-handed slaps to flatten it.

(2) Stand so that your shoulders are parallel with the edge of the working surface. Place the flattened dough about 12 inches directly in front of you. Grasp the pin at each extreme, extend your arms forward, and place the pin on the dough at the point where about ¾

of the dough is on your side and the rest is on the far side of the pin. Roll the pin away from you, using force but without leaning into the motion. The important idea here is to stretch the dough, not to compress it. Roll almost to the edge of the dough and then gently, without pressure, roll the pin backward to the point where you began. Quickly repeat this action four or five times. Without changing the position you are standing in, turn the dough 90° to the right, and roll that section of the dough as you did the first. Then turn it 90° more to the right and repeat the process, then 90° more and do the procedure once again. Now you should turn the dough a little more to the right and start rolling from closer to the center. Keep turning the dough slightly, and keep rolling outward with force and backward without. Stop when the circle of dough reaches about 8 inches in diameter.

(3) Until now we have concentrated on the extremes of the dough rather than the center. To extend the center you must do the following: With one hand, place the pin parallel to you at the far edge of the dough. Grasp the middle of the pin so that the tips of your fingers get a hold on the edge of the dough. Firmly press the heel of the palm of your other hand on the edge of the dough closest to you. Roll the pin toward you, bringing the dough with it. Keep rolling until dough wraps once around the pin. Do not wrap the dough over itself. Quickly unroll the dough—always keeping your other hand tight on the near edge of the dough—by pushing the pin away from you. Remember, push away, do not press down. Repeat the process, this time rolling more dough onto the pin than you did the first time. Roll and unroll very quickly so that the dough does not stick to itself. Finally, roll the dough completely around the pin, lift the ends of the pin in each hand, then turn the pin around so that each hand now

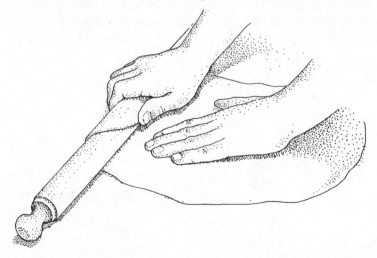

grasps the other end. Start to unfurl the dough by lodging the heel of your right hand against the exposed end of the dough and then roll the pin away from you across the working surface, stretching but being careful not to work too violently. Do this entire procedure once again, starting from the edge and gradually adding more. Remember, work quickly, and if you find that the dough is sticking, *lightly* flour your rolling pin. Working too slowly may mean that your dough will dry out.

(4) Now roll the far edge of the dough once around the pin, all the while gently smoothing the dough on the pin from the center to the 2 extremes. Roll more dough onto the pin and repeat the same motion. Work quickly. Then do this with the side of the dough closest to you.

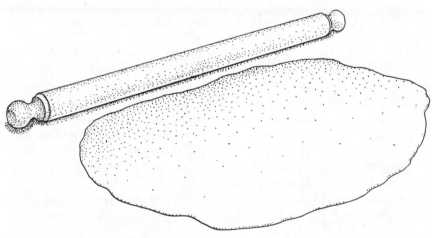

(5) Open the dough up again on the working surface and roll the pin a couple of times across the expanse of the dough. If you have done your job well, the dough will be about $\frac{1}{12}$ to $\frac{1}{16}$ of an inch thick. Some pasta cooks think it is necessary to see your hand through the pasta, but you need not worry about this sort of thing. If it is as thin as you want it, smooth and elastic, then you have done good work. Let the *sfoglia* dry on a clean towel or cloth.

ROLLING OUT THE DOUGH IN A MANUAL PASTA MACHINE: Divide the dough into 3 or 4 separate pieces. Remember to keep covered the pieces you are not working with. Set the machine on its widest setting and run the piece of dough quickly through the rollers a few times. Make the setting one notch smaller and run the dough through again. Keep narrowing the setting and running the dough through until it is as thin as you want it. Let the sheet dry on a clean towel and roll out the other pieces of dough. Machine-rolled dough dries out within 10 minutes, so you must work fast.

A FEW WORDS ABOUT FANCY ELECTRIC PASTA MAKERS: They produce decent pasta and are great conveniences for busy people. They also are occasionally noisy and often quite a nuisance to clean. Do not think that pasta from these machines can match handmade pasta. However, as I said, the results are pretty good, and if you don't choose to make pasta by hand, these machines might represent a good alternative if you want a ready supply of fresh pasta.

Cutting Sfoglia *to Make Various Pastas*

As I mentioned above, hand-rolled pasta does not dry quite as quickly as machine-rolled pasta. This is good, since it gives you a few minutes to take a breather after the rolling process. The pasta should be dry—but not dried out—before you cut it so that the noodles do not stick together. Remember that if you plan to stuff the *sfoglia*, that is, to make *pasta ripiena* such as ravioli, tortellini, and so on, you should not let the pasta dry since you need to fold it. You should have the filling before making the *sfoglia*. Read about making *pasta ripiena*, starting on page 62.

TAGLIATELLE: This is the logical choice to start any discussion on cutting pasta. It is the basic pasta of the Bolognese kitchen. They are

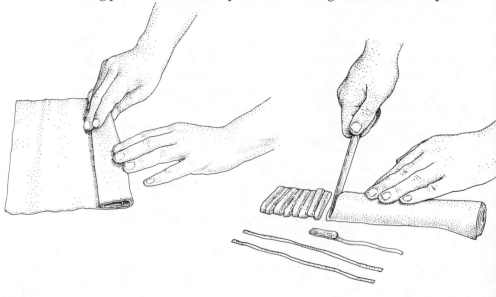

easy to produce. If you are cutting them by hand, make a *flat*, tight roll of the *sfoglia* about 2½ inches wide. Take a sharp knife and cut across the length of the roll, making cuts every ¼ inch. Lift each strip to let the noodles unfold. Let them dry for a few minutes before tossing them into boiling water. If you are using a manual pasta machine, slide each sheet of dough through the wide cutters, cranking the noodles out with the other hand. Separate them and let them briefly dry.

FETTUCCINE: Follow the same procedure as in cutting tagliatelle, except that the fettuccine should be about ⅛ of an inch wide. If you plan to make Fettuccine Alfredo (page 230) or some other cream-based sauce, do not roll out the *sfoglia* quite as thin as you generally would.

TAGLIARINI OR TAGLIOLINI OR TAGLIATELLINE): Follow the same procedure as in cutting tagliatelle, except that tagliarini should be about 1/16 of an inch wide. If you are using a manual pasta machine, slide the dough through the narrow cutters, cranking out the noodles with your other hand.

QUADRETTINI (OR QUADRUCCI): Fold and cut the *sfoglia* as you would for tagliatelle. Do not unfold the strips. Take 5 or 6 strips at a time and cut across them lengthwise in ¼-inch strips to produce little squares.

PIZZOCCHERI: Cut them as you would tagliatelle. For a further discussion of how to make the *sfoglia* for pizzoccheri, see page 152.

MALTAGLIATI: Roll the *sfoglia* as you would for tagliatelle, but cut in a zigzag fashion to obtain "badly cut" pieces of pasta.

PAPPARDELLE: Unlike the pre-ceding pastas, you should not fold the *sfoglia* into a flat roll to make these wide Tuscan noodles. In-stead, take a fluted pasta cutter and cut the sheet of *sfoglia* in 2, and then cut long strips at least ½ inch wide.

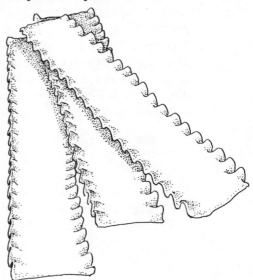

LASAGNE: Do not let the *sfoglia* get too dry before cutting it. Use a knife or a pasta wheel with either a straight or fluted edge. Your la-sagne should be 3 to 4 inches in width and as long as you would

like them to be. The average length is probably 4 to 8 inches, but sometimes it can be as much as 15 inches. Cut the sheet of *sfoglia* into widths and then cut in the other direction to produce the desired lengths.

CANNELLONI: Cut as you would lasagne, using a knife or a straight-edged pasta wheel, making squares or rectangles with sides of approximately 3 to 4 inches.

FARFALLE: Using a fluted pasta wheel, horizontally cut strips of *sfoglia* about ½ inch wide. Then, without moving the strips, cut them vertically 1½ inches apart. Pinch the center of each rectangle to produce the characteristic butterfly shape. Farfalline should be half this size, and farfalloni should be twice this size.

Pasta Verde

Spinach Pasta

All of the pasta shapes listed above are made with pasta all'uovo. *You can also make them with* pasta verde *or* pasta rossa *(red pasta), the recipe for which follows this one. Spinach pasta has become increasingly popular recently in the United States, though it has always been eaten with gusto in Italy, especially in Emilia-Romagna. Since spinach has fewer calories than flour, pasta verde also happens to be less fattening that egg pasta. The preparation of* pasta verde *will probably intimidate you at first, but soon you will find that it is an easy procedure and even pleasurable. The recipe here yields a little over 1 pound of pasta.*

  8 ounces fresh spinach
2½ cups unbleached flour
  2 large eggs

Wash the spinach well, making sure it is clean. Gently cook it in a pan, using only the water remaining on the spinach leaves. The spinach should be cooked just until it begins to turn soft. Remove the leaves from the pan and squeeze the spinach dry. You might want to keep the very nutritious spinach liquid for other uses. When the spinach is as dry as possible (wet spinach will need more flour in the pasta preparation—you don't want floury pasta), chop it and force it through a sieve. You might prefer to puree the spinach in a blender or a food processor. Put the flour on your working surface. Make a well *(la fontana)* in the flour, and add the eggs and spinach puree. Work these ingredients into the flour using the fingertips of one hand or a fork, making sure the spinach and eggs do not slip through the well to the working surface. Continue to work the ingredients together. If all the flour is not incorporated, add a few drops of olive oil or water. Add a bit more flour if the dough is too soft. Flour your hands and the working surface frequently as you make the dough. Knead it vigorously as you would in making *pasta all'uovo*. This process usually takes 10–20 minutes. Little air bubbles should begin to appear on the surface of the dough. Cut the dough into 2 or 3 pieces and roll them out, 1 at a time, to the thickness you prefer. Do not be surprised if *pasta verde* does not roll out quite as neatly as *pasta all'uovo*. It still makes wonderful pasta.

Pasta Rossa

Red Pasta

This is often referred to as tomato pasta, but as the ingredients below suggest, this is not an accurate appellation. I believe that green pasta can stand on its merits, but other colored pasta is a little pretentious. The flavor of tomato fares much better in sauce than it does in pasta. If you put a lot of tomato flavor into the flour, it will create a strong and, in my view, unappetizing taste. Since red pasta is aesthetically pleasing, especially when combined with green and yellow pasta (see Pasta al Tricolore on page 266) try the following, which has color and a pleasant taste.

8 ounces carrots	2 large eggs
2½ cups flour	1 teaspoon tomato paste

Wash and peel the carrots and cut in pieces. Boil them in a little water until relatively soft, then remove from the water and mash.

Return the mashed carrots to the pot (from which you have poured out the liquid) and add the tomato paste. Stir gently over a low flame until the ingredients are blended and the mixture is somewhat condensed. Let the mixture cool and then proceed as in the recipe for *pasta verde*, replacing the spinach with the carrot-tomato mixture.

Orecchiette

Orecchiette (little ears) are a specialty of Apulia. Their rounded shape nicely holds sauces, yet they are easy to eat. Many Italian children, once they graduate from pastina, start their pasta-eating careers with orecchiette.

MAKES 1 POUND

3½ cups semolina flour
  2 eggs
    Pinch of salt
¼ cup water, approximately (if necessary)

Make a small mountain of flour on a pastry board and form a well in the center. Add the eggs, salt, and water, and work the mixture with your hands until a relatively hard dough is formed (about 10 minutes). Take pieces of the dough, roll them out until you form long pencil-thin rods no more than ½ inch in diameter. With a rounded knife cut small pieces of the dough and press the pasta into your thumb in such a way that it takes the form of an ear or perhaps a shell. Let the orecchiette dry, covered lightly with a cloth, for 24 hours. Then you must use them because if they are kept longer, they will become too dry and will crumble.

Making Dough for Pasta Ripiena (Filled Pasta) (Agnolotti, Cappelletti, Ravioli, Tortellini, and So Forth)

Pasta ripiena is virtuous food best prepared by virtuous cooks. Therefore, making *pasta ripiena* builds not only muscles but character. The virtuous cook is loving, patient, attentive, practical, decisive and, when necessary, speedy. You must find all of these virtues within yourself; not only is pasta good for you but so is pasta preparation. Patience is required in the chopping, cutting, cooking, kneading, rolling, stuffing, and folding of the *pasta ripiena*. You must be attentive to assure that the pasta is neatly folded and sealed. Speed (though not haste) is a virtue in that you must make the pasta before the dough dries. Do not be intimidated; with virtue, practice, and time, you can become a *pasta ripiena* virtuoso.

Do not set about making dough *(la sfoglia)* for filled pasta until you have carefully read the instructions starting on page 52 for making fresh pasta. In fact, the processes are quite similar, but there are a few things to bear in mind when preparing pasta for filling. Pasta to be filled should be thinner and less eggy. In general, the number of eggs in the dough of a raviolo or tortellino is 50 percent less than in a tagliatella. If you find when making the *sfoglia* that it is too dry, add some form of liquid. I learned pasta making in Bologna, where the added liquid would be milk. In other parts of Italy, white wine, olive oil, or hot water is used. Since most stuffed pastas were created in Emilia-Romagna, it seems logical to prepare them with milk as the cooks of this region do. The amount you need will vary according to the type of flour you use and to how absorbent your eggs are. I have found, on the average, that one teaspoon of milk per cup of flour is about right.

The pasta should not be allowed to dry. Though this rule applies to the preparation of all fresh pasta, it is crucial here since you will need to roll and fold the *sfoglia*. If it dries, the pasta will crumble and your dish will be a failure. So be sure to work in an environment that is comfortably warm, though not hot, and completely free of drafts and air currents.

If you are making a large quantity of filled pasta, prepare only a small amount at a time, keeping the other sheets of dough covered with a cloth or with plastic wrap to prevent them from drying out. There are some cooks who roll out only as much dough as they need immediately. This extra work might result in a slightly more desirable product, but it is not necessary, especially if you are new at this.

Because it is necessary to work quickly with this type of dough, always prepare the filling *(il ripieno)* before making the *sfoglia*. Since most *ripieni* are uniform pastes of several ingredients, this process must be accomplished in advance, but even such simple *ripieni* as ricotta and parsley should be made before the pasta.

Making Ravioli, Agnolotti, and Anolini

According to many Italian food historians, there was once a clear distinction between agnolotti and ravioli. The former were filled with meat and the latter with fish, cheese, or vegetables. Agnolotti were made in the wealthy, meat-eating regions of the north while ravioli were eaten in the less affluent central and coastal parts of Italy. This sort of dish was almost nonexistent in the poorer south. These distinctions have blurred somewhat since World War II as improved communications and finances have made Italy slightly less regional.

Still, local names for very similar shapes of pasta persist. We have political history to thank for this. When the Piedmontese House of Savoy was given power in Sicily after the Treaty of Utrecht (1713), Vittorio Amedeo di Savoia introduced agnolotti to the island. Sicilians, ever aware of their own identity despite foreign domination, chose the word *agnillini* to describe the pasta, and they still do today. When Napoleon invaded Turin in 1806, King Vittorio Emanuele I di Savoia and his court took refuge in Cagliari, Sardinia. The royal family still wanted agnolotti, which their new Sardinian cooks called *angiulottus.* The original name for agnolotti came in the fourteenth century in Turin from the local word *anolot,* meaning a ring-shaped metal form used to cut the pasta. A smaller version of this pasta is known as anolini. Linguistic and gastronomic variations occur in Mantua, where they are called *agnolini;* in Parma, *anolen;* and in Piacenza, *anvein.*

The word *raviolo* comes from the Italian *ravvolgere* (to wrap up). The origin of the ravioli themselves is not quite as clear. Most historians agree that ravioli were made famous in Genoa, but some scholars doubt they were created in Liguria. I have read accounts of ravioli being served to Genoese sailors in medieval Sicilian prisons. By these accounts, the sailors did not enjoy being incarcerated, but they thought enough of ravioli to introduce them when they returned to Genoa. I am not certain this is true, but ravioli have been a favorite of seafaring Genoese for centuries. Columbus and other Ligurian sailors took dried cheese-filled ravioli to sea with them.

The fame of ravioli spread in the early Renaissance. Local chefs in towns throughout Italy used ingredients available to them to make their own versions of the Genoese classic. They gave these *paste ripiene* names derived from local dialects. These include: *casonsei* in Bergamo and Brescia; *casumziei* in Belluno; *cialzons* in the Friuli; *culingiones* in Cagliari; *culurjones* in Nuoro; *culurzones* in Sassari; *gobbein* ("little hunchbacks") in Tortona; *laianelle* in Molise; *marubini* in Cremona; *ofelle* in Trieste; *pansotti* in Rapallo; and *turtei* in Emilia. Some of these recipes appear in this book. Where instructions for shaping the pasta are slightly different, they are indicated in the individual recipes. Otherwise, for preparing these dishes as well as for classic agnolotti, anolini, and ravioli, read and follow the directions below.

In all cases, as I have already emphasized, make the *ripieno* first. Then make the *sfoglia*, that is, the pasta. Remember: Roll out only one sheet of *sfoglia* at a time so that it does not dry out. The *sfoglia* should be thinner than you would make it for tagliatelle. A thickness of ⅛ inch is a good average. Experiment until you discover what suits you best.

RAVIOLI: There are at least three procedures for making ravioli. I am listing them in the order I prefer.

METHOD 1

(1) Roll out a rectangular or square sheet of *sfoglia*.

(2) Distribute olive-sized portions (about ½ teaspoon) of *ripieno* about 1½ inches apart in a single line parallel to the edge of the sheet of *sfoglia*. The row of *ripieno* portions should be 1½ inches from the edge of the *sfoglia*.

(3) Carefully lift the edge of the *sfoglia* and fold it over the little balls of *ripieno* so that they are completely covered.

(4) Take a knife, fluted ravioli wheel, or small pastry wheel and cut along the line where the edge meets the *sfoglia*.

(5) Using your fingertips gently press down the pasta in between the balls of *ripieno* so that you have completely sealed them off from one another. (See Notes below.)

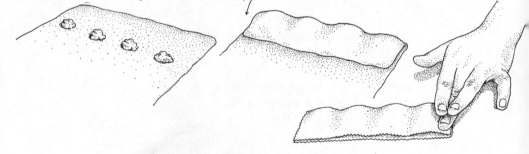

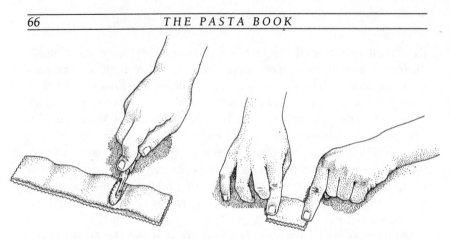

(6) Use the ravioli wheel to cut the rectangles of pasta which, as you now see, are ravioli.

(7) If necessary, gently press the edges of the ravioli with your fingertips to assure that they are sealed.

(8) Put the ravioli on a lightly floured dishcloth or towel, making sure that they do not touch one another. Sprinkle on a bit of flour so that they will not stick together and can dry (though not dry out) for 15 to 30 minutes.

Repeat the process until this sheet of *sfoglia* is used up. If you have more dough, roll out another sheet. Continue until all the materials *(ripieno* and *sfoglia)* are used.

Notes: You can do steps (1) through (3) and then form the ravioli with a ravioli press. These are available in square or round shapes for about $1.25 and can cut and crimp individual ravioli. If you use the round ravioli press, little scraps of *sfoglia* will be left over. You can use these as arc-shaped noodles in consomme.

For step (5) I keep a little dish of water nearby to moisten my fingertips.

METHOD 2

(1) Roll out 2 rectangular or square sheets of *sfoglia* of equal size.

(2) Distribute olive-sized portions (about ½ teaspoon) of *ripieno* in single lines. The balls of *ripieno* should be at least 1½ inches apart and no closer than ¾ inch from the edges of the *sfoglia.*

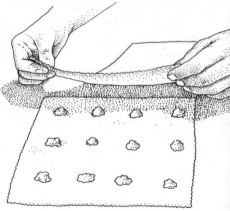

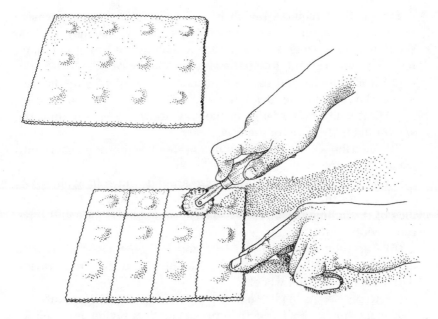

(3) Carefully place the second sheet of *sfoglia* on top of the first.

(4) Press down with your fingertips to separate the rows of *ripieno* so that individual ravioli may be formed.

(5) Cut along the rows with a knife or ravioli wheel in straight vertical and horizontal lines to produce the ravioli. You may also use a square ravioli press.

(6) If necessary, gently press the edges of the ravioli with your fingertips to assure that they are sealed.

(7) Place the ravioli on a lightly-floured dishcloth or towel, making sure that they do not touch one another.

(8) If you have enough dough to make 2 more sheets of *sfoglia*, roll them out and repeat steps (2) through (7). If not, make the rest of the ravioli according to the first method.

Note: This method may seem easier than the first. However, it requires much more precision in quickly cutting equal rectangular sheets of *sfoglia*, in lining up even rows of *ripieno* the proper distance apart, in quickly working so that the sheets of *sfoglia* do not dry out, and in accurately cutting the rows of ravioli so that they end up more or less equal in size.

METHOD 3

This method requires ravioli trays (or *raviolatrici*), inexpensive metal trays not unlike shallow ice trays except that they have 36 separate compartments. You can try a shallow ice tray if you don't have a ravioli tray, but I do not guarantee classic results.

(1) Roll out 2 equal-size rectangular sheets of *sfoglia* that are slightly larger than the ravioli tray.

(2) Put 1 layer of *sfoglia* in the tray and press gently until the *sfoglia* takes the form of the tray.

(3) Distribute little balls of *ripieno* (about ½ teaspoon each) into each compartment.

(4) Roll the second sheet of *sfoglia* around your rolling pin.

(5) Unroll the *sfoglia* over the tray, pressing down with the handles of the rolling pin until the 2 layers of *sfoglia* adhere and separate ravioli are formed.

(6) Carefully turn over the tray and let the ravioli fall onto a lightly-floured dishcloth or towel. Cut them into individual ravioli with a knife or ravioli wheel.

(7) Repeat steps (1) through (6) until all the materials are used.

This method yields perfectly formed, identical ravioli, but the process is slow and fussy.

Electric pasta machines feature attachments for ravioli making. You may use these if you like them, but I am a firm believer in making all *paste ripiene* by hand.

AGNOLOTTI: May be made following either the first or second methods for ravioli. However, agnolotti are larger than ravioli, 2 or even 3 inches square. Therefore, use more *ripieno* (about ¾ teaspoon to 1 teaspoon). Each portion of *ripieno* should be the size of a large olive. Also, the balls of *ripieno* should be 2 to 3 inches apart, since your agnolotti should have much more *sfoglia* surrounding the *ripieno* in the center.

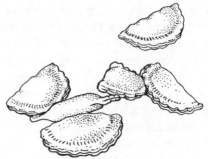

ANOLINI: Although there are triangular anolini, formed using the first steps for tortellini (page 72), the classic anolini are shaped like semicircles or half moons.

(1) Roll out a sheet of *sfoglia.*

(2) With a round ravioli press, biscuit cutter, or the mouth of a glass no more than 1½ inches in diameter, form separate discs of *sfoglia.*

(3) Put a small ball of *ripieno* (about ¼ teaspoon) in the center of each disc.

(4) Fold the discs to form semicircles.

(5) Gently seal the edges of the anolini with your fingertips. This is crucial to assure that the anolini do not open and release the *ripieno* during cooking.

Making Tortelli

To make tortelli, you should read about making anolini (above). You may use one of two methods:

(1) Cut out discs 2 inches in diameter with the rim of a glass or using a pasta wheel. Put some *ripieno* into the center of each disc and fold to form half-moons. Press down the edge to make sure they are totally sealed.

(2) Make 2 sheets of *sfoglia.* Dot one with rows of *ripieno* 2½ to 3 inches apart and carefully cover it with the other sheet. Press down between the balls of the *ripieno* and then cut out individual tortelli using a round ravioli press, the rim of a glass followed by a knife, or a ravioli wheel. Press down the edges to make sure they are totally sealed.

Tortelli should be boiled in a large pot of lightly salted water. Drain carefully with a slotted ladle or spoon. Tortelli are most frequently served with melted butter to which either sage, nutmeg, or cinnamon has been added. In Modena *tortelli di zucca* are often served with meat sauce.

If you are planning to serve tortelli to a large group of people and you are filled with ambition, adventure, and fantasy, I suggest the following: Make all three tortelli recipes—with fillings of potatoes, pumpkin, and spinach—and serve them together under lots of grated parmigiano, melted butter, and sage.

Making Cappelletti, Tortellini, and Tortelloni

These stuffed pastas would appear on anyone's short list of the great glories of the Italian kitchen. More specifically, they are the pride of the cuisine of Emilia-Romagna.

Tortellini are small, are usually stuffed with meat, and are made in Emilia. Cappelletti are basically the same size and shape as tortellini, yet they are not filled with meat and are made in Romagna. Tortelloni are larger versions of tortellini and are commonly stuffed with cheese, although it is also possible to find them filled with meat or even fish.

Among the things that make Bologna so special is that most of the great dishes of Emilia-Romagna are found there. While yelling *"bis"* ("encore") in most of Italy implies approval of a musician or opera singer, saying *"bis"* in Bologna will get you a plate of the foods the cook is most proud of—usually tortellini, tortelloni, and cappelletti, all in different sauces, and perhaps some Lasagne Verdi alla Bolognese or Tagliatelle al Ragù. The *bis*, as this platter is called, is served with freshly grated parmigiano, excellent red Lambrusco (not the sort sold for export), and the peculiar dry bread of Bologna that so effectively counteracts the richness of the food.

With a little practice you will be able to make fresh cappelletti, tortellini, and tortelloni that will have your dinner guests yelling *bis* and *bravo!* Before discussing how to make these pastas, a few reminders:

• Make the *ripieno* before starting with the *sfoglia*. If the pasta dries out, it is useless, so you should be ready to fill it once it is rolled out.
• Only roll out one sheet of *sfoglia* at a time so it does not dry out.
• You may use a *sfoglia* made either of egg pasta *(pasta all'uovo)* or spinach pasta *(pasta verde)*. This varies according to what *ripieno* you use and to your taste.
• The *sfoglia* should be rolled out as thin as possible: 1/16 of an inch would be ideal.

CAPPELLETTI AND TORTELLINI: The names mean "little hats" and "little tortelli" (similar to folded anolini). They were eaten by Bolognese university students in the Middle Ages, but people seem to think of modern tortellini as food from the Renaissance. The distinctive shape of these pastas is part of their charm. They can be taken as little hats, but I like the classic explanation more. Tortellini are traditionally eaten at Christmas dinner in Bologna, whose citizens would bring the freshly made pasta to their priests. My sacred Bolognese friends say the design was created by the church. My profane Bolognese friends disagree. The prevailing story is that a seventeenth-century Bolognese cook fell hopelessly in love with his master's wife. He once caught sight of her in the nude but could not act upon his desires. Instead, he rushed to the kitchen where he fashioned a *pasta ripiena* in the shape of the woman's navel. The following day he served 2 plates of these to his master and mistress who were each, in different ways, delighted, and the 3 lived happily ever after. A slightly different version of this story holds that tortellini were modelled after the navel of Venus, the goddess of love who has considerable influence in Bologna.

MAKING CAPPELLETTI:

(1) Make the *ripieno.*

(2) Roll out a rectangular or square sheet of *sfoglia*. If necessary, use a knife or pasta wheel to form the right angles on the *sfoglia.* The pasta you cut away may be used in soup or boiled and served with ragù.

(3) Measure in 1½ inches from the edge of the *sfoglia* and cut a strip that runs parallel to the edge. Cover the rest of the *sfoglia* with a towel to prevent it from drying out.

(4) Now cut the strip into 1½-inch lengths, thus forming perfect squares.

(5) Put a bit of *ripieno*, approximately ¼ to a scant ½ teaspoon, in the center of every square.

(6) Shape each square into a triangle by folding diagonally. The inside edge should reach *almost* to the outside edge. You should leave only a very thin border visible.

(7) Press down with your fingertips (which you might moisten with a bit of water if you think the *sfoglia* has dried) to perfectly seal the cappelletto.

(8) To make an individual cappelletto, wrap the triangle around your index finger so that the part containing the *ripieno* rests on your fingernail. Using your thumb, unite the 2 legs of the triangle under your index finger so that they overlap a little. Press to seal the legs.

(9) Place the cappelletto on a cloth to dry.

(10) Make the other triangles into cappelleti. Place them on the cloth, but do not pile on top of one another.

(11) Cut another 1½-wide strip of *sfoglia* and repeat the process.

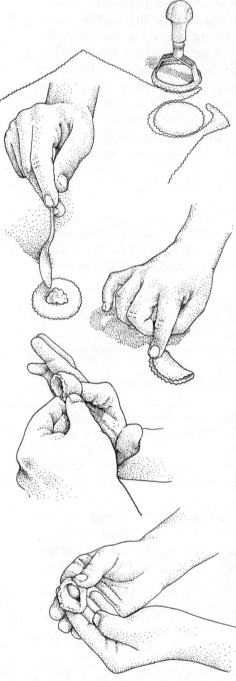

MAKING TORTELLINI:

Tortellino suggests a small *tortello*. A tortello is synonymous with an anolino (see page 69). Anolini are shaped like half-moons. To make tortellini in this fashion:

(1) Roll out a sheet of *sfoglia* to a thickness of ¹⁄₁₆ of an inch.

(2) Using a drinking glass or pasta cutter with a diameter of 1½ to 2 inches, cut out discs of *sfoglia*.

(3) Place ¼ to ½ teaspoon of *ripieno* in the center of each disc.

(4) Fold the discs to form half moons, making sure that the front edge does not quite line up with the rear edge. There should be a fraction of an inch of the rear border showing. Press down to seal the edges.

(5) To make an individual tortellino, wrap the half moon around the nail of your index finger so that the folded side faces upward.

(6) Join the ends of the half moon under your index finger. Press with your thumb to seal them.

(7) Set the tortellino on a cloth and make the others the same way. Do not pile the tortellini on top of one another.

(8) Continue until you have used up all the *sfoglia* and *ripieno*.

TORTELLONI: These are made the same way as tortellini except that the discs should be 3½ to 4 inches in diameter. If you choose to make tortelloni using squares of *sfoglia* (that is, the procedure for making cappelletti), the individual pieces of *sfoglia* should be cut 3½ to 4 inches square. You may put 1 teaspoon of *ripieno* or even a bit more in tortelloni.

Making Gnocchi

Gnocchi are Italy's version of dumplings. However, unlike most dumplings, which tend to stick to your ribs, gnocchi are usually delicate and airy, and make delightful foils for many good sauces. They can be served with tomato sauces, meat sauces, herb, vegetable, and cheese sauces. I like gnocchetti (small dumplings) with the Gorgonzola sauce used on rigatoni (page 143).

Nowadays most Italians think of gnocchi as being made with potatoes. Yet the potato was not introduced to Europe until the sixteenth century. During the Renaissance, gnocchi were often made with bread. In all likelihood, gnocchi appeared on tables centuries before the arrival of the potato, since they call for only the most basic ingredients: flour and water. They are easy to make, so if you are new to the world of homemade pasta, you might try your hand at gnocchi before advancing to orecchiette, corzetti, cannelloni, lasagne, tagliatelle and, finally, stuffed pastas such as ravioli and tortellini.

For the basic recipe for potato gnocchi, see Gnocchi di Patate alla Bava (page 161). Also read the recipes for Chicche Verdi del Nonno (page 184), Malloreddus (page 259), and Gnocchi Divino (page 274).

The process for shaping gnocchi or the smaller gnocchetti is the same no matter what ingredients are employed. The creation of the dough varies, so we will deal with each of those individually.

SHAPING GNOCCHI:

(1) Once the dough is made, separate it into several pieces.

(2) Take 1 piece and roll it out with your hands until you form a cordlike cylinder the thickness of your index finger.

(3) Take a sharp knife and cut pieces of the "cord" ½ to ¾ of an inch long. To make gnocchetti, cut pieces of the "cord" ¼ inch long.

(4) Take each gnocco and press it with your thumb against the back side of a cheese grater or the tines of a fork. These indentations

will become receptacles for sauce when you dress the gnocchi.

(5) Repeat this process until you have used all the dough. Let the gnocchi rest in a draft-free, cool place. Cover with a little more flour and do not pile them on top of one another.

COOKING GNOCCHI:

This is also an easy process. Bring a large pot of cold water to a boil, then toss in a small pinch of salt. As soon as the water returns to a rapid boil, add the gnocchi. Unlike most foods, gnocchi tell you when they are ready. Properly cooked gnocchi rise to the surface of the boiling water. You must then fish them out using a slotted ladle or spoon. I usually cut the first one in half to see if it is done to my liking, and then I taste it. If the doneness is right, I proceed as described. If the tasted gnocco is a bit grainy, I let them cook a bit longer. If it is mushy (this seldom happens), I try to retrieve them a bit sooner. Once you have removed the gnocchi, transfer them to a warm terrine or serving bowl that has been lightly buttered. When they are all in the serving bowl, add the sauce and serve immediately.

There are so many sauces that go well with Gnocchi di Patate. Try to be creative in selecting the ones you use. Some sauces are particularly suited to other pastas but also go well with gnocchi. In some cases you need to add a bit of butter to the gnocchi before adding the sauce. The following are a few suggestions:

Arugula, page 181
Asparagus, page 129
"Aurora," page 180
"Bassano del Grappa," page 130
Butter and Sage, page 156
"Fraddiavolo," page 249
Gorgonzola, page 143
Herbs, page 115
"Mare e Monti," page 261
Mascarpone, page 183

Pesto, page 168
Prosciutto, page 182
"Pummarola," page 110
Quattro Formaggi, page 122
Rabbit, page 216
Ragù Bolognese, page 178
Ragù di Castrato alla Marchigiana, page 204
Ragù di Maiale all'Umbra, page 209
Saffron, page 239

Making Crespelle

This is really a subdivision of pasta cookery, but it is included in this book because *crespelle* (crepes) are often used in recipes that call for either lasagne or cannelloni. You should not confuse *crespelle* with sweet crepes, pancakes, palacinky, and blintzes, all of which would not suit our needs here. About the only match are Russian blini, which are closer to *scripelle* (to be discussed later) than to traditional *crespelle*.

Unlike dessert crepes, *crespelle* have a little salt in the batter. They may be prepared with an assortment of fillings and sauces, and are often surrounded by besciamella (page 180) when they are baked.

With a bit of practice, *crespelle* are easy to make. The process is not unlike the one for preparing pancakes, except that you must be certain to make the *crespelle* very thin.

MAKES 16 CREPES

4 eggs or 2 eggs plus 1 cup whole milk
⅞ cup sifted unbleached flour
¼ teaspoon salt
2–3 tablespoons butter

Put either 2 eggs or the milk in a mixing bowl. If you are using eggs, beat them lightly with a whisk or fork. Add the flour a little at a time, beating the mixture gently to incorporate the flour with the liquid. Once you have used all the flour, add the salt and then the other 2 eggs, 1 at a time.

Take a 7-, 8-, or 9-inch skillet or frying pan (made of cast iron or having substantial weight) and heat it over a medium flame for a few seconds. It is important that the temperature be just right. If it is too hot, your *crespelle* will burn. If it is too cool, they will not adhere properly to the pan. Add a little butter and lift the pan, twisting with a motion of the wrist to spread the butter evenly. When the butter melts but has not turned brown, you should add batter to make a *crespella*. This varies according to the size of your pan. You might try the following amounts: half a ladleful or ⅛ cup or 2 tablespoons.

These have all worked for me. You should put the batter in the center of the pan and again lift the pan from the flame, twisting your wrist to distribute the batter evenly on the bottom of the pan.

As soon as the *crespella* has turned light brown on the bottom—you may check by lifting one side of the *crespella* delicately with a spatula or fork—flip the *crespella* over with the spatula and fry it briefly on the other side. Remove the *crespella* from the pan and transfer it to a plate. (You may stack the other *crespelle* on top of this one when they are ready.) Now take a little more butter—not as much as the first time—and melt it in the pan. Repeat the process until all the batter is exhausted.

You may use *crespelle* in 4 ways:
(1) Open and flat, as a substitute for lasagne.
(2) Filled and rolled over once in the shape of cannelloni.
(3) With sauce or stuffing spread lightly and evenly across the *crespella* within ½ inch of the edge. You then roll it up tightly and bake the cylinders side by side.
(4) Spread the sauce or stuffing as in (3) above, except that you fold the *crespella* into a half moon and then in half again, so that you have ¼ of a circle. Arrange these prettily in a buttered baking dish —perhaps in a floral design—and bake them topped with ragù, tomato sauce, or besciamella.

Ideas for Saucing Crespelle

Applying any of the 4 ways of using *crespelle*, you may consider any meat sauce in this book: Ragù alla Bolognese, Sugo di Coniglio alla Primetta, Ragù di Maiale, Sugo di Agnello alla Sarda, and so forth, and a sprinkling of parmigiano or pecorino. Bake them in a 350°F oven, surrounded and topped by 1 cup of besciamella until golden brown.

• For 16 *crespelle*, steam a firm, flavorful vegetable that appeals to you, such as asparagus, and then puree it. Make about 2 cups of besciamella. Fold the vegetable puree into 1¼ cups of besciamella and then fill the *crespelle* following method 3 or 4. Top each with a thin slice of Fontina, Bel Paese, or Swiss cheese before folding. Top with the other ¾ cup of besciamella and bake in a 350°F oven until golden brown.

• For 16 *crespelle*, combine 8 ounces of Gorgonzola and 1 cup of freshly grated parmigiano. Fill the *crespelle* with this mixture and fold them using either method 3 or 4. Top with 1 cup of besciamella and bake in a 350°F oven until golden brown.

• For 16 *crespelle*, wash 1 pound of fresh spinach well and steam it using only the water still clinging to the leaves. When the spinach is cooked, squeeze the liquid from it. Chop it well and sauté in butter. Add a bit of nutmeg and grated pecorino or parmigiano. Fold and fill the *crespelle* using method 2, 3, or 4 and arrange them in a buttered baking dish. Top with 1 cup of besciamella, fresh tomato sauce, or tomato cream sauce, and more grated cheese, and bake in a 350°F oven. Variation: Instead of sautéeing the spinach, combine it with 8 ounces of fresh ricotta.

• For 16 *crespelle*, sauté 1 pound of chopped escarole in olive oil with bits of garlic. Fill the *crespelle* using method 2 or 3 and top with fresh tomato sauce. Bake in a baking dish in a 350°F oven.

• For 16 *crespelle*, clean and chop 1 pound of fresh mushrooms. Sauté in butter, add ½ cup of cream, and fill the *crespelle* using method 3 or 4. Top with besciamella to which a generous pinch of nutmeg and, perhaps, 2 ounces of prosciutto slivers have been added. Sprinkle on 1 cup of parmigiano. Bake in a 350°F oven until golden brown.

• For 16 *crespelle*, sauté in olive oil and butter 1 pound of baby zucchini, baby eggplant, sweet onions, or a combination of the 3, sliced into thin discs. When they are golden in color, transfer to paper toweling. Grind on fresh pepper. Fold the vegetables into the *crespelle* using method 3 or 4. Before folding them, sprinkle on a generous amount of pecorino. Top with tomato sauce and more pecorino, and bake in a 350°F oven.

• For 16 *crespelle*, Gioacchino Rossini would have liked 12 ounces of foie gras, finely spread over the *crespelle* with 1 or 2 shavings of truffle over each. Fold them up using method 3 or 4, arrange in a baking dish, and top with 1 cup of besciamella and 1 cup of freshly grated parmigiano. Bake in a 350°F oven until golden brown.

VARIATION: *Scripelle* are a specialty of the Abruzzi. They are made with the same batter as the one for *crespelle*, often with 2 tablespoons of finely minced parsley and ½ teaspoon of black pepper tossed in. There are 2 differences between *scripelle* and *crespelle*: The former are small and fried in oil, and the latter are larger and fried in butter. Make them as you would *crespelle* except that the pan should be about 4 inches in diameter, lightly greased with oil, and 1 tablespoon of batter per *scripella*. These are usually fried to a greater degree of doneness than *crespelle*. The recipe for *crespelle* batter should yield about 32 *scripelle*. In the area around Teramo, *scripelle* are traditionally sprinkled with pecorino cheese, folded, and served in broth. Otherwise you may sprinkle the *scripelle* with grated pecorino and wrap them around spinach, escarole, sautéed chicken livers, ricotta, mozzarella, ham, or anything that strikes your fancy, baking everything topped with a ragù, a tomato sauce, or besciamella.

About
Cooking Pasta

The point at which your pasta reaches the perfect state of doneness as it cooks in boiling water is a highly subjective yet crucial issue. When Greeks cook maccheroni, for example, they like them much softer than any Italian would ever accept. Americans and Canadians also tend to overcook their pasta unintentionally.

Since this book is a collection of authentic Italian pasta recipes, you should prepare these dishes with the goal of achieving results comparable to those found in the kitchens of typical Italian homes. This is not difficult as long as you keep a close watch on what's cooking.

The key phrase here is AL DENTE. This is not the name of an Italian dentist; rather, it is a descriptive phrase suggesting the proper degree of doneness. Translated literally it means "to the tooth" or, more accurately, "to the bite" or "chewy." Essentially, pasta al dente should be cooked so that it is neither raw nor limp. You should feel it as you chew and swirl it across your tongue. Pasta al dente is still solid enough so that it can support a sauce instead of drown in it.

Not only is pasta al dente the most delicious, but it is also the most digestible. When pasta is undercooked, it still has a raw taste. Neapolitans favor slight undercooking but never to this extent. When pasta is overcooked, too much water has been absorbed. Instructions for cooking pasta correctly follow:

• Set a large pot of fresh, cold water to boil. Always use a minimum of 4 quarts of water, even if you are cooking only 4 ounces of spaghetti for yourself. The pot should be ¾ full at most, since the addition of the pasta will raise the water level, and you do not want it to spill over. To cook properly, even a small amount of pasta needs room to move in the pot. For cooking more than a pound of spaghetti, use at least 6 quarts of water. If you don't have 1 huge pot, use 2 pots of at least 4 quarts each.

• When the water reaches a boil, add a pinch of salt, or more if you like salt, but do not overdo it.

• As soon as the water has returned to a boil, add the pasta. Make sure it is fully immersed by stirring carefully with a large fork, preferably made of wood. When you add the pasta, the water will stop boiling as its temperature drops. Turn the flame to high to restore the boil. Then turn it down slightly so that the water does not boil out of the pot. A special note: NEVER break spaghetti or other long pasta before adding it to the pot. This is an affectation that in no way relates to authentic pasta preparation.

• Continue to stir every so often to make sure the pasta does not stick to the pot. This is particularly important for maccheroni. As pasta cooks it usually increases in size, often to 3 or 4 times its original dimensions. This is due primarily to absorption of water. It also absorbs the minerals in the water such as calcium and sodium chloride (salt).

• Do not follow the suggested cooking times on the pasta box too religiously. To know when the pasta is done, *you must taste it.* Sample a strand of spaghetti or a maccherono to see if it is cooked. If the pasta still tastes raw, continue to boil. Keep sampling until you have tried a pasta that is chewy and flavorful and not mushy. Then it is ready. Remember that fresh pasta such as tagliatelle is cooked almost as soon as it is immersed, so watch it very closely. Stuffed pastas you are boiling should be sampled as well. But there is another important consideration in cooking stuffed pastas, and that is the filling. A pork product may call for longer cooking than a cheese or spinach filling. In the case of gnocchi, they are ready when they rise to the top of the water. But taste one anyway to be sure.

Suggestion: Do not cook different types of pasta or even 2 brands of the same pasta shape together. There are usually differences among them, so if you taste a noodle that is cooked as you like it, this only means that *that* type is ready. The other type may be overcooked or undercooked.

• When the pasta is cooked sufficiently, it must be drained. There are 2 approaches to this. I have always wondered why so many Italian women have beautiful skin. Perhaps it is because of the mini-facials they receive standing over pots of boiling water cooking the pasta and then draining it. In Bologna pasta cooks often fish out tortellini and gnocchi using slotted spoons. They remove tagliatelle and other long pastas using pasta forks—wooden implements with long teeth to catch the strands. Fishing out pasta is more laborious than draining it in a colander, and if you do not work very quickly, some of the pasta in the pot will be overcooked. Yet by transferring it directly from pot to serving dish it may be eaten as hot as possible. Also—this is a fine point you need not worry about—by not draining a huge pot of pasta in a colander, you are saving the pasta from the trauma of roaring out of the pot with a lot of water and crashing into the colander. Spaghetti and tagliatelle that are fished out rather than drained are less likely to tangle, another consideration when it comes to saucing and eating.

The fishing method is something you can work on as you develop your pasta-cooking skills. However, it is absolutely acceptable to drain pasta in a colander. You should have a large, deep colander to catch the pasta. As you pour the pasta and water, try to tilt the pot so that much of the water rushes out first. This way you are not giving the pasta a bath when it comes out of the colander. Once you have emptied the contents, put the pot down right away and quickly lift the colander by its handles and give it a couple of quick shakes to rid the pasta of excess water.

Warning: It is a sin to rinse the pasta in cold water unless a particular recipe specifically tells you to do so!

Once the pasta is drained, transfer it to a serving dish, add a *little* butter and cheese if the recipe calls for it, top with some sauce, toss if necessary, and serve. However you drain pasta, work fast. If it is cold and limp, the pasta is not good.

About
Saucing Pasta

To some aesthetes, Italy exists as a gathering place for disparate and often chaotic elements that together produce a level of harmony and proportion known nowhere else. Most people do not bother to analyze this phenomenon, which I think is more in keeping with the spirit of the thing.

Everywhere you look in Italy, humans and nature blend with startling effect. Raw materials are crafted into things of beauty. Buildings are built to harmonize with their environment. Small towns such as Pienza in Tuscany are living works of art. In Italy, form and function are integrated rather than leading or following each other.

The same sense of proportion and harmony born of centuries of study and experimentation based on classic principles may be applied to pasta.

Long thin noodles such as spaghetti, vermicelli, and bigoli are suited to oil-based or seafood sauces because the strands wrap and hold these toppings well.

Broader flat noodles such as tagliatelle, fettuccine, pappardelle, and pizzoccheri are well paired with richer sauces based on meat, butter, cheese, or cream that coat their surfaces.

Rounded noodles, often with holes, such as maccheroni, penne, rigatoni, and fusilli have been created for meat ragùs and sauces with chunkier ingredients.

Read more about the many different types of pasta and their uses starting on page 97.

Americans who eat pasta make one mistake more often than any other: They put too much sauce on their pasta. In Italy when you get a plate of, for example, spaghetti with tomato sauce, your bowl has about 4 ounces of cooked pasta with a small ladleful of sauce in the center. There might be a dot of butter in the tomato sauce. You then toss the spaghetti, which becomes coated with sauce. There will be little or no sauce at the bottom of the dish. You might choose to add a little grated cheese, bearing in mind that this will be absorbed by the sauce, making the dish drier. You twirl a mouthful of properly cooked spaghetti around your fork. The sauce and cheese neatly cling to the pasta as you pop it into your mouth and chew rapturously.

The simplest ingredients achieve harmony and beauty when brought together in classic proportions. If too much sauce has been added, the dish becomes a soupy mess. Too much cheese in the correct amount of sauce dries it out and glues the spaghetti so that you cannot twirl it. Most importantly, it overpowers the flavor of the sauce and ruins the dish.

The lesson here is to use much less sauce that you expect to— only enough to flavor the pasta. Cheese should add flavor, not bulk.

Voltaire once said that England has 60 religions and 1 sauce. I would venture that in Italy the opposite is true, even if the few Italian Protestants, Jews, Moslems, and Buddhists wish to nitpick. There are over 60 pasta sauces in this book, and there are many more throughout Italy.

After you learn to make the recipes that appeal to you, I encourage you to experiment to create your own sauces. As you do this, remember what you have already learned. When I created the "Don Giovanni" sauce on page 262, for example, I knew that oysters would not be successful with lasagne or rigatoni; this sauce required a more delicate pasta such as vermicelli. Pair your newly created sauces with suitable pastas.

When you invent sauces, try to combine ingredients logically. When I added pear brandy and walnuts to the Gorgonzola sauce (page 143), this move was based on the knowledge that these ingredients have made successful appearances together on other culinary stages. Yet it is not that simple. Flavor is your first but not only consideration. You must also pay attention to variations in texture. Texturally, a pear stuffed with cheese and walnuts is a different sensation than a creamy pasta sauce. If a sauce has distinct ingredients that are all soft or all crunchy (both of these conditions occur frequently in bad versions of Pasta alla Primavera), you do not have interesting food. Another consideration is visual. Cutting ingredients such as green peppers into particular shapes adds effect. So does color. Pasta al Tricolore (page 266) and Fettuccine Antonia e Arabella (page 265) are examples of dishes that blend flavor, texture, and color with great effect.

Now that you are in the mood to create, where do you begin? I recommend doing what Italians have done since Etruscan times: Look to nature.

The next time you have a chance, listen to a performance of Vivaldi's *The Four Seasons*. We are often so dazzled by the brilliant intricacy of the music that we fail to note how supremely evocative it is of each season. Even within the movements, each an essay on the character of a particular season, there is a discernible shift, as there might be from early to late spring. Similarly, within each season some foods make brief appearances and then become memories. Enjoy them while they are there and incorporate them in your cooking.

Food is intimately tied to changes in weather. We eat differently not only because certain foods are or are not available but because of our mood. On a sultry August day you would probably not want a robust meat sauce on your pasta. In mid-winter such a sauce would answer a need for warmth and comfort against the cold.

Geography is also an important determining factor as far as foods available to you. Regional specialties in a country as small as Italy are due to the existence of special local foods. Truffles in Alba, buckwheat in the Valtellina, olives in Gaeta, onions and peperoncino in Calabria, and superb peppers and eggplants in Sicily have all been ingredients in recipes in their own locales. If you live in Maryland, for example, try to develop recipes with crab. If you live in Vermont or Wisconsin, try making sauces using your local cheeses. In Arizona try a sauce of sage and jackrabbit. This last one is not as strange as it might seem, but a legitimate variation on the game sauces popular in Tuscany that are served on pappardelle.

If you live in a city, away from the land, your sauces will be different. They may not seem as "natural" as those using ingredients fresh from the garden, but you have access to so many types of food that your potential for experimentation is virtually unlimited. You just need to develop a sense about when and where a particular ingredient is good. Use fresh herbs when they appear. If the market has nice fresh fish or a particularly appealing vegetable, go with that item. Italians shop daily (sometimes twice a day) and eat whatever suits their eyes, mood, stomach, and pocketbook. This is a good practice since you will be rewarded with instant gratification by eating what has pleased you. The shopping should not seem arduous. View it as 10 minutes of relaxation during which you can indulge yourself.

If you live in the country, your selection of ingredients may be more limited, but then they are likely to be absolutely fresh and delicious. Cook them in a simpler way than your city cousins might, exploiting their natural properties of flavor, texture, and color.

Feel free to experiment, to improvise, and to fail. Mistakes are instructive. You will be a happy creative cook if you permit yourself to integrate the rhythms of your moods and tastes with the rhythms of the elements that surround you. When we speak of creativity and pasta cooking, your room to experiment, always bearing in mind what you already know and what you sense, is vast.

Some
Thoughts
on Eating Pasta

The delights pasta gives to the eye and mouth appeal to almost everyone. Children love pasta as much as adults do because, above all, eating pasta is fun. As pasta, an old, simple, and good food, has been declared fashionable, some people seem more interested in being chic than in enjoying themselves. As I have mentioned elsewhere, I favor classicism to faddishness.

It is very popular in the United States, for example, to eat salads of cold fettuccine or tortellini. If you think about it, though, the idea of doughy, chilled pasta swimming in mayonnaise or chokingly redolent of vinegar is pretty awful. Similarly, tortellini that are chilled have the delicate flavors of their fillings rendered tasteless. So don't feel constrained by dictates of fashion and style; some pasta preparations are simply inappropriate.

This said, there are still certain rules that you should try to follow in order to eat pasta correctly.

When it comes to eating utensils, you need only a fork. Researchers tend to agree that the fork was first used in Venice during the Middle Ages. This finding conveniently coincides with the belief that pasta was introduced to Italy in Venice by Marco Polo in the late thirteenth century. Although we know that pasta existed in Italy long before then, the idea that a clever Venetian would realize that noodles could be effectively gathered in the tines of a fork is quite plausible.

The fork is the basic implement for eating pasta. You can easily eat 1 or 2 ravioli, tortellini, or gnocchi at a time by stabbing them with a fork. Cutting cannelloni, lasagne, or agnolotti with the side of the fork and then gathering the food across the plane of the fork is ideal. And poking a few maccheroni or rigatoni with a fork is easy. But what about spaghetti?

Italians, even as children, are remarkably dexterous at twirling spaghetti around a fork. This is the method: After you have tossed the spaghetti, slide your fork into a few strands near the side of the bowl. Twirl the fork against the bowl until you have gathered a small, tight ball of spaghetti near the end of your fork. As you lift the fork from the bowl, the strands that are not tightly wrapped around the fork will drop away. Lift the fork into your mouth and slide the fork out, keeping the spaghetti in your mouth. One mistake many spaghetti twirlers make is that they load too much on their forks. Take a small mouthful only, or you will make a mess of your face and your clothing.

Many people twirl spaghetti against a tablespoon—they actually believe that this is the more "authentic" technique, but this is not so. If you feel you must, go right ahead. But the spoon is really unnecessary since you have the side of the bowl for this purpose. Certain sinners actually cut their spaghetti with a fork or knife. This should *never* be done. Spaghetti is supposed to be twirled on a fork so that it gathers up sauce in the process. By cutting and scooping it, you are separating the pasta from the sauce.

The best dish for eating pasta is a broad, flat bowl that curves slightly on the edges. This way you can toss pasta without its slipping over the sides. High, rounded bowls are acceptable for spaghetti and maccheroni but are awkward for pastas such as tortelloni, lasagne, and cannelloni.

It is generally a good idea to warm the bowl before adding the pasta to it. This will maintain the temperature of the pasta and sauce, and will aid in the melting of added butter or cheese.

As to grating cheese, this should be done directly onto the pasta just prior to eating it. Never add salt to a completed dish of pasta. It is generally inadvisable to grind on fresh pepper, which can overpower the dish, unless the recipe calls for it, such as spaghetti alla carbonara.

Another issue is the use of grated cheese on pasta dishes with fish. The general rule is that cheese does not belong, yet there are a couple of exceptions. Ravioli stuffed with fish often have a touch of cheese added to the stuffing. But if you have any doubts, do not add cheese.

People differ on how to serve pasta with shellfish. In Naples and all along the Italian shoreline, it is common to find spaghetti topped with baby clams or mussels in their shells. Diners remove the meat and toss away the shell. They sometimes stab the seafood and then twirl some pasta around it. This is extra work, but most Italians don't seem to mind. American cooks tend to remove the cooked seafood from the shells and prepare the sauces using only the meat. This also is fine, but you must be extra careful not to overcook the seafood, which can happen in a matter of seconds. Clams or mussels can be steamed in their sauce—adding the flavor of their juices—and removed as they open. The meat can then be removed from the shells and added to the dish just before serving.

Beyond these pointers, you are on your own. Don't be intimidated or worried about what you think you should be doing. Simply relax and enjoy your bowl of pasta.

*Suggestions
for the Novice
Pasta Cook*

The following is a list of recipes in this book arranged especially for those cooks who are new to pasta. They can start with the sauces and work through the easier and more complicated *pastasciutta* recipes before graduating to gnocchi, then *pasta fresca, pasta al forno* and, finally, *pasta ripiena*. In this way, those new to pasta can become experts.

Twenty Sauces

Tomato Sauces

Sugo di Pomodoro Semplice
Pummarola
Per Chi non Vuole Ingrassare

Sugo di Pomodoro alla Svelta
Sugo di Pomodoro e Menta
Salsa Cruda con la Mozzarella

Cream Sauces

Sugo di Pomodoro e Panna
**Salsa alla Panna per i
   Tortellini**

Salsa Besciamella
Besciamella Magra

Meat Sauces

Ragù Bolognese
Ragù di Agnello alla Sarda
Ragù di Maiale all'Umbra

**Ragù di Castrato alla
   Marchigiana**

Herb and Nut Sauces

Salsa alle Erbe
Pesto alla Genovese
Pesto al Frullatore

Salsa di Maggiorana
Salsa di Pistacchi
Tocco de Noxe

Pastasciutta

Twenty Easy Dishes Using Pastasciutta

Spaghetti al Cacio e Pepe
Spaghetti con Aglio e Olio
Spaghetti Senza Insalata
Spaghetti con le Rucole
Spaghetti al Filetto

**Maccheroni Calabresi alla
   Cipolla**
Pasta Corta alla Contadina
Chiama Vinu

Spaghetti alla Carbonara di
  Luciano Pavarotti
Rigatoni con Uova e Salsiccia
Penne all'Arrabbiata
Pasta con Caviale
Spaghetti Fraddiavolo
Spaghetti ai Funghi Freschi
Farfalle allo Zafferano
Maccheroni Tartufati

Linguine al Morino
Spaghetti con Ricotta e
  Cannella
Pasta al Mascarpone
Capellini "Bassano del
  Grappa"
  plus Tito Gobbi's "Luncheon
  Package Deal for One"

Profumi del Mare e della Terra

(Pastasciutta *Dishes Using the Best Food
from Italian Seas and Soils*)

Spaghetti Mare e Monti
Spaghetti with Green Prawns
Scampi in Busera
Vermicelli "Don Giovanni"
Bucatini all'Alioto
Spaghetti con le Cozze
Spaghetti alla Tarantina
Spaghetti coi Polipi alla
  Gigliese
Spaghetti coi Polipi
  all'Elbanese
Bigoli Neri in Salsa
Vermicelli a Surchio
Spaghetti con Tonno
  Acciugato
Conchiglie Estive di
  Magda Olivero

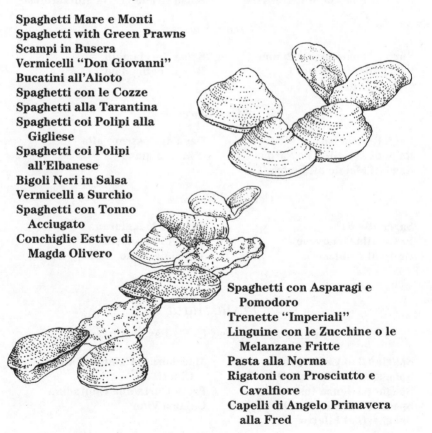

Spaghetti con Asparagi e
  Pomodoro
Trenette "Imperiali"
Linguine con le Zucchine o le
  Melanzane Fritte
Pasta alla Norma
Rigatoni con Prosciutto e
  Cavalfiore
Capelli di Angelo Primavera
  alla Fred

Maccheroni alla Ivana
Vermicelli alla Puttanesca
Bucatini all'Amatriciana
Rigatoni all'Amatriciana di
  Renata Scotto
Spaghetti Orlando e Rinaldo
Orecchiette alla Salsa di
  Verdura
Orecchiette alla Cicolella
Rigatoni al Gorgonzola
Farfalloni con Stracchino e
  Gorgonzola Dolce

Linguette Rustiche
Penne agli 8 "P"
Conchiglie al Dragoncello
Pasta con Avanzi di Pollo
Maccheroni al Sugo di Coniglio
  della "Primetta"
La Torchiata
Timballo di Mezzani
  all'Albanese
Pasticcio di Maccheroni
  Padovano

Gnocchi

Gnocchi di Patate alla Bava
Gnocchi Divino

Malloreddus
Chicche Verdi del Nonno

Pasta Fresca: Tagliatelle and Fettuccine and More

Tagliatelle al Prosciutto
Tagliatelle alla Scaligera
Tagliatelle alla Panoc
Tagliatelle Ernani
Pasta con Formaggio di Capra
Tagliatelle ai Quattro
  Formaggi
Tagliatelle ai Tre Formaggi
  Americani
Fettuccine Alfredo
Fettuccine Antonia e Arabella
Fettuccine al Radicchio
Fettuccine alla Papalina
Fettuccine di Trastevere
Pasta al Tricolore

Tagliolini con Asparagi e Panna
Tagliolini Enrico Caruso
Tagliolini Beniamino Gigli
Paglia e Fieno di Bologna
Pasta con Salmone e Fontina
Paglia e Fieno con Salmone
  Affumicato
Pappardelle all'Aretina
Pappardelle al Cinghiale
Pappardelle di Prato
Pappardelle alla Senese
Pizzoccheri alla Chiavennesca
Pizzoccheri di Teglio
Pizzoccheri di Tirano

Pasta al Forno (Baked Pasta)

Cannelloni con Provolone
Cannelloni alla Rigoletto
Cannelloni di Carne, Version 1
Cannelloni di Carne, Version 2
Cannelloni di Carne, Version 3
Cannelloni di Carne, Version 4
Lasagne Verdi alla Bolognese

Lasagne al Pesto
Lasagne alla Trapanese
Lasagne di Gubbio
Lasagne da Fornel
Sagne Chine
Pasta di Festa

Pasta Ripiena (Stuffed Pasta)

Ravioli di Ricotta
Ravioli ai Ciliegi
Ravioli di Melanzane
Ravioli con Sogliola
Agnolotti alla Piemontese,
  Version 1
Agnolotti alla Piemontese,
  Version 2
Agnolotti alla Piemontese,
  Version 3
Agnolotti alla Piemontese,
  Version 4
Agnolotti alla Savoiarda
Agnolotti al Tartufo Nero
Anolen alla Parmigiana
Marubini
Casonsei di Brescia
Culurzones
Sciatt
Pansôti

Casumziei Ampezzani
Türteln
Tortelli alla Piacentina
Tortelli di Patate
Tortelli di Zucca
Caramelle di Verdi
Tortellini alla Bolognese,
  Version 1
Tortellini alla Bolognese,
  Version 2
Tortellini alla Bolognese,
  Version 3
Cappelletti alla Romognola
Tortelloni della Vigilia
Tortelloni ai Quattro Formaggi
Balanzoni alla Delizia

Types of Pasta

Italy is known around the world as a nation of great style, creativity, and fantasy. It is a leader in every field of design, including clothing, automobiles, furniture, architecture, kitchen equipment, and so on. Therefore, you should not be surprised that there is an endless variety of shapes of pasta. Although there are pastas used throughout Italy, there are many more that were born in specific places and were designed to accompany local sauces.

Many names have disappeared. In Tuscany, cappelletti used to be called *nicchi*, but you only hear this usage in the remotest parts of the province. In Sicily many years ago there was a large variety of maccheroni similar to ziti and known as *Napoleoni*, in honor of Bonaparte. Around the same time, in parts of the Italian peninsula, a pasta similar to rigatoni was named *Cavour*, dedicated to one of the leading fighters for Italian national unity.

Keep in mind that particular pastas are suited to particular sauces. Long, thin spaghetti does not go well with rich meat sauces. These sauces need broader noodles such as tagliatelle or lasagne to embrace them, or curved or hollow noodles such as orecchiette, maccheroni, or penne that have spaces in which the meat can lodge itself. Conversely, thinner sauces such as those based on olive oil adhere to longer strands such as vermicelli, trenette, spaghetti, and capelli di angelo. In most cases, this book includes recommendations as to which sauce should be served with which pasta. *Pasta ripiena* suggests fresh pasta that has been filled and folded. What follows is a list of many of the most popular pastas currently used in Italy.

AGNOLOTTI: A stuffed pasta, similar to but larger than ravioli, popular in Piedmont and the Valle d'Aosta. The fillings vary from town to town, and the sauce is usually made of gravy from the meats used in the filling.

ANOLINI: Also known as *agnolini* in Mantua, *anvein* in Piacenza, and *anolen* in Parma. *Pasta ripiena* similar to tortellini.

BAVETTE: Flat or oval, these long Ligurian pasta strands are similar to *linguine* and are traditionally served with pesto.

BIGOLI: Also called *bigoi*. Homemade spaghetti produced in the 3 Veneto provinces and in Mantua. The longest of all pastas, they are served with sauces based on fish, onions, or tripe. The word probably comes from *bigato*, or worm, an apt description for these long noodles that wriggle as they are twirled on a fork or sucked into the mouth.

BUCATINI: The name used in Latium to describe the fat, hollow spaghetti (*buco* means hole) that is ideally suited for Salsa all'Amatriciana. Bucatini may be used for many of the sharp sauces used in central Italy.

CANNELLONI: Squares of fresh egg or spinach pasta wrapped around a filling and baked. Though they originated in northern Italy, probably in Piedmont, they are now prepared throughout Italy. Also see *crespelle* and *scripelle*. The word comes from cannello, which means welding torch or blow pipe. In Bologna they are traditionally called *borlenghi*, in Tuscany they are occasionally referred to as *ciaffagnoni*, and in areas near Rome they are known as *fregnacce*.

CAPELLI DI ANGELO: In English this means angel's hair. The thinnest of all fresh pastas, these fine strands are served in broth or *alla primavera*, with fresh vegetables. Also known as *capalvenere* (hair of Venus).

CAPPELLETTI: *Pasta ripiena* from Romagna; also found in Tuscany, Umbria, Emilia, and Lombardy. In Ferrara, as *cappellacci*, they are filled with pumpkin.

CAPPELLINI: Spaghetti-like strands of commercially made pasta, thinner than all but capelli di angelo.

CARAMELLE: *Pasta ripiena* from Emilia. Also known as *tortelli con la coda* or *turtei cu la cua* (stuffed pasta with a tail). These *paste ripiene* are twisted to look like wrapped candy.

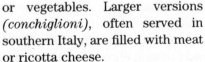

CASONSEI: Typical *pasta ripiena* of Brescia and Bergamo.

CASUMZIEI: Typical *pasta ripiena* of the Dolomite mountains. Also known as *casonziei*.

CHICCHE: The word comes from baby talk and means sweet or candy. This is also another word for gnocchi.

CONCHIGLIE: "Seashells" ideally suited for sauces containing meat or vegetables. Larger versions (*conchiglioni*), often served in southern Italy, are filled with meat or ricotta cheese.

CORZETTI: Typical Ligurian pasta shaped like a coin used in the Republic of Genoa.

CRESPELLE: Very thin crepes used in northern and central Italy to wrap fillings in a style similar to cannelloni. They are also occasionally used as substitutes for lasagne. Also see *scripelle*.

CULURZONES: Typical *pasta ripiena* of Sardinia.

DITALI: In English this means thimbles. They are popular in southern Italy served with meat or seafood sauces. *Ditalini* are smaller thimbles; in Sicily they are called *cannulicchi*.

FARFALLE: Butterfly-shaped pasta sometimes called bow ties. *Farfallette* are smaller farfalle; *farfalline* are smaller still. They are often served in broth. *Farfalloni* are large and frequently served with cream or tomato sauces.

FEDELINI OR **FIDELINI:** Spaghetti strands of pasta about as thick as capellini. The name comes either from the word *fedele* (faithful) or *filo* (thread or wire).

FETTUCCINE: A *fettuccia* is a tape or ribbon. These egg noodles are to Rome what tagliatelle are to Bologna, though they are not quite as wide.

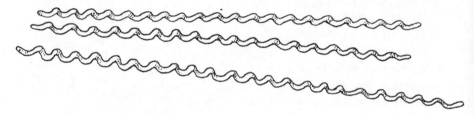

FUSILLI: Spiral-shaped pasta popular in southern Italy. They are frequently called *eliche* (helixes). Fusilli are called *turciniateddi e fusiddi* in Sicily, *ricci di donna* in Calabria, and *incannulate* in Apulia. Fusilli are suitable for rich creamy sauces with meat or vegetables.

GNOCCHI: Dumplings served in many versions throughout Italy. Usually made of potatoes or flour; sometimes flavored with vegetables such as spinach or pumpkin. *Gnocchetti* are small gnocchi.

LASAGNE: Long, broad rectangles of dough usually made with egg and perhaps spinach. They may be cut with a knife or a fluted pastry wheel. They are often baked with meat sauces and besciamella or served with cheese, vegetable, or herb sauces such as pesto. In some parts of Italy lasagne with fluted edges are called *lasagne ricce* or *reginelle*, which loosely translated means queen or belle (as in "of the ball"). Known as *lagana*, it was popular in ancient Rome.

LINGUE DI PASSERO: "Sparrow's tongues." Slightly thicker than linguine and broad as a sparrow's tongue.

LINGUETTE: Long, thin, flat pasta, thinner than linguine.

LINGUINE: Commercially produced strands of pasta that are flatter than spaghetti. Used for the same sauces as spaghetti.

LUMACHE: Pasta shaped like snails' shells. Similar in shape and application to conchiglie. *Lumachelle* are small lumache.

MACARONI: In English this suggests elbow-shaped pasta of different sizes. In Italian these are called maccheroni (see below). *Macaroni* in Italian comes from the Venetian dialect and referred centuries ago to gnocchi. The word is probably connected to macaroon.

MACCHERONI: Refers to a family of long, hollow noodles of varying sizes and thicknesses. Some, such as *penne*, are cut diagonally at their ends. Maccheroni may be either straight or elbow-shaped, ribbed or smooth, large or small. *Maccheroncini* are small maccheroni. The Italian *latino maccheronico* roughly translates as "pig Latin."

MACCHERONI ALLA CHITARRA: These "guitar-style" maccheroni are a specialty of the Abruzzi. Actually, they are shaped more like spaghetti than maccheroni. Maccheroni alla chitarra are made by forcing a thin sheet of pasta through a series of steel cords suspended tightly on a wooden utensil much as strings are strung on a guitar. Traditionally they are served with a dense sauce made of lamb and topped with grated pecorino cheese.

MALLOREDDUS: Typical gnocchi of Sardinia. They are made with saffron, and in parts of the island they are called *maccarrones caidos*.

MALTAGLIATI: Means "badly cut." In northern Italy these are usually pieces of pasta left over after making *pasta ripiena*. In the south they sometimes refer to penne. Northern maltagliati are usually served in vegetable soups. Cooks in Modena like to combine them with beans.

MARUBINI: Typical anolini of Cremona.

MEZZANI: Medium-thick maccheroni of varying lengths. Often used for baked dishes.

ORECCHIETTE: Ear-shaped pasta typical of Apulia. They are eaten all over southern Italy with meat, fish, or vegetables.

ORECCHIONI: These "large ears" are another name used in Romagna for cappelletti.

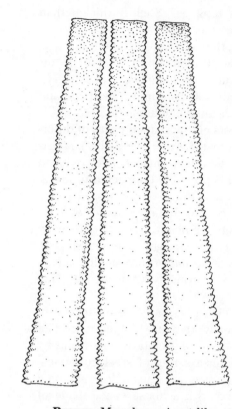

PAGLIA E FIENO: "Straw and hay." Green and white pasta, usually tagliolini, served with cream or tomato sauces.

PANSÔTI: Typical *pasta ripiena* of eastern Liguria. They are filled with wild greens and served with walnut sauce.

PAPPARDELLE: A broad noodle made of egg pasta and cut with a pastry wheel. These are especially popular in Tuscany where they are served with rich sauces of meat or game.

PASTINA: Refers to any. one of the many tiny pastas usually served in a rich broth with parmigiano. Among the many types are *stelline* (little stars), *perline* (little pearls), *ditalini* (little thimbles), *semi di mellone* (melon seeds), *anellini* (little rings), *margherite* (daisies), and *sorpresine* (little surprises).

PENNE: Maccheroni cut like quills or fountain pens. They come in various sizes, with or without ribs, and marry well with sauces of cream, meat, or vegetables.

PERCIATELLI: Hollow Sicilian spaghetti akin to Roman bucatini. The name comes from the Sicilian "pirciatu," which means it has a hole in it. They go well with vegetable and seafood sauces.

PIZZOCCHERI: These noodles from the Valtellina area of Lombardy, are made from a mixture of buckwheat and white flours, sometimes with a dash of brandy thrown in. They are served with rich local cheeses, cabbage, carrots, potatoes, and garlic.

QUADRUCCI OR QUADRETTI: Thick little squares of egg pasta usually served in beef broth.

RAVIOLI: These famous *paste ripiene* are of Genoese origin. The sauce you use depends upon what the ravioli are stuffed with.

RIGATONI: *Rigato* means with lines or ridges. These are among the largest of the maccheroni family and are ideal for meat sauces.

SCIATT: Typical *pasta ripiena* of the Valtellina. Stuffed with local cheese and briefly fried.

SCRIPELLE: Crepes popular in the Abruzzi. They usually have pepper in the batter and are fried in oil.

SEDANI: This is the plural of *sedano,* or celery. The Tuscans use this term for long, ribbed maccheroni that look like stalks of celery.

SPAGHETTI: The long, thin, cylindrical pasta that is one of the glories of the Neapolitan kitchen and probably the most famous of all pastas. The name comes from the word *spago,* meaning string or cord. Spaghetti are ideally suited to tomato sauces and sauces made with olive oil. *Spaghettini* are more delicate and go nicely with sauces made with small pieces of seafood. *Spaghettoni* are thicker and are a good match for salsa alla carbonara.

TAGLIATELLE: The name comes from the verb *tagliare,* to cut. Eminently Bolognese, they are served with meat sauce or prosciutto. Tagliatelle are made of egg pasta and are cut into noodles with a knife or straight blade. They may be made with spinach pasta as well.

TAGLIERINI: Fresh pasta cut much thinner than tagliatelle. In Piedmont they are called *tajarin.*

TAGLIOLINI: Another popular term for taglierini.

TONNARELLI: The Roman equivalent of maccheroni alla chitarra or spaghettoni.

TORTELLI: A popular *pasta ripiena* in Emilia and Lombardy, usually filled with cheese or vegetables.

TORTELLINI: The classic *pasta ripiena* of Bologna. These small, belly button-shaped creations are ideally matched with Bolognese ragù (meat sauce), cream sauce, or perhaps an herb sauce.

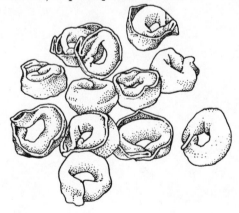

TORTELLONI: A larger version of tortellini. Usually filled with cheese.

TORTIGLIONI: Medium-length, spiral-shaped pasta well suited to meat sauces.

TRENETTE: Thin strands of pasta, like bavette or lingue di passero. They are popular in Liguria served with *pesto*.

TÜRTELN: Ravioli of the Dolomites. Filled with spinach, cabbage, or sauerkraut.

VERMICELLI: Another name, much used in Naples, for spaghetti. In English it means little worms.

ZITI: Neapolitan maccheroni similar to penne except cut in a straight line rather than at an angle. Ziti means grooms. *Maccheroni di zita* means the bride's maccheroni. Traditionally they were served in Naples as a first course at wedding feasts.

Recipes

INTERREGIONAL

Sughi di Pomodoro:
Sugo di Pomodoro Semplice   Pummarola
Per Chi Non Vuole Ingrassare   Sugo di Pomodoro alla Svelta
Sugo di Pomodoro e Menta   Salsa Cruda con la Mozzarella
Sugo di Pomodoro e Panna

Salsa alle Erbe · Spaghetti con Aglio e Olio ·
Spaghetti Senza Insalata · Rigatoni con Uova e Salsiccia ·
Pasta con Caviale · Spaghetti con Tonno Acciugato ·
Pasta con Formaggio di Capra · Tagliatelle ai Quattro Formaggi ·
Pasta con Salmone e Fontina ·
Paglia e Fieno con Salmone Affumicato ·
Cannelloni di Carne, Version 1 · Cannelloni di Carne, Version 2 ·
Cannelloni di Carne, Version 3 · Cannelloni di Carne, Version 4

Sughi di Pomodoro (Tomato Sauces)

When most people think of Italian cooking, and especially pasta, they see red; that is, they are convinced that everything Italian is covered with tomato sauce. As you will discover in this book, the great beauty of Italian cuisine is that it comes in so many colors and flavors. In fact, in looking over the history of food preparation in Italy, one finds that the tomato is a relative newcomer. It arrived after Spanish conquistadors brought it to Europe from Peru in the sixteenth century. Before that, pasta was cooked in meat broth or was sauced with cheeses, meats, and herbs. Many old recipes, such as those for *pappardelle sulla lepre* (hare sauce) and lasagne, used animal blood as a liquid before being replaced by the tomato. Though the tomato was written about in Italy during the 1550s, when it was called the *pomo d'oro* (golden apple), Italians did not really start eating them for another 200 years. Using the perspective of history, in a tradition of cooking that goes back thousands of years, the tomato can probably be considered an ingredient in Italian *cucina nuova*.

Yet the tomato has taken hold, and its influence, particularly in sauces for pasta, is enormous, especially in southern Italy. In Campania the wonderful San Marzano tomatoes grown there form the basis for the great Neapolitan sauces. When you make sauces at home using canned tomatoes, try to buy San Marzano-type tomatoes. They are juicy (not watery) and have delicious meat. Other imported tomatoes are seldom as good, and American canned tomatoes just don't compare. Try to buy canned tomatoes that are only that; avoid citric acid, preservatives, sugar, salt, and so forth. The tomatoes should be in their own liquid with perhaps a couple of basil leaves. That's it. You will find that in most cases the tomatoes are peeled *(pelati)* and have had the seeds removed. This is convenient because these are two processes you will therefore not have to perform. When you open the can, the tomatoes are ready to use.

I do not recall who once said that a person throwing an American tomato at an opera singer should be arrested for assault with a deadly weapon. Let me say first of all that I don't believe anything should be thrown at opera singers except kisses, but the point is well taken. Unfortunately, tomatoes grown in North America are prized more for their ability to travel than for being edible. Most are hard, mealy, and lacking in color, flavor, and personality. The only ones I would ever consider eating appear at local farms during the summer. They grow, ripen on the vine, are picked when mature, and should be eaten right away. For sauces you can use either the large fleshy beefsteak tomatoes or the smaller egg or plum tomatoes.

If you have access to good summer tomatoes and are skilled at putting up vegetables in mason jars, this is a good way to preserve the taste of summer for the colder seasons. You can remove the skins by immersing the tomato in boiling water for 30 seconds and then in cold water. When you remove it, you should be able to slip the skin right off. Cut the peeled tomato in half over a strainer so that you can save the juice while getting rid of the seeds. Conserve the tomatoes in their own liquid, adding a few leaves of fresh basil, which will liven up a *sugo di pomodoro* on a dreary winter day. Calculate about 3 pounds of tomatoes per quart. You can also put up tomato puree if you choose to. But before you attempt preserving of any sort, learn the correct and safest method.

If you make a tomato sauce but do not use all of it immediately, it can only be safely stored in a jar in the refrigerator for a couple of days. You will often find that a recipe calls for a little tomato sauce —especially if you are cooking for one—and you do not want to whip up a whole pot of fresh sauce. Nor do you wish to use an inferior commercial sauce from a can or jar that contains starch, extenders, gums, and all sorts of junk. How do you solve the problem? In Bologna I learned this trick: When I make a large batch of sauce, I use what I need and let the rest cool. I then put the sauce in ice trays and freeze them. If you try this, do not fill the ice tray all the way to the top since the liquid expands as it freezes. When the cubes are frozen, wrap each one individually in aluminum foil. In my ice tray each cube contains exactly 2 tablespoons of sauce. Measure your own and use it as a guide in cooking. If you plan to use more sauce at one time, put several cubes together in a plastic bag. If each cube is 2 tablespoons, 8 cubes will equal 1 cup of sauce. Remember that in freezing the sauce in this manner, it should just be tomato sauce and basic flavorings, without additional ingredients such as onions, meat, and so forth. If a food such as carrots or celery has disintegrated in the sauce after long cooking, then there is no problem.

A note about tomato paste: In Italy it is called *concentrato di pomodoro.* It is used sparingly to impart the rich flavor of tomato to a dish that calls for a bit of it. It also may be used to thicken or enliven sauces if the tomatoes you are using are not meaty or tasty enough. In Italy tomato paste is sold in cans or tubes. I use the convenient tubes, which I store in the refrigerator after opening.

What follows are a few recipes for tomato sauces. Some require cooking and can be eaten at any time of the year. The sauces calling for raw tomatoes should be made only when you have superb specimens of the genuine article.

Sugo di Pomodoro Semplice

Simple Tomato Sauce

This is the most basic sauce imaginable. You may use it to lend tomato flavor to other dishes or, if you have excellent tomatoes, to eat as a spaghetti sauce with a bit of grated cheese. Note that this sauce has no fats. An average portion contains about 35 calories.

6 SERVINGS

2 pounds fresh or canned tomatoes
  Pinch of salt (optional)

If you are using fresh tomatoes, peel and remove their seeds as indicated on pages 107–108. Pass the tomatoes through a sieve or strainer, or puree quickly in a blender. Add the salt and heat the tomatoes in a saucepan over a moderately high flame for 1 hour, stirring occasionally. The sauce should condense significantly. If you think it is too thin, add a bit of tomato paste after 30 minutes of cooking. This sauce may be served with spaghetti. In Bologna they add a little sweet butter and the sauce is called *burro e oro*. This, of course, also makes the sauce more fattening.

VARIATIONS: If you want the sauce to have any distinct flavor in addition to the tomatoes, other ingredients may be added when you start heating the pureed tomatoes. Try any one of the following: 2 cloves of garlic, crushed; 1 medium onion, minced; pinch of thyme; large pinch of oregano; bunch of fresh parsley, chopped; 2 bay leaves; 1 small peperoncino, minced; 2 anchovy fillets, mashed; pinch of sage; fresh basil leaves, whole or torn.

NOTE: If you want to enrich the flavor and substance of this sauce, add ¼ cup of olive oil as you start cooking the tomato puree.

Pummarola

Neapolitan Tomato Sauce

This is the classic, full-bodied, gutsy tomato sauce that makes one think of Naples. Accept no substitute, especially the so-called spaghetti sauces on supermarket shelves. Serve with vermicelli, spaghetti, or bucatini, and lots of grated cheese.

4 SERVINGS

1 pound fresh or canned
  tomatoes, drained
2 tablespoons sweet butter
1 tablespoon olive oil
1 small onion, minced
1 medium carrot, minced

1 stalk celery, minced
  Few sprigs of parsley, minced
2 cloves garlic, minced
  Few fresh basil leaves, wiped
  clean with a cloth
  Salt and fresh pepper to taste

Cut the tomatoes into quarters. Do not remove the skin or seeds. Heat the butter and oil in a pot and add the onion, carrot, celery, parsley, and garlic. When the onion turns slightly golden in color, add the tomatoes. (If you are using canned peeled tomatoes rather than fresh ones, add 2 teaspoons of tomato paste.) Stir with a wooden spoon for a few minutes. When the tomatoes start to fall apart, add the basil. Cover the pot and cook over a very low flame for 20 minutes. Add salt and fresh pepper to taste and cook uncovered for 10 minutes more or until the sauce is thick. Pass the sauce through a vegetable sieve into a serving bowl, to which you should add 1 pound of freshly cooked al dente pasta.

Per Chi non Vuole Ingrassare

For He Who Does Not Want to Get Fat

This recipe was given to me by Ruggero Raimondi, the marvelous bass-baritone from Bologna. Signor Raimondi is lean and elegant, so this must be part of the reason why. He has sung in major opera houses around the world in many roles, including the great Verdi parts and Rossini's Barber of Seville. *He had the title role in Joseph Losey's film version of* Don Giovanni, *featuring Kiri Te Kanawa,*

Teresa Berganza, Edda Moser, and Jose van Dam. He is Escamillo
in Francesco Rosi's Carmen *film and has begun an acting career in*
nonmusical cinema as well.

2 SERVINGS

2 large ripe tomatoes	Salt and fresh pepper to taste
½ onion	1 tablespoon extra-virgin olive
1 clove garlic	oil

Put the tomatoes, onion, and garlic in a mortar and crush until a
sauce is formed. If you do not have a mortar and pestle, you may
use a blender or food processor briefly on high speed; but the dish
is better made by hand, and the work will help you burn calories.
Add salt and pepper and stir in the oil. This sauce can be served over
any dried pasta (that is, spaghetti or maccheroni) that has been
cooked al dente. Do not, however, heat the sauce.

VARIATIONS: You might want to add fresh herbs such as basil or
rosemary.

🐌 WINE: Any delicate wine, white or red, will do. Young Chianti,
slightly chilled, is especially nice.

Sugo di Pomodoro alla Svelta
Very Fast Tomato Sauce for Pasta

Alla svelta *does not imply svelte or thin—it means in a hurry. I*
learned this procedure in fast-paced Milan, where people might
only take 60 or 90 minutes for lunch instead of the 2 or 3 hours
taken by the Bolognesi and the Romans. Though I wouldn't use this
sauce in elaborate preparations such as lasagne, it is fine for mak-
ing a quick one-course meal of pasta, salad, and a glass of wine.
Incidentally, I would never *think of using this sauce when good*
fresh tomatoes are at hand, since even quality tomato paste does
not measure up to the real thing. Therefore, I usually make this
sauce in the winter.

1 SERVING

2 tablespoons sweet butter	White wine or water
1 teaspoon olive oil	1–2 teaspoons tomato paste to
1 clove garlic, crushed	taste (see note on tomato
Freshly ground pepper	paste on page 293)

Heat 1 tablespoon of butter and the oil in a small saucepan, making sure the butter does not burn. Add the garlic and give the pan a couple of good shakes. Add pepper to taste. Pour in a small amount of wine or water (at most ¼ cup; less if you ultimately want a thicker sauce) and simmer for 30 seconds. Add tomato paste in the desired amount and stir. You should produce a sauce that is thick and flavored though not overpowered by the tomato paste. If the sauce is too thick, add more wine or water. If it is too thin, add a bit more tomato paste. I usually find that 3 squirts from a tube of tomato paste or ¾ teaspoon from a can is sufficient. Adjust the ratio to your own taste. Once the sauce is ready, melt in the other tablespoon of butter and serve on top of freshly cooked pasta with lots of grated cheese.

VARIATIONS: I have given you the most basic recipe. I improvise all the time, usually adding leftovers I find in my refrigerator. The most frequent addition is chopped onion, which I put in at the same time as the garlic. If I have fresh mushrooms, I chop them and cook them with the garlic. I frequently add leftover canned or frozen peas at the same time as the tomato paste. Also, I use the pea liquid instead of water. A bay leaf or fresh basil will always enliven the sauce. Minced celery, added to the sauce at the garlic stage, will give a slight saltiness, if that is your pleasure. Friends of mine use oregano in this sauce, but I do not, since I think that herb needs more time to impart its special flavor. Another good addition to this sauce would be slivered spicy salami (Milanese, Genovese, Calabrese, and so forth) which would go into the pot right after the garlic. As for cheese to grate on top, any fine hard Italian grating cheese will do. I often go for pecorino romano, Asiago, or even one of the Italian grating cheeses that contains whole peppercorns that grate along with the cheese. Grana is a fine choice also, though a bit too elegant here for my taste. I prefer something gutsier. In general I would recommend store-bought dry pasta for this sauce instead of fresh pasta, only because if you labor to produce fresh pasta, you owe it to yourself to make a very special sauce.

Sugo di Pomodoro e Menta

Tomato Sauce with Mint

An easy, delicious sauce if you have fresh mint.

2 SERVINGS

1 clove garlic
2 mint sprigs
8 ounces tomatoes, peeled and
  seeded

8 ounces spaghetti or
  vermicelli
1 teaspoon olive oil

Set a large pot of cold water to boil. Mince the garlic and 1 sprig of mint. Heat the tomatoes in a saucepan, gently breaking them up with a fork or wooden spoon. Add the garlic and mint. Cook for 5 minutes. At this point the water should be boiling. Toss in a pinch of salt, let come to boil again, and then start cooking the pasta. Keep stirring the sauce. When the pasta is al dente, drain well and transfer to a serving dish containing a teaspoon of olive oil. Tear the leaves off the other sprig of mint and put on the pasta. Add the sauce, toss well, and serve.

❧ WINE: Lacryma Christi white.

Salsa Cruda con la Mozzarella

Raw Tomato Sauce with Mozzarella

This recipe was given to me by Pier Luigi Pizzi, whose excellent recipe for Tortelli di Zucca appears on page 159. The amounts listed here are for 1 person, but it is easy to multiply by the number of people you are feeding. You may use spaghetti, maccheroni, or any kind of pasta of decent size.

1 SERVING

Several basil leaves
2 tablespoons olive oil
1 large tomato or 2 plum
  tomatoes
  Pinch of salt
  Generous sprinkling of
  oregano

2 tablespoons mozzarella, cut
  into ½-inch cubes
4 ounces spaghetti or other
  dried pasta

Set a large pot of cold water to boil.

In the meantime, clean the basil leaves if necessary by wiping with a clean cloth. Do not wash them.

Put the olive oil in a large bowl. Briefly immerse the tomato in the boiling water, using a ladle or slotted spoon. Remove and then slip off the skin. Put the tomato in the bowl and break it up with a fork. Add the salt, oregano, basil, and mozzarella. Toss briefly to combine the ingredients and then allow to sit for 15–20 minutes.

About 5 minutes before you are ready to eat, toss a pinch of salt into the boiling water, let come to boil again, add the pasta and cook until it is al dente. Drain well and transfer to the bowl with the sauce. Toss well so that the mozzarella melts from the heat of the pasta. Serve immediately.

🍷 WINE: Any fresh young wine, red or white. I might drink a Bardolino, slightly chilled.

Sugo di Pomodoro e Panna

Tomato and Cream Sauce

This sauce is suited to richer pastas such as tortelloni or cappelletti, as well as for use in certain baked pastas that call for tomato sauce. Cannelloni or lasagne with this sauce will become even richer, which might suit your taste.

MAKES 5 CUPS

4 cups tomato sauce (page 109)
1 cup heavy cream

Make Sugo di Pomodoro Semplice or any of the tomato sauces in this book that use tomatoes, herbs, onions, carrots, and celery. Note 2 important differences: Do not use garlic or peperoncino, and where other recipes call for olive oil, substitute an equal amount of sweet butter. Once the sauce is ready, add the cream and continue heating in a saucepan for 1–2 minutes, stirring continuously.

You do not have to bypass this recipe if you are dealing with smaller amounts. Simply maintain a ratio of 4 to 1. For example, for 6 tablespoons of tomato sauce, add 1½ tablespoons of cream.

When serving this sauce on freshly cooked pasta, you might want to add a pat of sweet butter. Then the sauce is called *burro e oro* (butter and gold).

Salsa alle Erbe

Herb Sauce for Pasta

This sauce goes well with meat-filled tortellini, cheese-filled tortelloni, or tagliatelle. Do not even attempt Salsa alla Erbe if fresh herbs are not available.

4 SERVINGS

4 ounces (1 stick) sweet butter
1 tablespoon rosemary
1 tablespoon minced sage
1½ tablespoons minced parsley

1½ tablespoons chopped basil
1 cup heavy cream
Freshly ground pepper

Start cooking the pasta. Five minutes before the pasta is al dente, melt the butter in a large saucepan. Add the herbs and let them flavor the butter for 3 minutes over a very low flame. Then pour in ⅓ cup of the cream and let the sauce heat gently over the flame. By now the pasta should be done. Drain it and add it to the sauce. Combine well and then add the rest of the cream. Briefly turn up the flame so the whole mixture is thoroughly heated but do not boil. Transfer to a serving dish, grind on some pepper, and serve. Grated cheese is not required.

❧ WINE: Depending on the pasta you make, you will want either white or red. Do not use any wine that will overpower the delicate flavors of the herbs. An Orvieto or a young Chianti would go well.

Spaghetti con Aglio e Olio

Spaghetti with Garlic and Oil

This is one of the simplest, most inexpensive, and most popular of pasta dishes in Italy. It is eaten throughout the country, and several regions claim it as their own. This is likely since any area in Italy that produces olive oil and garlic could have invented this recipe, and those two ingredients are ubiquitous. In Rome the dish is called spaghetti alla prestinara. *This goes back to the vulgarized Latin word* prestinarious, *meaning baker. Perhaps a woman baker (*prestinara *is feminine) invented this dish long ago in Rome. This* *recipe is for a very copious serving, but people seem to like to eat a great deal of this spaghetti while drinking lots of fresh young white wine.*

1 SERVING

⅓ pound spaghetti
¼ cup olive oil
1 clove garlic, cut in half
¼ hot chili pepper pod (more if your taste can stand it)

3 parsley sprigs, finely chopped
Pepper to taste

For cooking the pasta, bring a large pot (at least 6 quarts) of cold water to a boil. Lightly salt. When water comes to a boil again, add the spaghetti and cook until *al dente.* While the spaghetti is cooking, heat the oil and add the garlic, chili pepper, and parsley. As soon as the garlic begins to turn brown, remove it along with the chili pepper. When the spaghetti is ready, drain and put it in a bowl. Pour the oil over the pasta, grind on fresh pepper to taste, toss well, and eat.

VARIATIONS: There is a lot of room for variety in this dish, but the variety comes mostly in answer to one question: How hot do you want it? The above recipe is the least hot possible, though it still has zing. As I traveled further south in Italy, I often found cooks who didn't remove the garlic and chili pepper. If left in, it is better that the garlic be crushed and the chili pepper minced. Remember, do not burn the garlic—it will turn bitter. You can always make the dish hotter by using more garlic, chili pepper, and black pepper. A variation I once sampled in Assisi is worth mentioning. The cooks of Umbria seem to fancy ginger, and this particular chef put some in his Spaghetti con Aglio e Olio. He prepared the dish as above, except that a piece of ginger was substituted for the chili pepper. If you try this version, a piece of peeled fresh ginger about ½ inch long will do the job. I have even made this dish using a dash of ground ginger when a whole piece was not available.

🍇 WINE: Roman white or Orvieto.

Spaghetti Senza Insalata

Spaghetti with Oil, Lemon, and Garlic

I refer to this dish as "spaghetti without salad" because the sauce is actually a simple salad dressing. There are no greens in sight, though you may change that if you consult the variations listed below. This dish is fast, easy, and delicious. Use the best oil you can find.

1 SERVING

4 ounces spaghetti
3 tablespoons extra-virgin olive oil
Juice of ½ lemon

1 grinding of fresh pepper
1 small clove garlic, cut in slivers

Set a large pot of fresh water to boil. When it reaches a boil, toss in a pinch of salt. Wait 1 minute, then add the spaghetti.

While the pasta is cooking, prepare the other ingredients. When the pasta is al dente, drain thoroughly and transfer to a bowl. Pour on the oil with one hand as you squeeze or pour the lemon juice with the other. Grind in the pepper, sprinkle on the garlic slivers, toss well, and serve.

VARIATIONS: If you have spinach spaghetti, now available in stores, this adds color and flavor, and reduces the number of calories in the dish. Do not use pasta that is too thin—it will swim in the sauce. If you want to go further on the salad dressing theme, you may add a ½ teaspoon of Dijon mustard to the lemon juice before pouring it on the pasta; make sure the mustard and lemon juice are thoroughly combined. If you have a few cherry tomatoes, wash and slice them in half, making sure the liquid does not spill out, and add with the garlic.

🍷 WINE: Any fresh young wine, such as Chianti, Frascati, Merlot, or Bianco di Custoza.

Rigatoni con Uova e Salsiccia

Rigatoni with Egg and Sausage

This is an easy dish, but it does require careful attention. The sausage should not burn, and the eggs should not get too thick when heated. Rigatoni con Uova e Salsiccia is healthy and restorative. Served with a salad it makes a complete meal. It is also a good foil for drinking lots of wine.

1½ tablespoons olive oil	1 egg
8 ounces fresh lean sausage, skinned and crumbled	1 egg yolk Salt and pepper to taste
¼ cup red or white wine	1 tablespoon milk
8 ounces rigatoni	2 tablespoons grated cheese

Set a large pot of water to boil.

In the meantime, heat the oil for 30 seconds in a medium-sized pot with a handle. Add the sausage and continue cooking for 15 seconds. Pour in the wine, cover, and heat until the sausage is completely cooked, stirring occasionally.

When the water in the large pot is boiling, lightly salt. When it returns to boil, add the rigatoni and cook until al dente.

While the sausage and rigatoni are cooking, beat the egg and the egg yolk in a bowl and add the salt, pepper, milk, and cheese, beating the mixture only until thoroughly combined.

When the pasta is done, drain well. By this time the sausage should be ready. Working quickly and carefully, add the rigatoni to the sausage and toss briefly. Then, in one motion, lift the pot from the flame with one hand while pouring in the egg mixture with the other. Put down the egg bowl and take a fork or spoon. Toss the ingredients in the pot and move toward the bowls you will eat from. Once it appears that the egg is starting to stiffen, serve out the rigatoni immediately. Have additional grated cheese available.

VARIATIONS: There is much room for variation and experimentation in this dish. It depends on the ingredients available to you. I once ate this dish in Domodossola, on the Swiss border, with sausage made of chamois. In Tuscany they might use sausage made of wild boar. If you live in the northern United States, you might find sausage made of venison during hunting season. Experiment as much as possible. The same thing goes for the cheese. Different hard grating cheeses will yield different flavors: try parmigiano, pecorino, Asiago, Toscanello, Ragusano, caciocavallo, canestrato, and so forth. I once made a Milanese version of this dish: luganega sausage with softened Gorgonzola cheese—different but wonderful.

ə WINE: Try to match the region of origin to that of the cheese. Any young, eminent, drinkable wine will do.

Pasta con Caviale

Pasta with Caviar

I am not certain where in Italy this recipe originated. It is one of those delicious dishes found throughout the peninsula. If I were to guess, I would say that it began somewhere between Ferrara and the place where the Po River empties into the Adriatic. The Po is filled with excellent sturgeon that yield fine caviar. In the Middle Ages, Jewish fishermen in Ferrara were the only people who ate caviar. Only later did all Italians develop a taste for it. This recipe was given to me by Giovanna Montgomery, who is half Tuscan, half Venetian, very worldly, and utterly charming. Giovanna does special projects and documentaries for the New York office of RAI, the Italian state television network.

2 SERVINGS

3 tablespoons sweet butter   1 ounce fresh caviar
¼ cup heavy cream
8 ounces spaghettini or
  tagliolini

Set a large pot of cold water to boil. When the water reaches a full boil toss in a pinch of salt.

In a saucepan, melt the butter over low heat until foamy and add the cream. At this point start cooking the pasta. When the cream and butter are well blended, *add the caviar* and continue to stir gently. When the pasta is al dente, drain and transfer to a warm dish. Add the sauce, toss well, and serve.

VARIATION: Grate a tiny amount of onion into the butter as you melt it.

NOTE: It is not necessary to use the most expensive caviar in order for this dish to succeed.

⁊ WINE: Dry Champagne or Spumante. You may also drink vodka or a very dry white wine such as Verdicchio.

Spaghetti con Tonno Acciugato
Spaghetti with Tuna and Anchovies

This dish is popular throughout Italy, and every household has its own version. This one is from the Caviglia family of Rome, whose son Massimo is a good friend. My own variations follow.

4 SERVINGS

½ cup olive oil
1 clove garlic, minced
1½ ounces salted anchovy fillets, rinsed, and chopped in pieces
2 pounds tomatoes, peeled and seeded (or canned)
Freshly ground pepper to taste
1 pound spaghetti
7 ounces tuna, chopped in small pieces
1 tablespoon minced parsley

Put the oil in a pot and heat it over a medium flame. Add the garlic. When it turns a light golden color, put in the pieces of anchovy. A moment later, add the tomatoes and pepper, and cook for 30 minutes, stirring occasionally.

About 5 minutes before the sauce mixture is ready, start cooking the spaghetti in lightly salted boiling water. At the same time add the tuna to the tomatoes.

When the spaghetti are al dente, drain thoroughly and top with the tuna sauce. Sprinkle on the parsley and serve.

VARIATIONS: You may add ½ teaspoon of capers and 3 tablespoons of pitted black or green olives. Or try what I did when I had half a yellow pepper. I cut it into strips and added them to the boiling pasta water 30 seconds before draining. The sweetness and crunch added something special to this dish. A green pepper might also work. In Livorno a pinch of ginger is often added with the tomatoes.

&◆ WINE: Frascati or Bianco dei Colli Albani.

Pasta con Formaggio di Capra

Pasta with Goat Cheese

Here is an example of a dish that may or may not be Italian in origin, though it is popular in Italy, France, and some American homes. I prepare this recipe using smooth young French cheese rather than sharper aged cheese. There is Italian goat cheese similar to the French type I use, but it is not easy to come by in America.

1 SERVING

½ cup light or heavy cream (your choice)
2–3 ounces goat cheese, rind removed
Pepper to taste

4 ounces pasta (tagliatelle or some other fresh egg pasta are recommended)
3 tablespoons finely chopped fresh basil or parsley

For cooking the pasta, bring a large pot (at least 6 quarts) of cold water to a boil. Lightly salt, and let it come to a boil again. In a saucepan mix the cream, crumbled goat cheese, and pepper over a medium flame for 8–10 minutes, stirring gently with a wooden spoon to prevent sticking. Time the cooking of the pasta to coincide with the preparation of the sauce (dry pasta will take longer to cook than fresh pasta). When the pasta is ready, drain very well, and put in a bowl. Pour on the sauce, add the basil, toss well, and eat.

VARIATIONS: This dish can have an infinite number of variations because there are so many different types of goat cheese. I use fresh young cheese because I like how it tastes with basil. You may prefer a more distinctive cheese as the base of your sauce. If a sharper cheese is used, you might opt to leave out the herbs.

NOTE: I have had this dish with and without grated grana. It is good either way.

ᴥ WINE: I once read that sauternes go well with Roquefort cheese, so I tried a glass with this dish and liked it. But Sauterne is just too costly to have all the time. Since then, I have tried several German whites and enjoyed them with Pasta con Formaggio di Capra, but finally I settled on an Italian wine: Orvieto Abboccato. Be sure it says *abboccato* (loosely translated: "It takes to the mouth well") and not *secco* (dry), which I prefer with fish and seafood.

Tagliatelle ai Quattro Formaggi

Tagliatelle with Four Cheeses

Here is a dish which, by its very nature, is ideally suited for experimentation. Essentially its sauce is composed of 4 cheeses. The recipe I list below is the classic, but you can combine any cheeses you like. Just follow your instinct. I find, for example, that veined cheeses are not successful in this dish. Although single portions can easily be made by halving the ingredients, I am providng a recipe for 2 servings since I like this recipe for gastronomic tête-à-têtes.

2 SERVINGS

8 ounces tagliatelle (tagliolini or rigatoni will also do)
⅓ cup light cream
¼ cup grated Emmenthal (Swiss) cheese
¼ cup grated Edam or Gouda cheese

⅓ cup grated mozzarella (see note about this cheese on page 286)
⅓ cup freshly grated grana
Pepper

For cooking the pasta, bring a large pot (at least 6 quarts) of cold water to a boil. Toss in a pinch of salt and bring to a boil again. If you are using dry pasta, begin to cook it now. If you are using fresh pasta, try to time things so that the pasta and sauce are ready at the same moment.

Put the cream in a saucepan or double boiler over a low flame. Add all of the first 3 cheeses and half of the grana little by little, stirring the mixture gently with a wooden spoon as you do. Reserve the remaining grana. Continue to simmer and stir over a very low flame. Once the mixture is smooth, add freshly ground pepper to taste. When the pasta is ready, drain quickly and add to the cheese sauce. Mix quickly until the sauce coats the pasta well. Serve and top with the remaining grana.

VARIATIONS: There are many cheeses you can use in this dish. My own preference runs to balancing sharp and mild cheeses, and I almost always make grana one of them. Combinations I like include: Taleggio, Fontina, Emmenthal, grana; provolone, pecorino, mozzarella, grana; pecorino, Bel Paese, Gouda, grana; caciocavallo, mozzarella, pecorino, grana; Asiago, Emmenthal, Gouda, grana.

🏖 WINE: Rich wine goes well with rich food. A Barolo or a Sassella would make a good choice, as would an older Chianti Classico.

Pasta con Salmone e Fontina

Pasta with Salmon and Fontina Cheese

This recipe was given to me by Giulietta Simionato, the great mezzo-soprano from Forlì, in Romagna. Madame Simionato has recorded many of her finest roles, including Amneris in Aida, *Ulrica in* Un Ballo in Maschera, *Azucena in* Il Trovatore, *Rosina in* Il Barbiere di Siviglia, *and as* La Cenerentola. *I also love her rendition of "Anything You Can Do" from* Annie Get Your Gun, *recorded with Ettore Bastianini and accompanied by Herbert von Karajan and the Vienna Philharmonic!*

In this dish, unlike in Paglia e Fieno con Salmone Affumicato (page 124), I recommend using poached fresh salmon or well drained canned salmon which would impart a more distinctive flavor. For the pasta, I recommend paglia e fieno (page 102), tagliatelle (page 103), or large maccheroni.

2 SERVINGS

8 ounces pasta, homemade or store-bought (see above)
⅓ cup heavy cream
4 ounces cooked salmon, cubed or in rather large pieces (see above)

Pepper to taste
4 ounces Fontina, diced

Set a large pot of cold water to boil. When it reaches a full boil, toss in a pinch of salt, and when the water returns to a boil, start cooking the pasta. In the meantime, in a saucepan heat the cream, salmon, and pepper for a few minutes.

When the pasta is al dente, drain well and return to its pot. Immediately toss on the cubes of Fontina and pour on the cream sauce. Heat thoroughly for a few moments, tossing so that the Fontina melts into creamy strands. Serve immediately.

🏖 WINE: A good red might be Freisa, a rosé could be Chiaretto del Garda and, among the whites, a Gavi or Bianco della Valtellina would be excellent.

Paglia e Fieno con Salmone Affumicato

Paglia e Fieno with Smoked Salmon

*Another good preparation using fresh green and white tagliolini.
Of course, either green or white pasta alone also is fine.*

1 SERVING

4 ounces paglia e fieno, (page
     102), fresh or store-bought
1 tablespoon sweet butter
2 ounces smoked salmon, cut in
     2-inch strips

¼ cup heavy cream
   Pepper
1 tablespoon freshly grated
     parmigiano

Set a large pot of water to boil. When it comes to a full boil, toss in
a pinch of salt. Start cooking the pasta when water returns to a boil,
and prepare the sauce.

Melt the butter in a saucepan over a low flame. Do not let it brown.
Add the salmon and give the pan a good shake. Pour in the cream
and grate in a pinch of pepper. Continue to heat the sauce gently—
do not let it boil—stirring with a wooden spoon.

When the pasta is al dente, drain thoroughly and add to the sauce
along with the parmigiano. Toss quickly and serve immediately.

VARIATION: I once added a *dot* of tomato paste along with the cream.
It gave the sauce color and a touch of sweetness. Be very sparing.

& WINE: Perhaps a dry Spumante or Prosecco. A pinot grigio from
the Friuli is another good selection.

Cannelloni di Carne

Meat-filled Cannelloni

*The following is a basic version, but I also recommend trying the
alternate fillings that follow. After that, use your imagination in
filling these cannelloni.*

4–6 SERVINGS

Sfoglia
3½ cups unbleached flour
  4 eggs

VERSION 1
Ripieno

2 ounces (½ stick) sweet butter	4 ounces fresh mushrooms, sliced
1 clove garlic (optional)	½ cup dry white wine
4 ounces ground pork	3 tablespoons minced fresh parsley
8 ounces ground veal	
4 ounces ground beef	2 cups tomato cream sauce (page 114)
8 ounces chicken breast, chopped finely	1 cup freshly grated parmigiano
Salt and pepper to taste	

Prepare the dough for the *sfoglia* as indicated on pages 52–58. Wrap it in a towel or cloth and set aside in a draft-free spot.

Melt the butter and add the garlic if you are using it. A moment later add the pork and sauté for a few minutes. Add the veal, beef, chicken, salt, pepper, and mushrooms. Sauté for 5 minutes. Pour in the wine and let it evaporate. Continue cooking another 10 minutes or until the meat is well cooked.

While the meat is cooking, set a large pot of water to boil. When it reaches a boil, toss in a pinch of salt.

Roll out the dough to about ¼ inch thickness. Cut the *sfoglia* into 12 squares about 4–5 inches square.

When the meat is cooked, drain any liquid from the pan. Stir in the parsley.

Boil the squares of *sfoglia* 3 at a time until half cooked. Remove them carefully from the pot and dry on a towel. Continue until all the squares are done. Place a large spoonful or 2 of *ripieno* lengthwise in the center of each square. Distribute any leftover *ripieno* evenly among the squares. Roll each square over loosely to form the cannelloni.

Place the cannelloni in a large buttered baking dish next to one another but not touching.

Pour the tomato cream sauce over the cannelloni and dust the top with the parmigiano. Bake in a preheated 375°F oven for 15–20 minutes.

VERSION 2

1 clove garlic, minced	4 ounces mushrooms, sliced
1 small onion, minced	½ cup dry white wine
2 ounces (½ stick) sweet butter	3 tablespoons fresh parsley
1 pound ground lamb	2 cups tomato sauce
8 ounces ground veal	1 cup freshly grated pecorino
Salt and pepper to taste	

In making the *sfoglia* and forming the cannelloni, proceed as in Version 1.

In preparing the *ripieno*, first sauté the garlic and onion in the butter, then add the lamb and veal at the same time. (Pecorino is used instead of parmigiano).

VERSION 3

2 ounces (½ stick) sweet butter	Salt and pepper to taste
8 ounces spicy sausage, skinned and crumbled	4 ounces mushrooms, sliced
	½ cup dry white wine
8 ounces chicken breast, minced	3 tablespoons fresh parsley
	2 cups tomato sauce
8 ounces ground veal	1 cup freshly grated parmigiano

In making the *sfoglia* and forming the cannelloni, proceed as in Version 1.

In making the *ripieno*, cook the sausage alone for 3 minutes before adding the chicken, veal, and mushrooms.

VERSION 4

2 ounces (½ stick) sweet butter	½ cup dry white wine
8 ounces turkey breast, minced	Pinch of sage
8 ounces *mortadella*, minced	2 cups tomato cream sauce (page 114)
8 ounces chicken livers	
4 ounces mushrooms	1 cup freshly grated parmigiano
Salt and pepper to taste	

In making the *sfoglia* and preparing the cannelloni, proceed as in Version 1.

To make the *ripieno*, melt the butter and cook the turkey and *mortadella* for 5 minutes. Add the chicken livers, mushrooms, salt, and pepper. Three minutes later add the wine. When it evaporates add the sage and continue cooking until the livers are done. You may chop the livers loosely with a fork.

VARIATION: You may make the dish richer and more flavorful by putting a thin slice of Fontina, mozzarella, or Bel Paese cheese on each square before adding the *ripieno*.

➛ WINE: Any medium-bodied or full-bodied red. Try Chianti, Valpolicella, Inferno, Merlot, Rosso Conero, Barbera, or Montepulciano d'Abruzzo.

THE THREE VENETI:
Venezia Euganea, Friuli-Venezia Giulia, and the Trentino-Alto Adige

**Spaghetti con Ricotta e Cannella · Tagliatelle alla Scaligera ·
Tagliolini con Asparagi e Panna ·
Capellini "Bassano del Grappa" ·
Tito Gobbi's "Luncheon Package Deal for One" ·
Scampi in Busera ·
Bigoli Neri in Salsa · La Torchiata ·
Pasticcio di Maccheroni Padovano · Lasagne da Fornel ·
Casumziei Ampezzani · Türteln**

Spaghetti con Ricotta e Cannella

Spaghetti with Ricotta and Cinnamon

*When Venice was the world's largest spice market, about 6 centuries
ago, its cuisine reflected the desire of its citizens to try exotic new
flavors. Cinnamon became very popular, and it still turns up occasionally in the foods of the Veneto. Other major Italian port cities
—especially Palermo—have dishes that call for cinnamon. Actually, I ate this dish in Moena, a ski resort high in the Dolomite
mountains north of Venice.*

1 SERVING

4 ounces spaghetti	¼ teaspoon sugar
4 ounces fresh unsalted ricotta cheese	½ teaspoon cinnamon

Set a large pot of water to boil. When boiling, toss in a pinch of salt. Start cooking the spaghetti when the water boils again.

In the meantime, put the cheese, sugar, and cinnamon in a dish and add 1½ teaspoons of hot water from the spaghetti pot. Stir so that the cheese becomes creamier and the sugar and cinnamon are fully incorporated. When the pasta is al dente, drain well, put on top of the cheese sauce, and toss thoroughly. I was offered grated parmigiano but decided not to use it. The choice is yours.

ಿ WINE: Tocai del Friuli.

Tagliatelle alla Scaligera

Tagliatelle with Prosciutto, Peas, and Wild Mushrooms

Although this combination is found throughout Italy, I have particularly enjoyed it in trattorias and locandas in and around Verona in the early spring. Verona has been an important commercial crossroads since Roman times when the city's famous arena was built. The arena is 500 feet long, 420 feet wide, and 100 feet high, and today is the home of one of Europe's most important opera festivals. The story of 2 of Verona's most famous citizens, Romeo and Juliet, became the basis for Shakespeare's famous play, of course, but also for operas by Bellini (I Capuleti e i Montecchi), *Berlioz, Gounod, and Zandonai and for a wonderful ballet score by Prokofiev.*

The Scaligeri were the great Veronese princes in the thirteenth and fourteenth centuries when the town was at its most glorious. Verona fell under Milanese control from 1387 to 1405 before being taken over by Venice, which ruled Verona for 400 years. The city produced 2 important figures in music history. Gaetano Rossi (1774–1855) wrote the librettos for Rossini's La Cambiale di Matrimonio, La Scala di Seta, Semiramide, *and* Tancredi *and Donizetti's* Linda di Chamounix. *Antonio Salieri (1750–1825) was born in Legnago in the province of Verona. Thanks to Peter Shaffer's great play,* Amadeus, *he is known nowadays as the jealous man who possibly poisoned Mozart. Yet Salieri was also a major musical figure in his time. His opera,* L'Europa Riconosciuta, *was written for the inauguration of Milan's La Scala in 1778. He later became*

Kappelmeister *of Vienna's imperial court and took on many stu-*
dents, including Beethoven, Meyerbeer, Liszt, and Schubert.

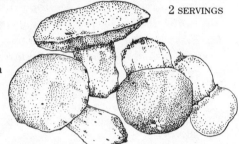

2 SERVINGS

½ ounce dried funghi porcini or
  2 ounces fresh mushrooms
4 ounces prosciutto
4 ounces fresh peas (use frozen
  peas if necessary)
  Freshly grated parmigiano
2 tablespoons sweet butter
8 ounces tagliatelle
⅓ cup cream

If you are using dried mushrooms, soak them for a couple of hours
in advance. Strain and conserve the liquid.

When you are ready to cook, set a large pot of water to boil. When
boiling, toss in a pinch of salt. Bring to boil again.

In the meantime, cut the prosciutto into small cubes, cook the
peas gently, slice the mushrooms and grate the parmigiano. Melt 1
tablespoon of butter in a saucepan and add the prosciutto. Cook
gently for 30 seconds, then add the mushrooms. Cook for 30 seconds
more and then add another tablespoon of butter and the peas. (At
this point, start boiling the tagliatelle until they are al dente). When
the butter melts, add the cream and simmer the ingredients gently
until the pasta is cooked. If you are using dried mushrooms, strain
the liquid they soaked in and add a tablespoon or so to the sauce at
the same time you add the cream.

Drain the tagliatelle well and add to the sauce. Toss briefly with a
fork and transfer to warm bowls. Give the pasta a generous dusting
of good parmigiano and serve.

€ WINE: Valpolicella.

Tagliolini con Asparagi e Panna

Tagliolini with Asparagus Cream Sauce

Another good recipe using asparagus. I tried it in Udine in the
Friuli. Aside from the asparagus, this pasta was outstanding be-
cause it contained the superb prosciutto di San Daniele which is
one of the stars of the Friuli kitchen. Udine was the birthplace of

Giulio Gatti-Casazza (1869–1940), who headed La Scala from 1898 to 1908 when he came to New York to become the first salaried general manager of the Metropolitan Opera. He remained at the Met until 1935. During his 27 years, while conducting all of his business in Italian, Gatti-Casazza presented most of the world's greatest singers on the Metropolitan's stage.

2 SERVINGS

8 ounces pencil-thin asparagus	½ cup cream
2 tablespoons sweet butter	Pinch of nutmeg (optional)
2 ounces lean prosciutto, cut in slivers	8 ounces tagliolini
	Grated parmigiano

Set a large pot of cold water to boil. Wash the asparagus and cut off the tough ends. Boil the tender stalks until they are barely al dente. Remove the asparagus without draining the pot of water, which you will use later to cook the pasta. Cut off the asparagus tips and then chop the rest of the stalks into small pieces. Melt the butter until it is foamy. Add the prosciutto and give the pan a couple of shakes. Add the asparagus, cream, and nutmeg. Toss a pinch of salt into the boiling water. When the water returns to the boil, start cooking the tagliolini. In the meantime, heat the sauce gently, stirring occasionally. When the pasta is al dente, drain thoroughly and transfer to a warm serving dish. Add the sauce, grate on some parmigiano, toss well, and serve.

🍂 WINE: Cabernet del Friuli or Merlot del Friuli.

Capellini "Bassano del Grappa"

Capellini with Apple and Brandy

This dish was served to me by the mother of a schoolmate from Bassano del Grappa. She named the recipe after her hometown to remind the cook that to make the dish authentically one must use Bassano's most famous product—grappa brandy. It is now possible to find this potent drink in the United States, but you can also use cognac. Bassano, in the province of Vicenza, also produces fine pottery and excellent Asiago cheese. It was the birthplace of Jacopo da Ponte, the sixteenth century artist whose luminous use of color and light started what is called the Bassanist school of painting.

*Opera lovers know that Tito Gobbi (1913–1984), one of this cen-
tury's great baritones, was from Bassano because of the singing
competition he sponsored annually near his native city. Though
Gobbi sang all of the important baritone roles, few people would
dispute the statement that his great role was Scarpia in* Tosca. *He
was a superb singer, actor, and stage director.*

2 SERVINGS

1 large flavorful apple
1 tablespoon lemon juice
3½ tablespoons sweet butter
　 Pinch of nutmeg
⅓ cup sweet cream
　 Pepper

1 tablespoon grappa
8 ounces capellini or other thin
　 pasta such as fedelini or
　 linguette
　 Additional butter (optional)

Set a large pot of water to boil. When boiling, toss in a pinch of salt
and bring to boil again. Peel and core the apple and grate into a
bowl. Stir in the lemon juice to prevent the apple from oxidizing.
Melt the butter in a saucepan and add the apple and nutmeg. As soon
as the apple turns a bit golden, pour in the cream and gently bring
the sauce almost to a boil. Grind in a little pepper to taste and stir in
the grappa. Turn off the flame.

Cook the thin pasta quickly in the boiling water until it is al dente.
Drain thoroughly and combine with the sauce. Add a dot of butter
and serve immediately.

VARIATIONS: I have tried this dish using different types of fruit. Pears
were, as you might expect, a success. Apricots worked well too, and
peaches were pretty good. Melons, grapes, berries, and plums were
dismal failures. One day I will try cherries, for which I hold some
hope, but I don't think I will attempt bananas.

❧ WINE: I don't like wine with this dish and would sooner suggest a
shot of grappa. Also, I like to serve Capellini "Bassano del Grappa"
with slices of Asiago cheese to nibble on while eating the pasta.

Tito Gobbi's "Luncheon Package Deal for One"

*I wrote to Tito Gobbi in February 1984 to ask if he would contribute
a pasta recipe for this book. At the time I did not know that he was
gravely ill; he died on March 5, 1984. Gobbi, who had a repertoire*

*of over 80 roles, was a great favorite of mine, and he was on my
mind when I wrote the recipe for* Capellini "Bassano del Grappa"
*(page 130) on the morning of May 1, 1984. A few hours later there
was a lovely letter in my mailbox from Gobbi's wife, Tilde. He did,
in fact, write and sign a recipe which Signora Gobbi sent, and
though it is not for pasta, I feel very honored to be able to include
it in this book.*

1 SERVING

5 drops olive oil	Slice of fresh tomato
Slice of toasted and buttered bread	Salt and pepper or seasoning salt
Slice of prosciutto	2 slices of mozzarella cheese out of which you have cut a disc in the center 1 inch in diameter
Slice of fresh tomato	
Salt and pepper	
Slice of mozzarella cheese	
Slice of toasted and buttered bread	Egg

Put the olive oil in the center of a square-foot sheet of aluminum foil
and pile up the other ingredients except egg. Lift the foil all around
the toast. Drop a fresh egg in the cheese hole. Join and twist the 4
corners of the foil and bake in a 375° F oven for 30 minutes. Serve
as is.

Scampi in Busera

Spaghetti with Shrimp

*This excellent and different recipe is from Liliana and Silvio Par-
enzan who operate the Tavernetta da Silvio in Trieste, the largest
port on the Adriatic. As you would expect, the Parenzans specialize
in seafood. If you do not love garlic, go on to another recipe.*

4 SERVINGS

⅓ cup olive oil	Salt and pepper to taste
15 cloves garlic, finely minced	2 pounds (approximately 16 to 20) large fresh shrimp, peeled and cleaned
1 teaspoon tomato paste	
1 cup bread crumbs	
1¼ cups dry white wine	¼ cup finely minced parsley
¼ cup cognac	1 pound spaghetti
1 lemon peel, grated	

In a deep pot place the oil, garlic, and tomato paste. Cook gently, stirring with a wooden spoon. When bits of garlic start to attach themselves to the bottom of the pot, add the bread crumbs and, in the following order, wine, cognac, lemon peel, salt, pepper, shrimp, and parsley. Cook at relatively high heat (near boiling) for about 15 minutes. If the sauce becomes too thick, add a bit of water or, if you have it, fish broth. Turn off the heat, cover, and let sit for 2 hours.

When ready to serve, cook the spaghetti in 6 quarts of boiling water. When the pasta is almost al dente, gently reheat the sauce. Toss the pasta with the sauce; decoratively place 4 or 5 shrimp on top of each serving.

VARIATION: I once made the sauce without the shrimp, which I added when I reheated the sauce after its 2-hour rest. This meant a longer reheating to cook the shrimp through and the sauce condensed somewhat, but this can be alleviated by adding a bit more water or fish broth.

🦐 WINE: Tocai, Pinot Bianco, or Pinot Grigio from the Friuli region.

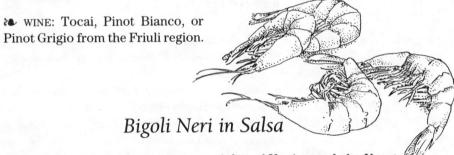

Bigoli Neri in Salsa

Bigoli, also called bigoi, are a specialty of Venice and the Veneto and are unusual for two reasons: They are made of whole wheat and are the longest of all pasta, as much as 15 inches long. Bigoli are otherwise similar to spaghetti, so if you have an attachment on your pasta machine to cut spaghetti, you can make bigoli as well. In the Veneto they use a cylindrical piece of equipment called the bigolaro to cut bigoli. The bigolaro is open at one end and has many small holes at the other, through which the pasta is forced to make the bigoli. Commerically prepared bigoli from Italy are now available in a few specialty shops in large American cities.

5 SERVINGS

Bigoli

3 cups whole wheat flour	1 teaspoon salt
4 eggs	1 tablespoon milk
2 tablespoons softened sweet butter	

Sauce

3 ounces canned sardines, anchovy fillets, or anchovy paste	8 ounces white onions, very thinly sliced
4 ounces extra-virgin olive oil	2 grindings of fresh pepper

To prepare the bigoli: Put the flour on a large flat surface, preferably of unvarnished wood. Make a well in the center of the flour, add the eggs, butter (which should be as soft as possible but not oily, so that it can combine easily with the flour), salt, and just enough milk to produce a relatively solid dough. Work the dough for about 15 minutes, then set aside, covered with a cloth, for about 30 minutes.

Roll out the dough, fold it over once or twice, and then roll it out again so that you can easily feed it into your pasta machine. Pass the dough through the machine, cutting the strands no shorter than 12 inches in length. Stretch out the bigoli to dry on a lightly floured surface.

Put a large pot of water on to boil.

TO MAKE THE SAUCE: Rinse the sardines or anchovies in cold water, removing any heads, tails, or bones. You should be left with at least 6 ounces of fish. Cut the fish into small pieces.

In a pot (Venetians use terracotta) heat half the oil over a low flame, then add the onions, which should be cooked until they are lightly colored. Put in a couple of drops of water and cover the pot. Cook until the onions have completely disintegrated, about 20 minutes. Now add the fish, breaking the pieces up further with a wooden spoon. Continue cooking another 2 minutes. Grind in the pepper and pour in the rest of the oil. Give the sauce another good stir, cover the pot, and turn off the flame.

Bring a large pot of water to the boil. Toss in a pinch of salt. Bring to boil again and start cooking the bigoli in the boiling water.

When the pasta is al dente, drain and transfer to a large bowl. Pour on the sauce and toss thoroughly. The classic way to eat Bigoli Neri in Salsa—as Vivaldi or Goldoni might have in an old Venetian *osteria* —is tepid or even cold. This dish improves in flavor as it cools.

NOTE: Anchovy paste is an acceptable time-saving substitute, though using canned fish is preferable.

&❧ WINE: Soave or Trebbiano Bianco.

La Torchiata

Bigoli with Tripe

This recipe comes from the Sandoli family, who operate the Risto-
rante Due Leoni in Ariano nel Polesine in the province of Rovigo.
This region, near where the Po River empties into the Adriatic,
combines the cuisine of Emilia Romagna and the Veneto. "La Tor-
chiata" comes from torchio, the Italian word for a press used to
crush foods or to pass them through a particular form or mold. In
this case we are talking about a bigolaro (page 133). This recipe
requires a great deal of work, particularly if you have not pur-
chased tripe that has already been cleaned and cooked.

6 SERVINGS

Pasta

3½ cups whole wheat flour
4 eggs
Pinch of salt

or

Commercially made bigoli

Sauce

8 ounces tripe
1 lemon, quartered (if cooking the tripe)
8 tablespoons olive oil
1 tablespoon sweet butter
1 medium onion, minced
2 carrots, minced
1 pound tomatoes, peeled and pureed

2 bay leaves
Pinch of salt
1 small peperoncino, cut in pieces, or 1 teaspoon dried chili pepper
1 cup freshly grated grana

If you are not using precooked tripe, you must engage in the long process of preparing it. It should be rinsed well and then soaked overnight. In the morning, wash it in several waters and at least once in white wine vinegar. Be sure to rinse the tripe well with water after the vinegar wash. Cut the tripe into large pieces and put into a large pot filled with fresh water. Make sure the tripe is totally immersed in water. Add the quartered lemon to the water. Cover the pot and cook over a low flame for 10–12 hours, then drain thoroughly. My advice is that you avoid this process by purchasing tripe that has already been cooked. This way you can devote your energy to the pasta.

If you are planning to make your own bigoli, use the amounts indicated in this recipe and follow the process described on page 134. Once the pasta is in hand, start making the sauce.

Cut the cooked tripe into tiny pieces. Heat 4 tablespoons of olive oil and the butter in a heavy-bottomed pot. Add the onion, carrots, and tripe, and sauté for 30 seconds. Add the tomatoes, bay leaves, and salt, and simmer, covered, for 40 minutes, stirring occasionally so that the ingredients do not stick to the bottom of the pot.

In the meantime, put 4 tablespoons of olive oil into a glass and add the peperoncino. Set aside.

Set a large pot of water to boil. Add a pinch of salt and bring to boil again. About 5 minutes before the sauce is done, cook the bigoli in the boiling water. Cook until al dente—dried bigoli will require a bit more cooking time than freshly made—drain well, and put into the pot with the tripe sauce. Bit by bit, start adding the grated cheese to the pot, tossing all the while over a very low flame. When all the cheese is used, transfer the pasta to a warm serving dish, pour over the piquant oil, and toss thoroughly. Serve immediately.

NOTE: I strain the oil so that the pieces of peperoncino do not go into the food.

🍷 WINE: A good Merlot or Cabernet from the Veneto or, if you prefer white wine, a Tocai di Lison.

Pasticcio di Maccheroni Padovano

Paduan Maccheroni Pie

This exquisite preparation is from the city of Padua in the Veneto, the place where Petruchio and Katharina spar in The Taming of the Shrew. *Padua is known for St. Anthony (who actually was born in Lisbon) and for its famous university where Galileo taught, Dante, Petrarch, and Tasso studied, and Vesalius did his pioneering work in anatomy. The city was the birthplace of Arrigo Boito (1842–1918) who is famous for composing the opera* Mefistofele *but is even better known as the librettist for Verdi's great* Otello *and* Falstaff *and of Ponchielli's* La Gioconda; *he was so ashamed of the latter that he insisted on being billed as Tobia Gorrio, an anagram of his real name. Padua is also the hometown of Lucia Valentini Terrani, a mezzo-soprano whose sweet full voice and wonderful phrasing have made her an outstanding interpreter of Rossini, especially his* La Cenerentola, *and of roles such as Charlotte in* Werther *and Marina in* Boris Godunov.

This recipe was kindly given to me by Miss Valentini-Terrani, who also sent the following words: "In an old Paduan house of grand tradition I once enjoyed this fragrant and tasty Pasticcio di Maccheroni which, according to custom, is served to celebrate joyous family occasions. I too, when I returned to my city of Padua to sing La Cenerentola, *wanted to serve this fabulous dish to my friends. This way we paid tribute to Rossini the gourmet after having admired his music."*

6 SERVINGS

1 ounce dried funghi porcini, soaked in tepid water
4 ounces (1 stick) sweet butter
2 ounces prosciutto, minced
½ onion, finely minced
1 small carrot, finely minced
1 stalk celery, finely minced
3 meaty squabs, cleaned and quartered
Salt and pepper to taste
¾ cup Marsala
¼ cup beef broth (or beef extract dissolved in boiling water to make ¼ cup)
12 ounces penne (or medium-sized maccheroni)
4 ounces prosciutto, cut in slivers
A few slices of truffle (see Variations)
1½ cups freshly grated parmigiano
1 egg, beaten

Pie Crust
3 cups unbleached flour
6 ounces (1½ sticks) sweet butter
1 egg
1 egg yolk
3 large pinches of salt
2 level tablespoons sugar

Besciamella
3 tablespoons sweet butter
1 tablespoon flour
1 cup milk
Pinch of nutmeg

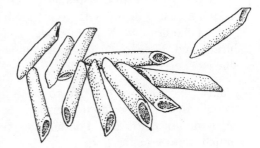

Two hours before cooking, soak the funghi porcini. Combine the ingredients for the pie crust to make a dough and refrigerate for 30 minutes.

To make the filling for the pie, melt 2 ounces of butter in a large pan or casserole and add the minced prosciutto, onion, carrot, and celery. Sauté briefly and then add the pieces of squab and a little salt and pepper. Cook the pieces slowly and carefully, turning to make sure they are cooking evenly. When the squab sections are golden brown, pour over the Marsala and continue cooking until most of the wine evaporates. Then add a little tepid water—enough to barely cover the bottom of the pan. Cover and cook very gently for 30 minutes or a little more, until the squab is cooked and the pan juices are rather condensed.

While the squabs are cooking, perform the following tasks: Remove the funghi porcini from the soaking water and squeeze them dry. Strain the water they soaked in. Sauté the funghi in a little butter and set aside. Bring a large pot of water to a boil. Toss in a pinch of salt. When water returns to boil, cook the penne in the boiling water until nearly al dente. Drain well and set aside. Make the besciamella (page 180).

When the squabs are cooked, remove from the pan and cool until comfortable to handle. Remove the meat from the bones and cut it into bite-sized pieces. Add the broth, salt, and pepper to the ingredients in the pan and then add the penne, pieces of squab, slivered prosciutto, funghi, truffle slices, remaining 2 ounces of butter, parmigiano and, finally, the besciamella. Cover and set aside.

Take the pie dough and divide into 2 pieces, one a little bit bigger than the other. Roll out into circles to fit a 10-inch pie dish. Butter the dish and line with the larger crust. Now add the penne-squab mixture and distribute the ingredients evenly on the pie crust. Carefully cover this with the smaller pie crust and join the 2 crusts at the seam, pressing firmly with your thumb to flute the edges. Brush the top of the crust with a beaten egg to give it more luster. Bake in a preheated 375°F oven for 45 minutes or until the crust is golden brown. Serve very hot.

VARIATIONS: Do not hesitate to make this dish if you do not have squab. Instead, use about 2½ pounds of any poultry you choose. Also, do not worry if you do not have truffles. Use the most flavorful mushrooms you can find.

🍷 WINE: Near Padua, a light red wine is made with a grape of American origin, the Clinton. It is probably difficult to find elsewhere, even in Italy, but locally it is quite popular. For this *pasticcio* I would recommend something more noble: perhaps Amarone from the Veneto or a great Piedmontese red such as Barbaresco, Gattinara, or Barolo.

Lasagne da Fornel

This dish is traditionally served on Christmas Eve in the Valle del Cordevole in the Dolomites. I tasted it in the town of Vittorio Veneto a bit further south. Vittorio Veneto used to be known as Ceneda and was the birthplace of one of the most fascinating characters in musical history. Lorenzo da Ponte (1749–1838) converted from Judaism to Catholicism at the age of 14 and took the holy sacraments 10 years later. He traveled around Italy for about 15 years, leading the life of a libertine, and then went to Vienna. There he met Mozart, for whom he wrote 3 of the greatest librettos in opera: Le Nozze di Figaro, Don Giovanni, *and* Così Fan Tutte. *During the same period he wrote 4 librettos for Antonio Salieri, Mozart's rival. Da Ponte moved to New York in 1819, where he wrote his charming and occasionally apocryphal memoirs while spending the last years of his life as an instructor of Italian at Columbia University. He is buried in New York.*

6 SERVINGS

4 apples	1 pound egg lasagne
2 teaspoons lemon juice	6 ounces (1½ sticks) sweet
4 ounces dried figs, cut in bits	butter
½ cup sultanas	4 tablespoons poppy seeds
4 ounces walnuts, crushed	3 tablespoons sugar

Set a very large pot of water to boil. Toss in a pinch of salt and bring to a boil again.

Peel and core the apples and grate into a mixing bowl. Add the lemon juice to prevent oxidation. Add the figs, sultanas, and walnuts.

When the water is actively boiling, cook the lasagne a few at a time until they are ¾ done. Drain on a clean cloth or towel.

Melt the butter in a double boiler and add the poppy seeds.

When all the elements are prepared, take a buttered baking dish and place a layer of lasagne on the bottom. Add some of the apple mixture, then some melted butter. Repeat in the same order. Finish with a top layer of lasagne, then butter. On top of this sprinkle the sugar. Bake in a preheated 375°F oven for 15 minutes and serve.

❧ WINE: A Prosecco Spumante di Conegliano for sparkling wine, a Cabernet del Veneto for a red, or a Tocai for a white.

Casumziei Ampezzani

This recipe is from the Valle d'Ampezzo, of which Cortina d'Ampezzo is the focal point. The Tofana di Mezzo, 10,673 feet high and northwest of Cortina, offers some of the best skiing in the Dolomites. The use of poppy seeds in the sauce should not come as a surprise, given Cortina's proximity to Austria. Casumziei are large half-moon anolini.

4 SERVINGS

Ripieno
1¼ pounds cooked fresh beets
  6 tablespoons (1½ sticks)
    butter
  4 ounces fresh ricotta

1 egg
½ cup bread crumbs,
  approximately
Salt and pepper to taste

Sfoglia:
  3½ cups flour
  2–3 eggs
  Milk or water, if necessary

Sauce
  4 ounces (1 stick) butter
1½ tablespoons poppy seeds
  Parmigiano

Cut the beets into wedges. Melt the butter in a pan and add the beets, mashing them with a fork or large metal spoon; the beets will absorb the flavor of the butter.

When the beets have become a coarse, chunky pulp, turn off the flame and add to the pan the ricotta, egg, bread crumbs, salt, and pepper. Combine the mixture well with a fork. If you think the *ripieno* is too soft to put into the *sfoglia*, add more bread crumbs, a little at a time. Set the *ripieno* aside.

Make the *sfoglia* as indicated on pages 52–58. Roll out the *sfoglia*. Using a round pasta press, biscuit cutter, or drinking glass about 3½ to 4 inches in diameter, press individual rounds of *sfoglia*. (Any leftover pieces may be used in soup.) Into each circle place a heaping teaspoon of *ripieno*. Fold the circle in half and press firmly around the seam to seal the pasta tight. If you wish to have a decorative edge use a ravioli wheel to give a perforated look. Bring a large pot of water to a boil. Add a pinch of salt. When water boils again, add the casumziei and cook according to the directions for cooking pasta on pages 79–82.

In the meantime, melt the butter, then turn off the flame and spoon in poppy seeds. Keep in a warm spot. As soon as the casumziei are cooked (6–8 minutes) drain thoroughly and transfer to a warm dish. Grate on some fresh parmigiano and top with the melted butter and poppy seeds. Serve immediately.

𝕒 WINE: If you can locate it, the ideal wine would be Lagrein rosato or Lagrein scuro. Each is a red wine produced near Bolzano. The rosato is lighter than the scuro and, for this dish, the best choice. A heavier red from the region is Santa Maddalena. If you cannot find any of these, try Chiaretto del Garda or Bardolino.

Türteln

If you drop the umlaut, the word goes from Italian local dialect to proper German. Türteln suggests the billing and cooing of birds. This lovely sound is very much in evidence in the Trentino-Alto Adige, where this recipe is from. Türteln borrow at least as much from the Tyrolean kitchen as from the Italian one. I tried them twice in the Dolomite mountains near Austria. The first time was in the smiling town of Ortisei, not far from Val Gardena which is the summer retreat of Italy's President Sandro Pertini. In Ortisei the türteln were filled with cabbage. In Pieve di Cadore, birthplace of Titian, the ones I sampled were stuffed with spinach. I am told that in the villages near the Austrian border the türteln are filled with sauerkraut.

6 SERVINGS

Ripieno
- 2 pounds cabbage, spinach, or sauerkraut
- 2 tablespoons sweet butter
- ½ onion or 2 cloves garlic, minced
  (do not use if the *ripieno* has sauerkraut)

- 1 teaspoon freshly grated pepper
- ½ teaspoon marjoram
- 4 tablespoons grated grana

Sfoglia
- 1¼ pounds rye flour
- 1 egg
- ¾ cup milk, approximately

- 3 tablespoons caraway seeds
- Peanut oil

If you are using cabbage or spinach, wash the vegetable and steam until tender. Drain thoroughly and chop well. Melt the butter in a pan, add onion or garlic, and sauté for 1 minute. Add the vegetable, pepper, and marjoram, and toss in the pan only until completely flavored. Do not overcook. Transfer to a bowl and combine with the cheese.

If you are using sauerkraut, do not combine with other ingredients. Simply drain well and stuff as is.

Make the *sfoglia:* As usual, start by making a mountain of flour and forming a well in the middle so that it looks like a volcano (page 53). Add the egg and pour in the milk *gradually* so that the flour will absorb the liquid evenly. Work the dough and roll it out until it is quite thin. Sprinkle the caraway seeds evenly over the *sfoglia* and cut into 2-inch squares using a ravioli wheel. Spoon olive-sized portions of *ripieno* onto the centers of half the squares. Cover with the other halves and press down firmly on the edges to seal the türteln.

In a deep fry pot put in enough oil to fry the türteln. If possible, use a wire fry basket. When the oil is hot, add the türteln a few at a time. When they are golden brown, lift the basket and let the türteln drain thoroughly. If you are not using a basket, remove them with a slotted spoon and drain on absorbent paper. Serve immediately. I like to squeeze on a bit of lemon juice.

🍇 WINE: A Sylvaner or Gerürztraminer, preferably from the Trentino-Alto Adige.

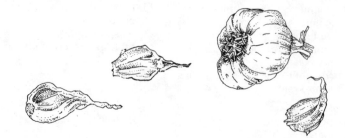

LOMBARDIA (LOMBARDY)

Rigatoni al Gorgonzola

This is an easy and elegant dish that happens to be wickedly delicious. You can make it for yourself in just a few minutes. It's also a great pasta for guests: simply multiply the ingredients' quantities by the number of guests.

Gorgonzola, a wonderful blue-veined cheese produced just outside of Milan, has frequently been compared to Roquefort cheese. This is a mistake. The French cheese is coarse and grainy, and derives from goat's milk. Gorgonzola is from cow's milk and is rich and creamy. It is available in 2 types: dolce (sweet) and piccante (sharp). Either is suitable to this dish. The sweet type is actually a bit sharp, so don't be deceived. Many years ago, before the days of urban sprawl, the village of Gorgonzola was a major stop for herdsmen with their migratory cattle. The cows gave the town an abundant supply of milk, all of which could not be immediately consumed. So it was stored, and after a while made the great leap to immortality, becoming Gorgonzola cheese. By the way, the town of Gorgonzola is now reachable on the green line of Milan's subway.

1 SERVING

4 ounces imported Gorgonzola
4 ounces rigatoni

¼ cup light or heavy cream or whole milk (your choice)
1 teaspoon sweet butter
3 sharp grindings of pepper
⅛ teaspoon nutmeg
Freshly grated grana to taste

Bring a large pot (at least 6 quarts) of cold water to a boil.

Toss in a pinch of salt and bring to a boil again. In the meantime, crumble the Gorgonzola into small pieces.

Cook the rigatoni for the specified time—until al dente.

While the pasta is cooking, heat the cream and butter in a saucepan on a low flame, almost to the point of simmering, but do not let the mixture boil. Add the Gorgonzola, pepper, and nutmeg. Stir with a wooden spoon until the sauce is velvety, and don't let it stick to the pan. When the rigatoni are cooked, drain well and mix with the sauce. Serve immediately, topped with grated grana.

VARIATIONS: Years ago, on a foggy winter afternoon in Milan, I was walking in the Zona Garibaldi, an old and very typical Milanese district not far from La Scala. I was hungry, and as the skies suddenly changed from ominous to aggressive, I ducked into an old trattoria. After a fine lunch of risotto alla milanese, cotoletta alla milanese, and the house red wine, I asked the *padrona* if she had an equally Milanese specialty for dessert. She brought a fresh juicy pear stuffed with Gorgonzola and chopped walnuts, a luscious dessert that made me forget the gloomy weather.

As delicious as it was, that pear was also very instructive. It was the first time I realized that a dish could be truly outstanding if it is a combination of perfectly matching flavors, textures, smells, and colors. The reddish skin and amber flesh of the pear was nicely offset by the white and brown cheese and nut mixture. The crunch of the nuts, the tangy creamy cheese, and the sweet meaty pear blended as beautifully as voices in bel canto opera.

When I became relatively adept at preparing Rigatoni alla Gorgonzola, I was eager to improvise and remembered that pear. You can add crunchiness and a dry sweetness to this dish by garnishing it with chopped walnuts. On another occasion I put a couple of drops (that's all that was needed) of pear brandy from Switzerland in the sauce as I added the Gorgonzola. I toned down the pepper a bit and increased the nutmeg. I've never divulged (until now) what that added ingredient was. I find that both the brandy and the nuts in the sauce are not successful, but you may like it.

Another variation is to melt the grana with the Gorgonzola rather than grating it later over the finished dish. This will produce a creamier texture but will make the independent flavors of the two cheeses less distinct.

   ❒ WINE: Any from the Valtellina (preferably red) will suit this dish.

Farfalloni con Stracchino e Gorgonzola Dolce

Large Butterflies with Stracchino and Sweet Gorgonzola

Stracchino *is a general term denoting several types of Lombard cheeses. Typically, they are straw-colored and buttery. The flavor varies from farm to farm. They are popular as breakfast cheeses and are becoming more readily available in the United States. The name comes from the Italian word* stracco, *which can best be translated as "dead tired." The cows in Lombardy, at least in former times, made long journeys from the Alps down to the plain. When they arrived they were on their last moo, so to speak, and it is at this point that they were milked to make* stracchino. *Two combined milkings are required to produce authentic* stracchino.

2 SERVINGS

8 ounces *stracchino*, cut in pieces, at room temperature
1 ounce Gorgonzola dolce, crumbled
   Pepper to taste
8 ounces farfalloni (or rigatoni or tagliatelle)

Set a large pot of water to boil.

In the meantime, put the cheeses in a serving dish and grind on some pepper. When the water is boiling, toss in a pinch of salt and again bring to a boil. Take a spoon and add a bit of water to the cheeses. Using a fork, combine the cheeses and water until you have a rich, creamy sauce; adjust the thickness to your own taste.

Boil the farfalloni until al dente. Drain, but do not go out of your way to shake off the extra water. Add the pasta to the sauce, mix well, and serve.

VARIATIONS: As indicated above, if you do not have farfalloni, you may also use rigatoni or tagliatelle. Instead of Gorgonzola, you may use a good, aged grana. The taste will not be as distinctive, but it is also quite nice.

❧ WINE: Buttafuoco or Barbera from the Oltrepo Pavese, Gutturnio from Piacenza, or any medium-bodied red.

Maccheroni Tartufati

Maccheroni with a Truffle Cream Sauce

This dish is popular with Milanesi who enjoy truffles but don't have the time to prepare a complicated dish.

1 SERVING

4 ounces maccheroni	2 tablespoons grated parmigiano
½ cup heavy cream	2 ounces shaved white truffle

Bring a large pot of water to a boil. Add a pinch of salt. When it again reaches a full boil, cook the maccheroni until al dente.

Drain well and put in a medium-sized pot. Add the cream, parmigiano, and truffle. Cover and let the ingredients warm over a very low flame for 1 minute. Uncover and stir continuously until the sauce is hot, though not boiling, and the pasta is thoroughly coated.

❧ WINE: A good red such as Sfursat from the Valtellina or a Barbera from either Piedmont or Lombardy.

Conchiglie Estive di Magda Olivero

Magda Olivero's Summer Seashells

Magda Olivero is a singer whose reputation in America has reached the status of legend. Her performances in Europe as such Puccini heroines as Mimi, Manon Lescaut, Minnie, Cio-Cio-San,

Liu, and Tosca were highly acclaimed, yet her debut at the Metropolitan Opera (as Tosca) came quite late in her career. Miss Olivero's interpretations of many of the great soprano roles are always stylish and distinctive, and her fans are among the most ardent I've ever encountered. Miss Olivero, who was born near Turin, lives in Milan and especially recommends this dish for a hot summer day of the type that city is known for.

6 SERVINGS

2 pounds fresh ripe tomatoes
2 large bunches of fresh basil, washed and torn into pieces by hand
4 ounces pickled gherkins, cut into tiny bits

3 cloves garlic
6 tablespoons olive oil
1 pound conchiglie or other dried pasta
Freshly grated parmigiano

Peel and drain the tomatoes of their juice and seeds. Puree and place in a large bowl. Add the basil, gherkin bits, garlic cloves, and oil. Cover the dish and let it sit for at least 2 hours; 4 hours would be better still.

Bring a large pot of water to a boil. Toss in a pinch of salt and add the pasta when the water comes to a boil again. Cook until al dente, drain well, and put in a serving dish. Remove the garlic cloves from the fragrant sauce. Pour the sauce onto the pasta, sprinkle on some freshly grated parmigiano, and serve.

ᴥ WINE: A fresh young wine is recommended: reds such as Chianti Novello Bardolino, and Rosato di Garda, or whites such as Erbaluce di Caluso and Bianco della Valtellina.

Spaghetti ai Funghi Freschi
Spaghetti with Fresh Mushrooms

When you enter a bookshop in Italy, there are shelves containing books on all the usual subjects: history, politics, literature, cuisine, travel, and so forth. What is notable, though, is that many major bookshops now devote an entire wall to the subject of mushrooms. The study, hunt, cultivation, dangers, and virtues of mushrooms have become a major interest for Italian hobbyists and food lovers alike. Perhaps no other edible item has had more written about it in Italy than the mushroom. This is not surprising, since the quality and variety of mushrooms found throughout the country are astounding.

In areas such as Bergamo, at the foothills of the Alps, many dishes are based on the delicious mushrooms that are so abundantly available. This recipe comes from Vittorio Cerea of the Ristorante da Vittorio in Bergamo. If you can acquire safe, edible wild mushrooms, make this dish with whatever type is available. Otherwise, use dried funghi porcini or any other flavored dried mushrooms you like. You may want to extend the recipe by adding a few cultivated mushrooms of the type found in most markets, but remember that you can only expect these to add bulk rather than a distinctive flavor.

4 SERVINGS

10	ounces fresh wild mushrooms or 3–4 ounces dried funghi porcini or other special mushrooms	2	slivers fresh garlic (optional)
		8	ounces spaghetti
		3–4	tablespoons sweet butter
3–4	tablespoons olive oil	2	tablespoons minced fresh parsley
	Salt and pepper to taste		Freshly grated parmigiano

If using dried mushrooms, rinse gently and then soak in water for at least 2 hours. If you are using fresh mushrooms, wipe them clean with a damp cloth or paper towel, then cut up coarsely. Put in a largish pan with 1 scant cup of water, oil, salt, pepper, and garlic, and cook partially covered over medium heat for 15 minutes.

In the meantime, bring a large pot of water to a boil. Toss in a pinch of salt. When water again comes to a boil, add the spaghetti and cook until ¾ done. Drain well and add to the mushroom sauce. Cook 3–4 minutes more. Before serving, add the butter and parsley, toss lightly, and then sprinkle on the parmigiano.

VARIATIONS: This dish works well using fettuccine, which is what a Roman cook would do. Also, when I have made this dish using dried funghi porcini, I have strained the water they soaked in of all sediment and used that water as part of the scant cup needed for the sauce.

ઠ WINE: This dish goes well with a medium-bodied red such as Inferno or Grignolino. If you want white wine, a Chardonnay from the Veneto would go nicely.

Orecchiette alla Salsa di Verdura

Orecchiette with Vegetable Sauce

This recipe has been in use for more than a century in a family I know in Como. This may strike you as unusual on two counts. One is that orecchiette are traditional pasta in Apulia, which is a long way from Como. This is very true; the answer is that one of the great-grandmothers was from Lecce, but she married a comasco. The other oddity is that a recipe would be in use continuously for generations by one family. In Italy, many families keep albums of recipes handed down through the years. They often eat certain dishes on particular days—such as the birthdays of the recipes' creators—to honor a member of the family. Many of the recipes in this book come from albums of families I know throughout Italy. I am grateful to them for sharing their treasures.

3–4 SERVINGS

1 carrot, cut in small pieces
1 red or yellow pepper, cut in small pieces
1 zucchini, about 4 ounces, quartered lengthwise and cut in 1-inch strips
1 small ripe tomato, cut in small pieces, drained, and seeds removed
2 tablespoons olive oil

1 clove garlic, minced
1 medium onion, minced
½ teaspoon flour
Salt and pepper to taste
¾ cup water or vegetable broth
6 fresh basil leaves, torn into small pieces
2½ cups orecchiette (page 62), fresh or store-bought
Grated parmigiano

Cut the carrot, pepper, zucchini, and tomato to your liking. Heat the oil in a medium-sized pot and add the garlic and onion. After 30 seconds put in the pepper, wait a few more seconds and then add the carrot, zucchini, and tomato. Stir a few moments to thoroughly combine the ingredients. Now sprinkle on the flour, salt, and pepper, and pour in the water or broth. Stir again, cover the pot, and cook over a very low flame for 35–40 minutes. The result will be a relatively thick sauce. When it is done, turn off the flame and sprinkle on the torn basil leaves.

Bring a large pot of cold water to a boil. Add a pinch of salt. Return to a boil.

A few minutes before the sauce is finished, cook the orecchiette in the rapidly boiling water until al dente, allowing a few extra minutes for the dried, store-bought type. Drain thoroughly, transfer to a warm dish, and top with the vegetable sauce. Toss well and serve immediately with grated parmigiano.

NOTE: Even within the confines of using particular ingredients and amounts, there is much room for fantasy in the preparation of this recipe. You can make a dazzling visual impact by cutting the vegetables in unusual shapes. With a little extra work you can make star-shaped pieces of carrot and zucchini. Also, since you do not peel the tomato, each plate will have several luminous flecks of red. Be sure to save the liquid from the tomato when you remove the seeds. I often cut the pepper into little diamonds.

& WINE: My friends serve Cellatica, a red from near Brescia. Any medium-bodied red will do.

Maccheroni alla Ivana

This recipe is from Enzo Dara, a fine basso who is a specialist in opera buffa. Signor Dara has gained wide acclaim for his Rossini roles, including Dr. Bartolo in Il Barbiere di Siviglia, *Dandini in* La Cenerentola, *and Don Geronio in* The Turk in Italy. *He is also well known as Dulcamara in* L'Elisir d'Amore *and as Puccini's Gianni Schicchi. Signor Dara is a resident of Mantua, and in giving me this recipe said that "Mantuan cuisine is very refined, since it was influenced by the Austrians and the French." The recipe is rather different from the usual, and though it requires a fair amount of work, the results are pleasing.*

4 SERVINGS

1 ounce dried mushrooms, preferably funghi porcini
1 8-ounce can borlotti beans (see Note) or ½ cup dried beans
5 tablespoons seed oil or any light cooking oil

4 ounces (1 stick) sweet butter
1 carrot, coarsely chopped
1 onion, coarsely chopped
1 stalk celery, cut into chunks
3 sage leaves
1 teaspoon rosemary

¼ beef or vegetable bouillon cube	1 tablespoon tomato sauce
	1 pound maccheroni
Salt	Grated parmigiano

Two hours before cooking, soak the dried mushrooms in tepid water.

If you are using dried beans, prepare them by covering well with cold water and bringing to a boil over medium-high heat. Boil for exactly 2 minutes. Remove pot from the heat and set aside for 1 hour.

Put the oil and butter into a large pot, preferably earthenware. Add the carrot, onion, celery, sage, rosemary, bouillon cube, and a bit of salt. Cover and cook over the lowest flame possible until the vegetables are well cooked; this may take up to 1 hour. Stir the contents of the pot occasionally.

Remove pot from the stove and pass all the cooked vegetables, along with half the beans, through a sieve or puree them in a blender or food processor.

Return puree to the pot, spoon in the tomato sauce, and place the pot back over a very low flame. Remove the mushrooms from their soaking liquid with a slotted spoon and add to the pot. Reserve the liquid. Stir the mixture continuously to prevent sticking; if the sauce seems too thick, thin with 1 or 2 teaspoons of mushroom water, but take care not to include any sediment that may have soaked out of the mushrooms.

Add remaining beans to the sauce and continue to cook at the lowest possible temperature, stirring occasionally, until the beans are cooked to the point of tenderness, but do not let them become mushy. This will take about 1 hour more.

In the meantime, bring a large pot of water to a boil. Add a pinch of salt and bring to a boil again. When the sauce is almost ready, cook the maccheroni in the boiling water until al dente. Drain the pasta well and place in a large bowl. Spinkle generously with grated parmigiano, pour on the sauce, and mix well. Top with more cheese or pass some at the table.

NOTE: Borolotti are large, round, reddish beans found in Lombardy. The name comes from the Milanese dialect: borlot. You can occasionally find a can of borlotti in specialty shops, but you may substitute either kidney beans or white beans. I used a combination of both varieties, dried, with excellent results.

🍷 WINE: Franciacorta Rosso or Gutturnio dei Colli Piacentini.

Pizzoccheri alla Chiavennesca

Pizzoccheri from Chiavenna

Though the adjective "rustic" is suffering from a bad case of over-use, there can be no question that it is a word well suited to the description of pizzoccheri. This is good, old-fashioned food from Lombardy's alpine region of the Valtellina. Even in this relatively small, secluded area, there is great variation. You will also find here 2 other versions of pizzoccheri. The town of Chiavenna is in a region of valleys, forests, and mountain passes, including the Splügen pass to Switzerland to which Chiavenna is the chiave *(key). This recipe comes from the Ristorante al Cenacolo-Antica Trattoria Fagetti, which has a small terrace perched high over the Mera River and a stunning view of the nearby mountains. The owner told me that the word* pizzoccheri *means a mixture of flours put together on the spot. He said that the white flour comes from the lower Valtellina while the buckwheat comes from elevations of at least 900 meters (2,970 feet).*

4 SERVINGS

2¾ cups buckwheat flour
1¼ cups unbleached, all-purpose flour
Pinch of salt (optional)
⅓ cup cool water

2–3 medium-sized potatoes
4 ounces (1 stick) plus 2 tablespoons sweet butter

1 clove garlic, cut in slivers (optional)
Salt and pepper to taste
4 sage leaves
6 ounces Bitto, Fontina, or Taleggio cheese, thinly sliced
4 tablespoons freshly grated parmigiano

Sift the 2 flours together on your working surface. Add the salt, if you wish. Form a well in the middle and pour in some of the water. Start working the flour and water into a dough, adding more water if you think it is required. This depends on altitude—you would need more water in Denver or Chiavenna than in New York or Milan. Work the dough for about 15 minutes, until it is smooth and firm.

Roll out the dough to form a *sfoglia* thicker than usual (about ¼ inch). Using a sharp knife, cut the *sfolgia* into strips about ⅜ inch wide. When this is done, cut the *sfoglia* in the other direction to form noodles 2 to 2½ inches long.

When the pizzoccheri are made, set a large pot containing 3–4 quarts of water or beef broth to boil.

In the meantime, peel the potatoes and cut into bite-sized pieces. When the liquid is boiling, add the potatoes. When the potatoes are barely cooked, add the pizzoccheri.

In another pot, carefully melt the butter and add the garlic, salt, pepper, and sage. Make sure the butter and garlic do not turn brown.

The pizzoccheri are ready when they rise to the top of the liquid. They should be al dente. Drain the potatoes and the pizzoccheri and put half of them in a serving dish. Top with some cheese, pour on more butter, then the rest of the potatoes and pizzoccheri, the rest of the cheese, all the parmigiano, and the rest of the butter. Toss briefly, allowing the cheese to melt. Serve immediately in warm dishes.

NOTE: It is possible to purchase commercially prepared pizzoccheri. These require a longer cooking time than fresh pasta.

ᔠ WINE: Valtellina Superiore, Sassella, Grumello, Inferno, Valgella, or Sfursat.

Pizzoccheri di Teglio

Another version of this Valtellinese classic, from the town of Teglio.

4–6 SERVINGS

2¾ cups buckwheat flour
1¼ cups unbleached, all-purpose
    flour
⅓ cup cool water
8 ounces cabbage
6 ounces (1½ sticks) sweet
    butter

3 cloves garlic, slivered
12 ounces Bitto, Fontina, or
    Taleggio cheese, thinly sliced
1 cup grated parmigiano
    Freshly ground pepper

Prepare the pizzoccheri as indicated in the recipe for Pizzoccheri alla Chiavennesca, page 152.

Wash the cabbage and tear into large bite-sized pieces, or cut it into long strips. Put the cabbage into a large pot of boiling water. Cook for 3 minutes, toss in a pinch of salt, and then add the pizzoccheri. Cook until al dente, about 7 minutes.

While the pasta is cooking, melt the butter in a pot and add garlic slivers. Do not let them turn brown.

When the pasta is ready, drain well and put part of the pizzoccheri and cabbage in a terrine or serving dish. Top with some butter, cheese, and parmigiano. Repeat until you have exhausted all of the ingredients. Add freshly ground pepper to taste. Toss when the cheese has begun to melt. Serve immediately in warm bowls.

🍷 WINE: Any red from the Valtellina.

Pizzoccheri di Tirano

Tirano is a charming town in the Valtellina. From here you can catch a train to St. Moritz over the Bernina Pass (7,586 feet). This version of pizzoccheri is the most colorful one I tried in the Valtellina.

4–6 SERVINGS

2¾ cups buckwheat flour
1¼ cups unbleached, all-purpose flour
⅓ cup water

2 medium-sized potatoes
2 leeks
4 ounces string beans
2 small carrots, cut in discs
4 ounces (1 stick) plus 3 tablespoons sweet butter

2 cloves garlic, cut in slivers
A generous pinch of fresh sage
3 cabbage leaves, torn in large pieces
8 ounces Bitto, Fontina, or Taleggio cheese, thinly sliced
4 tablespoons freshly grated parmigiano

Make the pizzoccheri as indicated in the recipe for Pizzoccheri alla Chiavennesca, page 152.

Peel the potatoes and cut into bite-sized pieces. Wash the leeks well and cut the white portion into bite-sized pieces. Wash the string beans, cutting off the tough ends.

In a large pot of lightly salted boiling water, cook the potatoes and leeks until about half done. Add the string beans and, 2 minutes later, the pizzoccheri and carrots. While these are cooking, melt the butter in another pot and add the garlic and sage. Three minutes before you think the pizzoccheri will be al dente, drop the cabbage leaves into the boiling water. They should still be slightly crunchy when you eat them.

When the pizzoccheri are ready, drain the pot well. Pour a bit of melted butter into a terrine or large serving bowl. Put down a layer of pizzoccheri and vegetables, a layer of thin cheese slices, more butter and garlic, and so on, making layers until all the ingredients are exhausted. Sprinkle the parmigiano on top. Toss when the cheese has begun to melt. Serve immediately in warm bowls.

🍷 WINE: Any Valtellina red.

Marubini

Marubini are the classic pasta ripiena of Cremona. Traditionally they are served in a rich beef broth with grated grana, but you may also try them with melted butter and sage. As I have mentioned elsewhere, Cremona is no ordinary town. This provincial capital in Lombardy has provided the musical world with some of its great figures. Claudio Monteverdi (1567–1643) wrote madrigals and vespers as well as the greatest early operas: Orfeo, Il Ritorno d'Ulisse in Patria and L'Incoronazione di Poppea. Antonio Stradivari (1644–1737) and his sons Francesco and Omobono were the most outstanding violin makers of all time. Amilcare Ponchielli (1834–1886), also Cremonese, might not be considered among the finest of operatic composers—only his La Gioconda is still regularly performed—but he was an influential teacher whose most famous pupils were Puccini and Mascagni.

4 SERVINGS

Ripieno

8 ounces braised beef, finely minced

4 ounces roast veal, finely minced

4 ounces roast pork, finely minced

4 ounces boiled calves brains, finely minced

1 egg

2 tablespoons softened sweet butter

2 tablespoons bread crumbs

3 ounces grated grana

Pinch of nutmeg

¼ teaspoon salt

½ teaspoon freshly grated pepper

Sfoglia

3½ cups flour

3–4 eggs

A bit of milk, perhaps

3–4 quarts of good beef broth

Prepare the *ripieno* by mixing the beef, veal, pork, and brains. Add the egg, butter, bread crumbs, cheese, and spices, and combine until a uniform filling is made. If the *ripieno* is too soft, add more bread crumbs. If it is too firm, add all or part of another egg.

Make the *sfoglia* (pages 52–58). Separate the dough into 2 pieces of equal size. Roll out 2 sheets of *sfoglia* and set 1 aside.

Dot 1 sheet of *sfoglia* with olive-sized balls of *ripieno* with space of 1–1½ inches between. Once this work is done, carefully cover the *sfoglia* with the other sheet. With a round perforated press, stamp each *marubino*. When you have done this, carefully lift the sheets of *sfoglia* and let the marubini drop back onto your working surface. (You may cut up the leftover *sfoglia* to use in soup or with a meat sauce.) Let the marubini rest for 30 minutes, covered with a cloth.

Boil the marubini in broth until they flower, that is, until they grow in size and thickness, and resemble large flowers. Serve the marubini in the broth topped with freshly grated parmigiano or drain and serve with melted butter and grated cheese.

VARIATIONS: If you do not have braised beef and roast veal and pork on hand, you may buy these meats already ground and sauté them in a pan. Use the leanest meat available and drain the pan of any liquid that has been rendered.

In one Cremonese family I know they separate the yolk from the egg white. The yolk is added to the *ripieno* and the white is brushed on the layers of *sfoglia* before the *ripieno* is added.

🍷 WINE: A Barbera or Buttafuoco from the Oltrepo Pavese would be ideal. Any medium- to full-bodied dry red will do.

Casonsei di Brescia

Brescia is an important industrial town in Lombardy. Its province includes the western shore of Lake Garda. The city dates back to Roman times, when it was known as Brixia. Throughout history, either as a free duchy or under foreign domination, Brescia has been Europe's leading producer of arms and armor. Italians refer to it as La Leonessa (the lioness), a name Brescia earned after it rose up against the Austrians in 1849. In Brescian dialect casonsei means shorts or, perhaps, knickers. This pasta looks like so many little pairs of shorts. They are not as difficult to prepare as these instructions may lead you to believe. With a little practice and dexterity, you will become quite expert.

4 SERVINGS

Ripieno
⅔ cup bread crumbs
   Enough milk to soak bread
   crumbs
10 ounces pork sausage (spicy or
   mild, without fennel),
   approximately, skinned and
   crumbled

1 cup grated parmigiano
   Salt and pepper to taste

Sfoglia
3½ cups flour
 3 eggs

Sauce
 4 ounces (1 stick) sweet butter
   Fresh sage leaves

   Freshly grated parmigiano

Soak the bread crumbs in the milk for a few minutes and then drain carefully. Combine the bread crumbs with the sausage, parmigiano, salt, and pepper. Work the mixture into a uniform paste and set aside.

Make a dough with the flour and eggs (see pages 52–58). Once it has become smooth and elastic, set aside for a few minutes in a draft-free place.

Next, roll out the *sfoglia* until is is rather thin. With a knife or, preferably, a ravioli wheel, cut rectangles 3 x 5 inches in size—you can use a 3 x 5-inch index card as a guide. Put approximately 1 tablespoon of *ripieno* in the center of each rectangle. Fold each rectangle in half lengthwise. Using both hands, press down on the *sfoglia* so that the *ripieno* is squeezed into the center of the rectangle, pressed against the folded edge. Seal the outer borders tight by pressing down with your fingertips. Finally, press your thumbs against the part where the *ripieno* is and, using your other fingers, guide the "legs" around to where your thumbs are.

Once your casonsei are ready, let them rest for a few minutes before boiling in abundant boiling salted water.

While the pasta is cooking, melt the butter in a pan and add the sage. When the casonei are thoroughly cooked (this will vary according to their size, 6–9 minutes), drain carefully, put in a very warm dish, and top with the melted butter and sage. Serve with freshly grated parmigiano.

🍂 WINE: Franciacorta rosso, from the hills near the Lago d'Iseo in the province of Brescia, is the classic match. Any other good full-bodied red will also go well with casonsei.

Sciatt

This recipe comes from Sondrio, the principal town in the Valtellina, the alpine region of Lombardy. The most famous Valtellinese dish is Pizzoccheri (page 152), yet there are many other fine preparations based on the typical ingredients of the area: buckwheat flour, semisoft cheese, cabbage, marvelous funghi porcini and, near the town of Madesimo on the Swiss border, wild blueberries. The Valtellina also produces the excellent red wines I drink most often.

Sciatt means tails in the local dialect; these pasta are tail-shaped ravioli fried in oil or fat. The typical cheese used in Sciatt is called Bitto, produced in a valley of the same name. Bitto is suited for Sciatt when it is about 3 years old and semihard. If you cannot locate it, try other alpine cheeses, even softer ones, such as Taleggio, Fontina, Valseriana, Robbiola della Valsassina, Montasio, or even Swiss cheese.

4 SERVINGS

2½ cups buckwheat flour
1¼ cups unbleached, all-purpose
    flour
½ cup aquavit, grappa, or
    cognac

6 ounces Bitto or other suitable
    cheese, cubed
    Corn or sunflower oil

Sift the 2 flours onto your working surface and make a well in the center. Add the aquavit and enough water (approximately 1 cup) to form a smooth, elastic dough. Work the dough until smooth and then shape into a ball. Cover with a cloth and set aside for 30 minutes. Roll out the dough until about ⅛ inch thick. Cut into squares 3 to 4 inches long. Put 2 or 3 cubes of cheese into each square. Fold each square in half to enclose the cheese, press down at the seams, then pick up and twist the 2 extremes, making it look like a wrapped hard candy. When you have prepared all of the *sciatt*, pour about ¼ inch of oil into a frying pan and, when hot, fry the *sciatt* until golden brown. Eat as hot as possible.

VARIATION: In folding the *sciatt* you may put the cheese in the middle of the square of dough, then gather the 4 ends together and twist the dough so that the *sciatt* looks like a tadpole instead of hard candy.

In the Valtellina many people dip the hot *sciatt* into granulated sugar, but I do not recommend this.

ই WINE: Valtellina Superiore, Grumello, Inferno, Sassella, or Valgella.

Tortelli di Zucca
Pumpkin Tortelli

*One of the most famous opening lines of an opera aria is, "Ah!...
che zucconi!" the start of the title character's agitated lament in
Puccini's comic Gianni Schicchi. Zucconi, literally translated,
means big pumpkins, but the real sense of this word implies block-
heads or dunces. Pumpkins have not received the exalted status in
Italy that they hold in the United States. Only in lower Lombardy
and upper Emilia are they at all esteemed. Italian pumpkin often
has a green shell and yellow meat. It is most frequently used for
this preparation, native to Cremona and Mantua, where it is traditional Christmas fare.*

*Pasta filled with pumpkin is food from the olden days. These
tortelli were served in the Renaissance ducal courts of Cremona,
Mantua, Parma, and Modena, where it was called tortelli di Novi,
presumably because they were created in the town of that name.
The combination of sweet and tart flavors—especially in the Cremonese version of this dish—is characteristic of many recipes of
the Renaissance.*

*This recipe was given to me by
Pier Luigi Pizzi, a Milan native
and one of Italy's most outstanding operatic stage directors and
designers. His work has been rep-
resented in practically every
major opera house in Europe and
North America.*

6 SERVINGS

Ripieno
- 2 pounds pumpkin or 2 cups canned pumpkin puree
- 4 ounces amaretti, pulverized
- ½ cup bread crumbs

Sfoglia
- 4½ cups unbleached flour
- 5 eggs

- 1¾ cups freshly grated parmigiano
- Pinch of salt
- Pinch of nutmeg
- 1 egg

- Drop of oil
- Pinch of salt

To make the *ripieno:* If using a fresh pumpkin, cut the top off and remove all the seeds. Cut into several pieces, and bake in a 350°F oven for 1½ to 2 hours, until the pumpkin is tender. Let cool and then remove the meat from the shell. Puree in a sieve, blender, or food processor.

Put the pumpkin puree into a mixing bowl and add remaining ingredients. Combine thoroughly and set aside.

Make the dough for the *sfoglia,* cover with a cloth, and let sit for a few hours. Roll out the dough into 2 very thin sheets. Prepare the tortelli using the second method described on page 69. Brush 1 sheet lightly with a little cold water before putting on the balls of *ripieno.* Once the tortelli are prepared, place them on a towel and sprinkle on a bit of flour. Let them rest for 45 minutes. Bring a large pot of water to a boil. Toss in a pinch of salt. Bring to a boil again. When the tortelli are ready, boil them in the lightly salted water, drain carefully, and transfer to a warm serving dish. Serve immediately with melted butter and parmigiano.

VARIATIONS: Traditionally the *ripieno* for this dish is made the day before and stored in the refrigerator. It often includes an ingredient known as *mostarda di Cremona,* a sort of fruit relish made of unripe fruit preserved with mustard seeds. *Mostarda di Cremona,* which might remind you of chutney, has been used since the Renaissance. Though it does taste best when served out of a barrel in Lombardy, you can find *mostarda* in jars in some food stores. If you like, add about 4 ounces to the *ripieno.* If you cannot find *mostarda,* grate a little lemon peel into the *ripieno.* You might also replace *mostarda* with quince preserves.

🍷 WINE: Since this dish is often served on festive occasions, champagne or good spumante would not be out of place. For a red wine, try Buttafuoco or Barbera from the Oltrepo Pavese. Other good choices are Ghemme, Gattinara, and Franciacorta.

PIEMONTE (PIEDMONT) AND THE VALLE D'AOSTA

Gnocchi di Patate alla Bava · Agnolotti alla Piemontese, Version 1 ·
Agnolotti alla Piemontese, Version 2 ·
Agnolotti alla Piemontese, Version 3 ·
Agnolotti alla Piemontese, Version 4 · Agnolotti alla Savoiarda

Gnocchi di Patate alla Bava

Potato Gnocchi as Prepared in the Valle d'Aosta

This is the basic recipe for potato gnocchi. They can be served with many types of sauces, so be creative and experimental. In Naples potato gnocchi served with meat sauce are called Strangolapreti *(the priest strangler) because of their effect on one cleric who loved them so. Fear not, just remember to chew.*

I first tasted gnocchi alla bava while on a skiing trip in Cour-mayeur, a sunny community on the French border at the foot of Mont Blanc. Bava *means floss or silk filament. As the fontina melts, it forms silken strands.*

4 SERVINGS

Gnocchi
1¼ pounds mealy potatoes
2½ cups unbleached, all-purpose
   flour

1 egg
   Pinch of nutmeg
   Pinch of salt

Sauce
- 8 ounces Fontina cheese, thinly sliced
- 3 ounces sweet butter
  Truffle shavings (optional)

Wash the potatoes and boil with their skins on. When cooked, peel and mash them. Form a mound of the potatoes on your working surface, combine with the flour, nutmeg, and salt, and make a well in the center. Add the egg and work the mixture together until you form a dough. Then shape the gnocchi as indicated on pages 73–74.

Grease a baking dish with 1 ounce of butter. When the gnocchi are cooked, put a layer in the baking dish, top with a layer of Fontina and, if you wish, some truffle shavings. Add more gnocchi, more cheese, and so forth, finishing with a layer of gnocchi. Dot with butter and bake in a preheated 375°F oven until the cheese melts.

VARIATION: In the Dolomites I have had something similar to Gnocchi di Patate alla Bava. The difference was that ¼ cup of grappa (another brandy can be used) and a little more flour is added to the dough. Instead of Fontina, a local cheese such as Taleggio is used.

🍷 WINE: Carema is an excellent red from the Valle d'Aosta. You may also drink Inferno from the Valtellina.

Agnolotti alla Piemontese

This is the classic pasta ripiena of Piedmont, served with great pride in Turin. You can walk up the Via Roma to the great Teatro Regio in the center of town, and little trattorie in the side streets will all be serving their own version of agnolotti. The ripieno varies somewhat in every Torinese kitchen—four versions are included below. Every smart cook knows that leftovers should never be wasted. You may use whatever leftover meat you have, but try to achieve a balance between delicacy and substance regarding both flavor and texture. I wonder if tenor Francesco Tamagno, who was born in Turin in 1850, longed for a soothing plate of agnolotti before stepping onstage at La Scala as Verdi's first Otello on February 5, 1887? Another great son of Turin was Giuseppe Giacosa (1847–1906), who collaborated with Luigi Illica on the libretti for Puccini's La Bohème, Tosca, *and* Madama Butterfly.

4 SERVINGS

VERSION 1

Ripieno

8 ounces braised beef	3 tablespoons grated grana
4 ounces roast pork	2 ounces (½ stick) sweet butter
4 ounces sausage (without fennel seeds), skinned and cooked	½ teaspoon nutmeg
	¼ teaspoon salt
	¼ teaspoon freshly ground pepper
4 ounces boiled calves brains	1 egg
10 ounces cooked spinach	

Sfoglia

3⅛ cups flour	Any braising liquids, gravy, or pan juices reserved from cooking the meats above (optional)
2 eggs	
⅜ cup milk or water, approximately	

After all the meats have been cooked as indicated, reserving the liquids, finely chop or grind them. Wash and cook the spinach only in the water left on the leaves. When cooked, drain the spinach of its liquid (which you may reserve for other uses) and chop the leaves well. Combine the meat and spinach, and add the cheese, butter, spices, and egg. The *ripieno* should be well blended and relatively soft. Set aside.

Using the amounts listed above, prepare the *sfoglia* as indicated on pages 52–58. Use only as much milk as necessary to make an elastic dough. If it seems too soft, add a bit more flour. Roll out 2 sheets of *sfoglia* and make the agnolotti as indicated on page 68, using either of the first two methods. Each agnolotto should be between 2 and 2½ inches in size, so space the balls of *ripieno* accordingly on the *sfoglia*.

Cook the agnolotti in broth or boiling water. Drain and transfer to a pan containing 2 tablespoons of melted butter and lots of whatever gravy from the braised beef or roasted meats is on hand. Cook over medium heat for 1 minute, shaking the pan continuously, and serve with grated grana. Or simply serve with melted butter and shaved truffle or, perhaps, with a simple fresh tomato sauce.

VERSION 2

Ripieno

1 small endive, about 4 ounces	¼ cup red wine
4 ounces (1 stick) sweet butter	1 tomato, peeled, seeded, and pureed
1 small onion, minced	½ cup boiled rice
1 small carrot, minced	Salt and pepper to taste
1 stalk of celery, minced	3 tablespoons grated grana
2 tablespoons minced fresh parsley	1 egg
8 ounces ground beef	

Boil the endive until soft (approximately 10 minutes), then mince well. Melt the butter in a saucepan and add the onion, carrot, celery, and parsley. When the onion turns golden, add the meat, sauté for a few seconds, and then pour in the wine. When the liquid reduces, add the tomato puree and rice. Stir with a wooden spoon and, when the meat is a bit more cooked (about 1 minute), add the endive, salt, and pepper. Raise the temperature until the liquid boils, then lower the flame as far as possible and cook for 25–30 minutes. Remove from heat and let cool to room temperature, then combine with the grana and egg.

Prepare the *sfoglia* and make the agnolotti as indicated in version 1.

VERSION 3

This version is especially tasty served with melted butter and shaved truffle.

Ripieno

8 ounces boiled chicken, minced
4 ounces cooked sweetbreads, minced
4 ounces prosciutto crudo, minced
4 ounces cabbage, blanched and finely chopped

2 ounces (½ stick) sweet butter
⅛ cup red wine
3 tablespoons minced fresh parsley
½ teaspoon nutmeg
Salt and pepper to taste
4 tablespoons grated grana
1 egg

After the meats and cabbage have been prepared, melt the butter in a saucepan and add the meats. Sauté briefly and pour in the wine. Once the alcohol has evaporated, add the parsley, cabbage, and spices. Cook for 2 minutes and turn off the flame. Allow the mixture to cool, then combine with the grana and egg. If it is too soft, add more grana and perhaps some bread crumbs. Set aside.

Prepare the *sfoglia* and make the agnolotti as indicated in version 1.

VERSION 4

This version requires no more than a simple sauce of melted butter and sage (page 156) plus a generous grating of grana.

Ripieno

8 ounces finely chopped beef, veal, pork, or chicken
2 ounces (½ stick) sweet butter
8 ounces boiled spinach, chopped
8 ounces boiled beetroot, chopped

½ cup boiled rice (see Note below)
½ teaspoon nutmeg
Salt and pepper to taste
4 tablespoons grated grana
1 egg

If the meat is not already cooked, sauté in butter. If it is cooked, melt the butter, then add the spinach and beetroot. Allow the greens to be infused with the sweetness of the butter and then add the meat, rice, and spices. Do not heat the combination long—the idea is that the ingredients impart their flavors to one another, not that they be cooked further. Allow the ingredients to cool, then combine with the grana and egg. Set the *ripieno* aside.

Prepare the *sfoglia* and make the agnolotti as indicated in version 1.

NOTE: The *piemontesi* sometimes cook their rice in milk, a method you might choose for this preparation as well.

&❧ WINE: Any of the great reds of Piedmont. These include Barbara, Barolo, Dolcetto, Freisa Gattinara, Ghemme, Grignolino, Nebbiolo, and Spanna.

Agnolotti alla Savoiarda

The dimensions of this recipe are awesome, but then so is the region it comes from. This dish is prepared at the Ristorante da Pierre in the town of Verres in the Valle d'Aosta. This is the region of Fontina cheese, chamois, Mont Blanc (Monte Bianco), and the Matterhorn (Monte Cervinia), nestled in the northwest corner of Italy, bordering on Switzerland and France. In many ways the Valle d'Aosta has more in common with these 2 countries than the region of Piedmont to its south.

You can try to reduce this recipe—or serve bigger portions—but Agnolotti alla Savoiarda seems suited to a big meal in the late fall or winter with abundant meats, cabbage, potatoes, carrots, alpine cheeses, and robust wines. In making your ripieno, *try to use different meats, such as venison and goat, balancing the filling with some fowl. According to Signor Pierre, this recipe would serve 20 persons, but I think the correct figure is about half that.*

8–10 SERVINGS

Ripieno

2 pounds roast meats (beef, turkey, game, and so forth), coarsely chopped
3 eggs

½ cup sultana raisins, washed
½ cup grated parmigiano
   Salt and pepper to taste

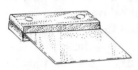

Sfoglia
   2 pounds flour
9–10 eggs

Sauce
2½ cups gravy or juices reserved
     from cooking the meats
  1 cup heavy cream

After chopping the various meats you are using (the liquids should be reserved for the sauce), combine with the eggs, sultanas, cheese, salt, and pepper to make a fairly stiff *ripieno*. Mold batches of *ripieno* into the shape of Havana cigars (advice of Signor Pierre). Or roll it into balls about the size of large olives in diameter. In either case, set aside.

Make the *sfoglia* (pages 52–58) and roll it out to form a rectangular sheet, about 3 times as long as it is wide. The *sfoglia* should be between ¼ and ½ inch thick. Lightly brush the entire surface of the *sfoglia* with egg. With a ravioli wheel, cut the *sfoglia* lengthwise straight down the middle, making 2 equal sheets.

Take a "cigar" of *ripieno* in your left hand and cut off balls of *ripieno* with your right, lining the balls parallel to the edge of the *sfoglia*, 1 inch in from the edge and 1 inch from one another. Or set out preformed balls in the same manner. In other words, make ravioli as described in method 1 on pages 65–66. Once each sheet of *sfoglia* is lined with a row of *ripieno* balls, fold them over and press firmly between each agnolotto. Cut them with the ravioli wheel and set aside, but not on top of one another.

Bring a large pot of cold water to a boil. Add a pinch of salt and bring to a boil again. Cook the agnolotti in the rapidly boiling water until al dente (8–9 minutes).

In the meantime, prepare the sauce by skimming any fat off the gravy or juice and then heating it together with the cream in a saucepan. When the agnolotti are done, drain well, transfer to a large warm dish, and pour on enough sauce to flavor the pasta without drowning it. Toss delicately and serve with grated parmigiano.

෨ WINE: Any robust red such as those suggested for Agnolotti alla Piemontese (page 162).

LIGURIA

**Corzetti · Pesto alla Genovese · Pesto al Frullatore ·
Salsa di Maggiorana · Tocco de Noxe · Trenette "Imperiali" ·
Lasagne al Pesto · Ravioli di Ricotta · Pansôti**

Corzetti

*Corzetti are one of the classic pastas of the Ligurian kitchen. I
sampled this dish in Moneglia, a seaside town on the border between the provinces of Genoa and La Spezia in an area filled with
olive groves. Felice Romani, a Genoese who produced some of the
most important libretti in Italian opera, died in Moneglia in 1865
at the age of 77. Romani wrote* Il Pirata, La Sonnambula, I Capuleti
e i Montecchi, *and* Norma *for Bellini;* Anna Bolena, L'Elisir d'Amore,
and Lucrezia Borgia *for Donizetti;* Il Turco in Italia *for Rossini and*
Un Giorno di Regno *for Verdi. Crosazzi were silver coins in use
during the Genoese Republic in the thirteenth and fourteenth centuries whose shape influenced the design of corzetti. In fact, the
coins themselves were pressed into the dough to form the shaped
pasta. The corzetti in this recipe originated in the Val Polcevara
near Genoa. They are shaped in a figure 8 and their name, in
dialect, is* corzetti tiae co-e-die. *You may serve these with Salsa di
Maggiorana (page 171) or a mushroom sauce such as the one in
Spaghetti ai Funghi Freschi (page 147). This is a good dish for
budding pasta cooks who are still getting used to working with
dough but are not yet confident about rolling and cutting.*

2½ cups flour
2–3 eggs

Form a mound of flour on a lightly floured working surface. Separate the flour in the center to form a shell; the sloping flour will resemble a volcano in shape. Break the eggs into the center of the flour. Beat well with a fork and add 1 tablespoon of lukewarm water. Start working the pasta with your hands until you form a firm and smooth dough.

Pull off a piece of dough the size of a cherry. Using both index fingers, flatten and stretch the dough lengthwise and then press down on either side to form a corzetto shaped like the number 8.

As you make the corzetti, set them out on your working surface, keeping them from touching. Let dry for several hours, even several days, before cooking.

Bring a large pot of water to a boil. Add a pinch of salt. When the water boils again, cook the corzetti until al dente. Drain well and combine with the sauce of your choice.

🐟 WINE: Depends on the sauce; see individual sauces.

Pesto alla Genovese

This is the classic pasta sauce of Genoa. Many Italians consider it the finest sauce of all. There are many variations, some of which are listed below, but the traditional ingredients are fresh basil, Sardinian pecorino cheese, Ligurian olive oil, and garlic. Pesto may be served with Ravioli alla Ricotta, spaghetti, trenette, bavette, or gnocchi. Pesto also is excellent in lasagne, and when stirred into vegetable soup makes Minestrone alla Genovese. It does not go with meat-filled pasta such as tortellini or on chicken breast with grapes, though I have actually seen these preparations in so-called gourmet food stores in New York. Pesto is the product of a particular region and should be served with specific foods from that region. The name of the sauce comes from the action required to produce it: using a pestle and mortar to mash the ingredients into a paste. Nowadays a blender is also used to make a good pesto, as you will see in the next recipe, Pesto al Frullatore.

4 SERVINGS

1 large bunch of fresh basil leaves	5–6 tablespoons extra-virgin olive oil, approximately
½ teaspoon salt	⅞ cup freshly grated sharp pecorino
3–4 cloves garlic	
1 teaspoon pinoli	

Ligurians say that basil should never be washed. Rather, wipe the leaves carefully but well with a clean cloth if they need cleaning. Discard the stems and put the basil leaves in a mortar. Add the salt and a clove of garlic and crush with the pestle against the sides of the mortar. When they have become mushy, add some more basil and another clove of garlic. Continue crushing until you have used all of the basil and garlic. Now put in the pinoli and continue the crushing until all the ingredients are well blended. Continue, adding a little olive oil to moisten the mixture. As the sauce grows creamier add the pecorino cheese little by little, mixing with a wooden spoon. Add the rest of the oil, a little at a time, continually blending with the pestle or wooden spoon. If you do not want to use all the oil, do not. If you think the sauce requires more oil, add it, but remember that the result should be creamy yet quite thick. You may want to dilute the *pesto* with a few spoonfuls of the boiling water you use for cooking the pasta.

VARIATIONS: In some parts of Liguria the sauce is made only partially with basil, the rest of the greens being a combination of marjoram, parsley, and spinach. You may use walnut meats instead of pinoli. This sauce used to be part of the rustic cooking of local people. Only pecorino was available to them. When people in Liguria started using grana cheeses such as parmi- giano from Emilia, they put them in their *pesto* as well. You may combine cheeses or use just one, though *pesto* made with pecorino is classic.

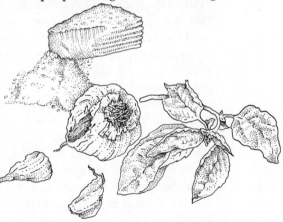

❧ WINE: A white such as Gavi or a red such as Dolcetto or Rossesse di Dolceacqua.

Pesto al Frullatore

Pesto Made in a Blender

This version of the Ligurian sauce was given to me by the excellent Genoese baritone, Giuseppe Taddei. He is well known in both romantic and comic roles, and is also admired for his beautiful phrasing and fine acting. Here, in his own words, are Taddei's thoughts and recipe for pesto: "Pasta is the prince of Italian cuisine and, for its pliability, is a bit of a symbol of fantasy, plasticity, and the capacity of this people to create much with very little. There are innumerable pasta recipes, new ones as well as classics. Among the classic recipes I like most, due in part to my Genoese origin, is pasta with pesto. Pesto is a green sauce based on basil. To obtain a good pesto the basil must be fresh. The ideal would be the very green, thick, extravagantly perfumed basil that grows on the sunny, rocky slopes of my Liguria, but since it is not always possible to find it, settle for the freshest, greenest basil available. This sauce, I think, is one that does not keep well and should never be stored in jars or cans.

4 SERVINGS

8 ounces fresh basil
8 ounces freshly grated parmigiano
2 ounces pinoli
3 cloves garlic
1 cup pure, high-quality olive oil
¾ cup heavy cream

"Put all the ingredients (except the cream) in a blender and mix until you have sort of a green cream. Add the heavy cream and mix only until the amalgam is perfect. The cream is my own personal addition. You can also do without it, but I think it makes the sauce creamier, smoother, and more uniform. The taste of the sauce becomes more delicate without its being robbed of the aroma.

"Put the sauce in a serving bowl (perhaps of earthenware—avoid plastic) and add freshly cooked pasta al dente or potato gnocchi. Personally, I prefer gnocchi with pesto, but these require long preparation. The type of pasta I recommend are bavette (similar to spaghetti but flat rather than round). I also suggest that you cook 3 or 4 potatoes, peeled and cut in several pieces, along with the pasta. When the pasta is al dente, drain with the potatoes and add both to the pesto.

"Before serving, add a bit of melted butter mixed with a few drops of water."

VARIATION: You may use pecorino instead of parmigiano or combine the 2 cheeses.

AUTHOR'S SUGGESTION: When using the blender, mix at maximum speed for 1 minute, then check the sauce, scraping the sides with a rubber spatula. Mix for another few seconds, and the sauce should be ready.

🍷 WINE: A white such as Gavi or a red such as Dolcetto or Rossesse di Dolceacqua.

Salsa di Maggiorana

Marjoram Sauce

This sauce may be used on corzetti (page 167) or Ravioli di Ricotta (page 174). Of course it will be much more successful if you use fresh marjoram. The name of this herb comes from the Greek; it means joy of the mountain, and it flourishes in the hills of Liguria.

4 SERVINGS

    4   ounces (1 stick) sweet butter
    2   tablespoons fresh marjoram or 1 teaspoon dried
    2   tablespoons pinoli
    ½   cup grated grana or pecorino

Gently melt the butter in a saucepan or double boiler. When thoroughly melted, add the marjoram and pinoli and let the combination heat slowly for 1 minute. When the pasta is ready, transfer it to a warm dish. Sprinkle on the grated cheese and then pour on the herb butter. Toss quickly and serve at once.

🍷 WINE: Dolceacqua from the province of Imperia, Polcevera from the province of Genoa, or Dolcetto Ligure are all classic choices. If you cannot locate these, a good red would be Dolcetto from Piedmont. For a white, drink Vernaccia di San Gimignano.

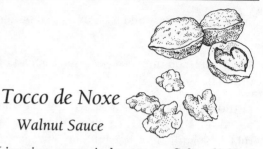

Tocco de Noxe

Walnut Sauce

In most of Italy, this Ligurian sauce is known as Salsa di Noci, but I call it by its name in dialect. This sauce has become quite chic in sophisticated food circles, though it does not marry well with all pasta dishes. It is required for Pansôti (page 176) and also goes well with cheese ravioli, tortelloni, tagliatelle, and some tortellini. Traditionally this sauce is made with curdled milk, known in Liguria as prescinseua, *but you may use milk or fresh ricotta diluted in water.*

4 SERVINGS

6 ounces walnut kernels
2 tablespoons plain bread
  crumbs
1 clove garlic, minced
  Salt (optional)
4 tablespoons olive oil

2 tablespoons freshly grated
  grana
  Pinch of marjoram
1 cup milk, or 6 ounces ricotta
  and a bit of water

Put the walnuts in a mortar with the bread crumbs, garlic, and salt and, using a pestle, grind to a fine paste. Or run everything together in a blender; what this method lacks in authenticity it compensates for in simplicity. If you use a blender, add the oil with the other ingredients. Another method is to finely chop the walnuts (with a good knife or in one of the new-fangled nut chopping toys now appearing on the market) and then combine with the above-mentioned ingredients to form a paste.

However the paste is made, add to it the grana and marjoram, and then pour in just enough milk to produce a semi-thick sauce. Unless you used the blender, you still have not added the oil. Fold it in now, a tablespoon at a time, stirring continuously with a wooden spoon.

VARIATION: Instead of all walnuts, use 4 ounces of walnuts and 2 ounces of pinoli.

🍷 WINE: This depends on what sauce is served on; see recommendations for filled pastas.

Trenette "Imperiali"

Trenette from Imperia

Imperia is the provincial capital of an area that includes much of the western coast of Liguria, the area also known as the Italian Riviera. The nearby Valle d'Impero produces a sensationally fruity olive oil. You should only attempt this recipe with fresh artichokes.

3–4 SERVINGS

½ ounce dried mushrooms
   Juice of ½ lemon
4 artichokes
1 clove garlic
½ small onion

4 tablespoons minced parsley
½ cup olive oil
4 large fresh tomatoes, pureed
   Salt and pepper (optional)
12 ounces trenette

Rinse the mushrooms carefully and then soak in cool water for at least 2 hours.

Fill a bowl with cold water and squeeze the lemon juice into the water. Remove the leaves and chokes from the artichokes, slice them and put into the lemon water. Slice the tender end of the artichoke stems and add to the lemon water.

Remove the mushrooms from their water, carefully squeeze out excess liquid, and mince along with the garlic, onion, and parsley. Heat the oil in a pot and add minced ingredients. Sauté for 3 minutes. Drain the artichoke hearts and add to the other ingredients along with the tomato puree. Add salt and pepper if you wish, cover the pot, and turn the flame down as low as possible. Cook for 15 minutes.

In the meantime, cook the trenette in abundant boiling water; try to time them to finish with the sauce. Just before serving pour a drop of white wine into the sauce and turn the flame up high for 15 seconds. Do not serve grated cheese.

🍷 WINE: Ligurian wine has not ventured to the United States. If you can find a Rossese or a Dolceacqua, they are recommended. In their absence, try a Dolcetto, a Freisa (both reds), or a white Cortese dell'Alto Monferrato from neighboring Piedmont.

Lasagne al Pesto

4–6 SERVINGS

VERSION 1
  1 pound lasagne
     Pesto (amount produced in recipe on page 168)
  ½ cup grated pecorino and/or parmigiano

Boil the lasagne in a large pot (or perhaps 2 pots) of lightly salted boiling water until al dente. Drain carefully so the lasagne do not break. Put a spoonful of *pesto* in the bottom of a very warm serving dish. Put in a few lasagne, top with a layer of *pesto* and grated cheese, then continue with more lasagne, *pesto*, and cheese, working quickly and making as many layers as you can.

Serve immediately. To keep the dish hot while building the layers, you might consider resting it over a pot of boiling water.

VERSION 2
Ingredients listed above
  ½ pound of fresh ricotta

Boil the lasagne until almost al dente. Drain carefully and place a layer in a lasagne pan or baking dish that has been greased with olive oil. Spoon on some *pesto* and spread it so that the entire sheet of pasta is covered. Top with bits of ricotta and sprinkle on some grated cheese. Cover with another layer of lasagne and continue making thin layers until you have exhausted all the ingredients. Finish with lasagne on top. Grate over this a good amount of pecorino or parmigiano, dot with butter and bake in a preheated 425°F oven for 10 minutes.

& WINE: A red Dolcetto or a white Gavi.

Ravioli di Ricotta

In North America these are called cheese ravioli, but that appellation fails to underscore what makes this such a popular pasta dish

in Italy: the presence of fresh, creamy ricotta romana. Though the
principal ingredient is from Rome, this dish is eaten in most of
Italy and is especially popular in Liguria.

4 SERVINGS

Ripieno
  1 egg
    Salt and pepper to taste
 12 ounces fresh ricotta

  4 tablespoons freshly grated
    parmigiano

Sfoglia
3½ cups unbleached, all-purpose
    flour
  3 eggs

Make the *ripieno* first. Beat the egg with salt and pepper, then add
the ricotta and parmigiano in a mixing bowl. Blend with a fork or
spoon until the ingredients are thoroughly combined.

Make the *sfoglia* according to the directions on pages 52–58. Prepare the ravioli using either method 1 or 2 as indicated on pages 65–
66 and 66–67. Let them rest a few minutes before cooking in a large
pot of boiling water until they balloon slightly or, as they say in
Rome, until the ravioli flower. Drain carefully but well, and serve
with one of the following sauces: tomato (page 109); tomato cream
(page 114); tomato with herbs (page 110); *pesto* (page 168); melted
butter with sage (page 156); and strips of prosciutto; any meat sauce;
walnut sauce (page 172); herb sauce (page 115).

VARIATIONS: Instead of using all ricotta, try 6 ounces combined with
6 ounces of any of the following: Stracchino, Bel Paese, Taleggio. Or,
instead of using ricotta you may use fresh goat's milk cheese or
fresh sheep's milk cheese. In Basilicata they use freshly grated aged
pecorino instead of parmigiano. In Bologna they add nutmeg and
cinnamon to the cheese. I once made it in the Bolognese fashion and
added raisins (about 2 ounces).

You may also make these ravioli with 8 ounces of fresh spinach
which has been washed, steamed, squeezed dry, finely minced and
blended with 6 ounces of ricotta.

&❧ WINE: This depends on which sauce you use
since the ripieno is neutral.

Pansôti

The name of this pasta ripiena *comes from the Ligurian dialect for the Italian word* panciuti, *which means pot-bellied. This great specialty of the Italian Riviera is difficult to reproduce due to the absence of the traditional ingredients. At the heart of the ripieno is the* preboggion, *an assortment of herbs that grow wild on the slopes of Liguria. These are combined with various minced greens and ricotta cheese to make the* ripieno. Pansôti *are always served with walnut sauce. I have adapted this recipe for our kitchens from the way pansôti are prepared in 2 fine Ligurian restaurants: Il Gigante in Monterosso in the Cinqueterre and Ca' Peo in Leivi in the province of Genoa.*

For your preboggion *and greens, use a combination of as many of these ingredients as you can find: spinach, watercress, arugula, fennel, chicory, escarole, savoy cabbage, a generous amount of chervil, beet greens, acacia, fresh marjoram, nettles, parsley, and a little basil. Do not use an overwhelming amount of any one of these. It is in combination that they become interesting. Only spinach, parsley, and chervil should appear in substantial amounts.*

4 SERVINGS

Ripieno
1½ pounds combined greens and
   herbs
  8 ounces fresh ricotta
  2 tablespoons freshly grated
    grana

2 eggs
1 clove garlic, finely minced
  (optional)
  Pinch of salt

Sfoglia
3½ cups unbleached, all-purpose
    flour
  2 eggs or some white wine (see
    below)
    Pinch of salt

Walnut Sauce (page 172)

Make the *ripieno* first. Wash and steam the greens and fresh herbs together; the water clinging to the vegetables is sufficient. When they are well cooked, drain and squeeze well, conserving the liquid, if you wish, for a soup. Mince. Combine the greens and herbs in a mixing bowl with the ricotta, grana, eggs, garlic, and salt until thoroughly combined. Set aside.

To make the *sfoglia*, put the flour in a mound on your working surface and form a well in the middle. Into the well put the eggs, salt, and enough water to make a rather solid dough.

Once the dough is ready, roll out to a thickness of ⅛ to ¼ inch. Cover with a towel or cloth to prevent from drying. Take a knife or pasta wheel and cut equilateral triangles of *sfoglia* with sides 2½–3 inches long. Put about ½ teaspoon of *ripieno* in the center of each triangle. Fold the triangles so that you join the 2 outermost points. Press all around to seal the *pansôto* tightly.

Once all the *pansôti* are made, let them sit on a board or baking sheet dusted with flour for 30–45 minutes in a draft-free place. Meanwhile, bring a large pot of water to a boil. Toss in a pinch of salt and bring to a boil again. Cook the pansôti in the boiling water until al dente, about 8–10 minutes. Serve with Walnut Sauce.

VARIATIONS: Instead of cutting the *sfoglia* into triangles, cut into squares with 2-inch sides. Put the ripieno in the center and fold the squares diagonally to form triangles. In making the *preboggion*, you may also steam the greens alone, adding minced fresh herbs after. This will result in a *ripieno* with more distinct herbal flavor and fragrance.

NOTE: The recipe for the *sfoglia* above is according to the method at both Il Gigante and Ca' Peo. However, in some areas of Liguria the *sfoglia* for *pansôti* is made by pouring some white wine into the well and adding a few tablespoons of tepid water, again to form a relatively solid dough.

❧ WINE: Vernaccia di San Gimignano or Orvieto.

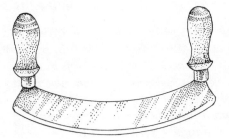

EMILIA-ROMAGNA

Ragù Bolognese · Salsa Besciamella · Besciamella Magra ·
Spaghetti con le Rucole · Tagliatelle al Prosciutto ·
Paglia e Fieno di Bologna · Pasta al Mascarpone ·
Chicche Verdi del Nonno · Cannelloni alla Rigoletto ·
Lasagne Verdi alla Bolognese · Pasta di Festa ·
Anolen alla Parmigiana ·
Tortelli alla Piacentina di Giorgio Armani ·
Tortelli di Patate · Caramelle di Verdi ·
Tortellini alla Bolognese, Version 1 ·
Tortellini alla Bolognese, Version 2 ·
Tortellini alla Bolognese, Version 3 ·
Salsa alla Panna per i Tortellini · Cappelletti alla Romagnola ·
Tortelloni della Vigilia · Tortelloni ai Quattro Formaggi ·
Balanzoni alla Delizia

Ragù Bolognese

Meat Sauce in the Style of Bologna

*This recipe is from Ruggero Raimondi, who also provided his own
creation, Per Chi non Vuole Ingrassare, on page 110. Signor Raimondi, who is Bolognese, says that ragù is his favorite sauce. When
I lived in Bologna, I could never get enough of this magnificent
sauce, which is ideally matched with fresh Bolognese tagliatelle.
With a light gilding of parmigiano, this is pasta eating at its best.
You may also serve Ragù Bolognese with maccheroni, tortellini, or*

tortelloni. For a more elaborate version, suited for boiled pastas, see the recipe for Lasagne Verdi alla Bolognese (page 187).

In examining the ingredients for this sauce, you may be surprised. Outside Italy, meat sauces are usually very liquidy. In Bologna the ragù (which does not mean stew as it does in French) is rich and condensed. The secret to success is slow cooking.

FOR 1 POUND OF PASTA

3 tablespoons sweet butter
3 tablespoons olive oil
2 carrots, coarsely chopped
2 stalks celery, coarsely
   chopped
½ medium onion, coarsely
   chopped
1 pound ground lean beef

⅛ to ¼ teaspoon nutmeg
Salt to taste
1 cup whole milk
1 tablespoon tomato paste,
   diluted with ½ to ¾ cup
   water
½ beef bouillon cube (optional)

Over a very low flame, gently melt the butter together with the oil in a heavy-bottomed deep pot. Add the carrots, celery, and onion, and sauté slowly and carefully, making sure they do not burn. When the vegetables are lightly sautéed, add the meat, nutmeg, and salt. Using a wooden spoon, combine all ingredients, cover the pot, and cook *very slowly*. When the meat is lightly cooked though not yet brown, add the milk, cover, and cook over the lowest possible heat for 45 minutes or until the milk has been absorbed. Mix every once in a while with the wooden spoon. When the milk has evaporated, add the diluted tomato paste. (If bouillon is used, first dissolve the bouillon in the water for diluting the tomato paste.) Continue cooking very slowly another 45 minutes.

VARIATIONS: Instead of tomato paste, add 1 pound of coarsely chopped fresh or canned peeled tomatoes with their liquid. In this case, cook for 3–4 more hours, until the tomato liquid has completely evaporated and the sauce is quite thick. When I make ragù this way, I use 4 carrots for extra texture and sweetness.

❧ WINE: A Bolognese would drink Lambrusco or Sangiovese di Romagna. The only Lambrusco I recommend is Lambrusco di Sorbara, which is hard to find outside Italy. You may also drink a Barbera or, failing all of these, an Inferno, Chianti, or Cabernet del Friuli.

Salsa Besciamella

Bechamel Sauce

This is one of the most frequently used sauces in pasta cookery. You find it throughout Italy but especially in Emilia-Romagna, where it is often referred to as balsamella. *It is used as a key ingredient in baked pasta dishes such as cannelloni and lasagne, as well as for enriching other sauces. A sauce of equal parts besciamella and tomato puree is called Salsa Aurora, a simple and tasty sauce for penne or maccheroni when served with lots of freshly grated grana.*

1–2 SERVINGS

½ cup whole milk
1 tablespoon sweet butter
1 tablespoon flour

An "idea" of nutmeg
Salt and pepper (optional)

Heat the milk in a pot until almost boiling. In the meantime, gently melt the butter in another pot. When it becomes foamy (make sure it does not turn color), add the flour, nutmeg, salt, and pepper, and stir so that the combination is completely free of lumps. Pour in the hot milk a little at a time, stirring all the while with a wooden spoon. Continue cooking for 8–10 minutes more, stirring constantly to prevent lumps. The result should be velvety and uniform.

NOTE: The desired thickness of besciamella changes according to the dish in which it is to be used. Therefore, in every recipe in this book that calls for besciamella, the proportions required are listed. The process is always the same.

Besciamella Magra

"Lean" Bechamel Sauce

I devised this sauce for those who want the richness of besciamella but still want to watch calories. Please understand that this is not the classic version of the sauce, but it is an acceptable substitute. You may use this for a Salsa Aurora with a clear conscience. When combining with heavier sauces, the besciamella will lend some richness and will benefit from the fats in the other sauces.

6 SERVINGS

2 cups whole milk
1½ tablespoons sweet butter

7 tablespoons flour
An "idea" of nutmeg

Heat the milk in a pot until scalding. In the meantime, gently melt the butter in another pot. When it becomes foamy (make sure it does not turn color), add the flour gradually while continuously stirring with a wooden spoon. Try to stir out all the lumps. Add the nutmeg and then a very small amount of milk. Stir until all the lumps are gone. Add milk gradually, stirring all the while. Heat for 8–10 minutes more, until you have a smooth, creamy sauce.

Spaghetti con le Rucole

Spaghetti with Arugula

This easy and delicious recipe was given to me by Ezio Salsini, proprietor of the Taverna alle Tre Frecce in Bologna. Signor Salsini is typically Bolognese: warm and expansive, enamored of good food, fine company, and high spirits. His restaurant specializes in the traditional dishes of Emilia-Romagna and dabbles in cucina nuova but is always mindful of the great gastronomic tradition of this region.

1 SERVING

4 ounces fresh arugula
4 ounces spaghetti
3 tablespoons extra-virgin olive
   oil

1 clove garlic, cut in half
1 small peperoncino, cut in 3
   pieces

Set a large pot of water to boil. When it boils, add salt.

Carefully wash the arugula, removing any discolored stems or leaves. Separate the stems if they are joined but do not tear the leaves from the stems. Put the spaghetti and arugula in the boiling water.

In a saucepan heat the oil with the garlic and peperoncino. Use moderate heat and make sure that the 2 "flavors" do not burn, which would give the oil a bitter taste. When the spaghetti are al dente, drain them and the arugula thoroughly, giving the colander several good shakes. Remove the garlic and peperoncino from the pan, add the spaghetti and arugula, and toss with a fork over moderate heat for 30 seconds. Serve immediately. Do not use cheese.

🍂 WINE: An amber-colored Albana or red Sangiovese, both from Emilia-Romagna, are ideal.

Tagliatelle al Prosciutto

An easy recipe whose success rests on the luxury of superb ingredients. When I lived in Bologna, eggy tagliatelle, nutty parmigiano, sweet butter, and sublime prosciutto were available in every pastificio and salumeria. The combined flavors are classic. One hint: Before boiling the tagliatelle make sure they are separated from one another. This will make them cook evenly, and they will be easier to sauce.

Use the best prosciutto available.

1 SERVING

4 ounces fresh tagliatelle (page 58), or store-bought	2–3 tablespoons freshly grated parmigiano
1½ tablespoons sweet butter	
2 ounces prosciutto, cut into small cubes	

Set a large pot of cold water to boil. When the water in the pot reaches a full boil, toss in a pinch of salt, bring to a boil again, and start cooking the tagliatelle.

At the same moment, melt the butter in a pan, add the prosciutto, and brown gently.

When the tagliatelle are al dente, drain thoroughly and transfer to a warm bowl. Sprinkle on 2 tablespoons of parmigiano, then add the prosciutto and butter sauce. Toss well, add the third tablespoon of cheese if you choose, and serve right away.

🍂 WINE: If you have an excellent Lambrusco di Sorbara, that would be ideal. Sangiovese is also fine.

Paglia e Fieno di Bologna

The combination of white and green pasta is popular throughout Italy but especially in Bologna and Rome. This pairing is known as paglia e fieno *(straw and hay).*

1 SERVING

1 tablespoon sweet butter	2–3 ounces light cream
1 small clove garlic	Nutmeg
6 fresh mushrooms, sliced	Pepper
3 ounces ground pork sausage	Grana
4 ounces fresh green and white pasta (tagliatelle or tagliolini)	

For cooking the pasta, bring a large pot (at least 6 quarts) of cold water to a boil, lightly salt, and bring to a boil again.

In a small pan melt the butter and sauté the garlic. Discard the garlic and sauté the mushrooms. At the same time, fry the sausage meat in another pan, making sure to cook it thoroughly. When the sausage is almost ready, start to cook the pasta.

Add the cream and a dash of nutmeg to the mushrooms and stir. Drain the pasta and put in a bowl. Add the heated mushroom-cream mixture and the sausage, and toss well. Grate on fresh pepper and grana to taste, and then eat.

VARIATION: In the springtime I often add young peas to this dish; they give it a touch of sweetness.

🐌 WINE: Sangiovese di Romagna, Rosso Conero, or Inferno.

Pasta al Mascarpone

Most of the dishes I have chosen for this book are healthy and sane, good for you and fine to eat at any time. But here is a dish that is wickedly delicious, much too fattening to comprehend, and yet ideal for a once-in-a-great-while special treat. Read about mascarpone on page 285. I have found, through much too frequent sampling, that the pastas most suited to this sauce are gnocchi and large maccheroni.

2 SERVINGS

8 ounces gnocchi (page 73)
  or maccheroni
7 tablespoons sweet butter
½ cup heavy cream
½ cup grated parmigiano or
  Gruyère

2 ounces (½ cup) mascarpone
1 egg yolk
  Salt and pepper to taste

Once the pasta is in hand, set a large pot of water to boil. When it boils, toss in a pinch of salt.

Melt the butter slowly in a pan and add the cream. Let the combination reduce for a couple of minutes.

Start cooking the pasta. The gnocchi are ready when they rise to the top of the boiling water. The maccheroni should be cooked al dente.

Once you have heated the cream and butter as directed, add the parmigiano or Gruyère and combine well with a wooden spoon. Let the cheese melt slowly over a moderate flame. In the meantime (while the pasta is cooking and the cheese is melting—stay alert!), put the mascarpone in a bowl and blend in the egg yolk with a wooden spoon until you have a velvety cream. Add a bit of salt and pepper.

Drain the pasta thoroughly and add to the pan with the cheese sauce. Toss over low heat for a few seconds until the sauce and pasta are combined. Remove from the heat and pour on the mascarpone. Combine quickly and thoroughly, and serve *immediately*.

NOTE: If you are increasing this recipe, incorporate the egg yolks one by one.

VARIATION: I have made this dish with a combination of Gruyère and parmigiano. This makes for a good mixture of sweetness and tang.

❧ WINE: A robust red is indicated. I suggest Nebbiolo d'Alba, Barbera, Carema, Sassella, or Franciacorta Rosso.

Chicche Verdi del Nonno

This recipe is from Carlo Bergonzi, the excellent Verdian tenor who was born in Vidalenzo in the province of Parma, not far from Giuseppe Verdi's birthplace in Roncole. Signor Bergonzi operates the Hotel I Due Foscari (named for a Verdi opera) in Busseto, the town where Verdi spent most of his life. This dish, along with Caramelle di Verdi *(page 195), are both specialties at I Due Foscari.* Chicche *are gnocchetti or small dumplings.*

8 SERVINGS

Pasta

1½ pounds medium-sized potatoes	2½ cups semolina flour, sifted
8 ounces spinach	2 eggs
	Pinch of salt

Sauce

4 ounces (1 stick) sweet butter	1½ cups heavy cream
1 tablespoon tomato puree	1 cup grated parmigiano

Make the *chicche:* Wash and boil the potatoes until tender, but not mushy (about 20 minutes). Peel the potatoes and then grate coarsely. Wash the spinach well and cook until tender using only the water clinging to the leaves. When cooked, drain of all excess liquid and chop very fine. On a pastry board combine the potato, flour, and spinach. Form a well in the center, add the eggs and salt, and work the whole mixture into a soft homogeneous dough. Divide the dough into several parts and roll into long cylinders about ¾ inch thick. Start cutting the dough into ¾-inch lengths so that you are left with little square dumplings. If you wish, you may roll each dumpling under a fork so that the tines give the *chicche* the distinctive gnocchi "look." This is not crucial, however.

Cook the *chicche* in a large pot of lightly salted boiling water. They are ready when they rise to the top of the boiling water. As they do, remove them with a wooden spoon to a large bowl of cold water.

When all the *chicche* are cooked, drain in a colander and start making the sauce.

Melt the butter in a large saucepan, spoon in the tomato puree to give the sauce a rosy tint, and add the cream. Heat gently for 3–4 minutes—*do not boil*—and add the *chicche.* Stir carefully for a few seconds and then add the grated cheese. Combine well, continuing to cook for 2–3 minutes. Serve immediately.

&. WINE: If you have access to an *excellent* Lambrusco, that would be ideal. If not, try Sangiovese di Romagna, Gutturnio dei Colli Piacentini, Freisa, or Ghemme.

Cannelloni alla Rigoletto

Occasionally I am asked what is the best meal I have ever eaten or what is the best restaurant I have ever been to. I will never respond to such a question because a memorable meal is a product of several tangible and intangible factors: excellent food, capably and imaginatively prepared; exciting company; a pleasing environment; and, I suppose, the mood of the eater. I can tell you that one of the most blissful combinations of these elements happened for me at the Ristorante Guareschi of Roncole Verdi in the serene countryside of the province of Parma. Alberto Guareschi, his lovely wife, and their beaming family take immense pride in their work. Their restaurant, down the street from the birthplace of Giuseppe Verdi, serves only food they grow and wine they produce themselves. They are even proud of the local water, which is served in large pitchers garnished with lemon slices and fresh mint from the Guareschi garden. Nowhere have I tasted better parmigiano, which is brought to the table in a large wedge accompanied by a grater, ready to gild a wonderful array of dishes. All of the pastas here are superb but, as an opera man, it was my correct hunch that Cannelloni alla Rigoletto would please me most.

4 SERVINGS

Sfoglia:
5 cups durum wheat flour (see Note)	3 eggs
	1–2 tablespoons water

Ripieno:
2 pounds fresh spinach	2 cups grated parmigiano
2 cups ricotta	Pinch of salt
1 egg	

Besciamella:
2 quarts whole milk	1½ cups all-purpose flour
8 ounces (2 sticks) sweet butter	Salt to taste

Prepare the pasta as explained on pages 52–58. Cut the sheets into 8 squares approximately 5 × 5 inches each. Boil the squares briefly in a large pot, 1 or 2 at a time, until they are less than half done. Drain and set aside to cool.

To make the filling, wash the spinach thoroughly and put in the pot you used to cook the pasta. Do not add water. When the spinach is cooked, drain well of any excess liquid and chop very fine. Put the spinach and all the other ingredients in a bowl and mix thoroughly until they form a lumpy paste.

Divide the paste into 8 equal portions and place one on each pasta square. Loosely fold over 2 sides of the squares to make cylinders.

Make the besciamella sauce. Heat the milk until almost boiling. At the same time melt the butter over medium heat in a heavy enameled saucepan. Stir the flour gradually into the butter using a wooden spoon until the combination becomes a thick, bubbling paste. Cook and stir 2 minutes more, taking great care not to scorch the mixture. Remove the saucepan from the heat and start adding the milk, 2 tablespoons at a time, stirring all the while. Continue until all the milk is completely blended into the sauce. Return the pan to low heat, add a bit of salt to taste, and stir until the mixture has the consistency of heavy cream.

Take a flat enameled baking dish large enough to hold all the cannelloni with room to spare. Pour in half the besciamella sauce, then arrange the cannelloni side by side but not touching. Top with the rest of the sauce. Give the pasta a dusting of gold by generously sprinkling parmigiano over the sauce. Bake in the center of a pre-heated 350°F oven for 20 minutes, by which time the sauce should be bubbling.

Immediately before serving, place the pan under a broiler and heat until the top is crusty and golden brown. Drizzle on a bit of melted butter and another dusting of parmigiano.

NOTE: This recipe makes more pasta than is required for this dish. Keep the rest to use as fettuccine or tagliatelle for another dish.

🞄 WINE: A rich, full-bodied red is called for. Amarone, Barolo, and a good Spanna are excellent choices.

Lasagne Verdi alla Bolognese

This is one of the glories of Italian cuisine. After tasting Bologna's green lasagne it was difficult for me to even consider lasagne from elsewhere in Italy or America. Of course, there are many fine lasagne (this word is the plural of lasagna), but the following recipe is clearly my favorite. Its preparation is painstaking, but I think you will agree that the effort is worth it.

6–8 SERVINGS

1 pound lasagne verdi (see recipe for *pasta verde*, page 60, or use store-bought green lasagne of high quality) Large piece, at least 10 ounces, parmigiano for grating

2 tablespoons butter

Ragù
2 ounces (½ stick) butter
1 onion, chopped
1 large carrot, finely grated
1 stalk celery, chopped
12 ounces lean ground beef
8 ounces ground veal
8 ounces ground lean pork
4 ounces chicken livers, chopped

¾ teaspoon salt
Pepper
½ cup fresh tomato sauce
¾ cup white wine
1½ cups stock or water

Besciamella
2 ounces (½ stick) butter
4 tablespoons flour
2 cups milk, at room temperature

2 pinches of freshly grated nutmeg
Salt

Prepare the *lasagne verdi* first if you are making fresh pasta. Let it dry according to the instructions.

Bring a large pot (at least 8 quarts) of cold water to a boil. Add a pinch of salt and bring again to a boil. Preheat oven to 375°F.

Prepare the ragù: Melt the butter in a saucepan and add the onion, carrot, and celery. Sauté the vegetables lightly. Add the beef, veal, and pork, and cook on a low flame for 10–15 minutes. Drain off any excess fat, leaving just a drop. Add the chicken livers, salt, and pepper to taste. Cook for 2 minutes. Pour in the tomato sauce, wine, and ½ cup stock or water. Simmer for 60–70 minutes and then add more stock, bit by bit. This sauce should be thick and concentrated, not a suspension of ingredients in a lot of liquid.

While the ragù is simmering, prepare the besciamella sauce: Melt the butter in a heavy saucepan. Just as the butter starts to foam (don't let it turn brown), add the flour, lower the heat, and beat steadily with a wire whisk, making sure there are no lumps in the mixture. When the mixture is smooth pour in the milk and continue beating with the whisk, being ever watchful for lumps. Cook for 3–4 minutes, then add the nutmeg and, if you wish, a bit of salt.

When the besciamella is ready, boil the lasagne sheets until a bit firmer than al dente—about 3 minutes (but keep vigilant watch since homemade pasta may cook faster or slower).

Cook only a few lasagne at a time and then drain. Boil only enough to use for 1 layer at a time, according to the directions below. Boil more only as needed. Once cooked, lay the lasagne on a moist towel, making sure they do not tear. Coat a 9 × 13-inch baking dish with 1 tablespoon of butter. (Do *not* use a thin aluminum lasagne pan.) Follow with a thin layer of ragù, then a dusting of fresh parmigiano. Dot with a little butter; then cover with a layer of lasagne.

Continue to add layers in the following sequence: ragù, besciamella, parmigiano, lasagne. Keep the layers thin: Try to repeat the sequence 5 or 6 times. This will make the dish more delicate and intriguing than heavily piled layers of sauce and pasta. Finish off the layers with some ragù, besciamella and a generous amount of parmigiano. Dot with a little more butter.

Bake for 20 minutes. The top should be golden and the lasagne bubbling hot; the edges should have shrunken away from the sides of the pan and be just a bit crisp. If you don't think it is ready, bake 5 to 10 minutes more until the lasagne is cooked as you like it. Allow to rest slightly, then cut wedges and serve with parmigiano for those who would like to grate some on. *Buon appetito!*

❧ WINE: Lambrusco di Sorbara or any full-bodied red wine.

Pasta di Festa

Holiday Pasta

This recipe calls for crespelle (crepes). You can make them according to the instructions on page 75. If you want to save time or if you are interested in a bit of variety, lasagne can be substituted with good results. Pasta di Festa is served by Tarcisio Raccagni at his Ristorante Gigole in the charming town of Brisighella, not far from Faenza in the province of Ravenna. This is an excellent example of la vera cucina romagnola *(true cuisine of Romagna).*

6 SERVINGS

12 crepes or 1 pound white lasagne	6 ounces grated parmigiano
12 ounces fresh spinach	Salt to taste
4 ounces prosciutto, cut in tiny cubes	Pinch of nutmeg
	1 pint fresh heavy cream

Make the crespelle and set aside.

If you are using lasagne, cook in abundant boiling water until al dente. Carefully set to dry on cloth toweling.

To prepare the sauce, wash the spinach well and then steam in a covered pot—do not add more water—until the leaves are soft. Squeeze excess water from the spinach and then chop very fine. Put the spinach in a mixing bowl and add the prosciutto, parmigiano, salt, and nutmeg. Beat the cream slightly with a whisk and pour into the bowl. Continue to beat until the mixture becomes slightly foamy.

Place a layer of crespelle (or lasagne) at the bottom of a buttered baking dish. Spoon over enough sauce to lightly cover the crespelle. Add another layer of crespelle, then sauce, and so forth, until you have used up all the ingredients. Dot the top layer with butter and grate another sprinkling of parmigiano over the dish.

Bake in a preheated 425°F oven for 15–20 minutes until golden brown on top. Allow to rest for a few minutes before serving.

🍷 WINE: Sangiovese di Romagna is a perfect match for this dish. Any medium-bodied red will do. For something special, try to find a Lambrusco di Sorbara. Most Lambruschi sold in America are like soda pop—definitely not like the Lambrusco consumed in Emilia-Romagna. But genuine Lambrusco, well chilled, would sparkle with this festive dish.

Anolen alla Parmigiana

Anolini from Parma

This recipe unquestionably dates from an era when people in Parma had time on their hands. It takes over 12 hours to prepare, and veri parmigiani *insist that the only authentic way is to make the* ripieno *one day and stuff the* sfoglia *the next. I wonder if Giuseppina Strepponi, the great diva who was Verdi's second wife, passed her extra time in the kitchen in Sant'Agata making Anolen alla Parmigiana while Verdi was in the next room writing* I Vespri Siciliani *and* Simon Boccanegra. *Sublime inspiration indeed.*

4–6 SERVINGS

Ripieno

6	ounces (1½ sticks) sweet butter	
1	onion, minced	
1	carrot, minced	
1	stalk celery, minced	
1	pound loin of beef	
3	cloves garlic, slivered	
1	cup red wine	
3	tablespoons tomato sauce	

3–4 cloves
2 teaspoons cinnamon
  Salt and pepper to taste
1 quart broth or hot water
¾ cup bread crumbs
2½ cups grated parmigiano
2 eggs
¼ teaspoon nutmeg

Sfoglia
3½ cups flour
3–4 eggs
  Milk, if necessary

Melt the butter in a medium-sized, heavy-bottomed pot. Sauté the onion, carrot, and celery. Cut slits into the beef and insert the garlic slivers; put the meat in the pot. Brown on all sides over a low flame for 10 minutes. Pour in the wine, raise the heat slightly, and let most of the wine evaporate. Add the tomato sauce, cloves, cinnamon, salt, pepper, and half the broth or water. Cover the pot and cook over the lowest flame possible for 10–12 hours.

You must check the pot every 20–30 minutes to make sure the liquid does not become too condensed. When necessary, add a little more broth, hot water, or red wine. The meat you are cooking is called *stracotto* (extra-cooked) and may be served as a second course after the pasta. When the *stracotto* is done, remove from the pot and strain the gravy.

Now comes a choice: In some Parma kitchens only the gravy is used; in others the *stracotto* is ground and added to the gravy. The decision is yours. Combine the gravy (and meat, if you choose) with the bread crumbs, parmigiano, eggs, and nutmeg until the ingredients are well blended.

If you are not including the meat, you will probably need more parmigiano and bread crumbs to make a firmer *ripieno*. Let the *ripieno* rest for a while. If you are planning to finish the *anolen* the next day, keep the ripieno in the refrigerator in a sealed container.

When you are ready to make the *sfoglia*, follow the directions on pages 52–58. Roll out a sheet of *sfoglia* and stamp out rounds 1–1½ inches in diameter using a drinking glass or a pasta press. Put a tablespoon of ripieno in the centers of half the *sfoglia* rounds. Cover with the remaining *sfoglia* rounds and press down around the edges of the *anolen* to seal.

Boil the *anolen* in a large pot of meat or chicken broth or lightly salted water. Serve either in broth with grated parmigiano, with a sauce of melted butter and sage plus parmigiano, or with Ragù Bolognese.

🥢 WINE: Drink the same wine you use for cooking. My first choice is Sangiovese, which is produced throughout Emilia-Romagna. Any Barbera from Piedmont, Lombardy, or Emilia-Romagna is fine. One particular wine that would be a special treat if you can find it is Vien Tosc Rosso, a fresh wine similar to Sangiovese that is produced high up in the Apennines. The special flavor is due not only to the mountain soil but to the grape used. It is known as Tosca, and it obviously appeals to any opera lover.

Tortelli alla Piacentina di Giorgio Armani
Spinach and Cheese Tortelli from Piacenza

I asked Giorgio Armani for this excellent recipe from his native Piacenza, not only because these tortelli are delicious but because Armani embodies many of the virtues so particular to the aesthetic of Italy: intimate knowledge of the materials at hand; an emphasis on quality, elegance, and practicality; and a startling individuality that is somehow in harmony with its surroundings. Armani's work is at the same time classical in feeling yet influenced by his own creative perspective. These virtues, evident in many areas of Italian life, should be applied to Italian cooking as well. Classic recipes should be learned, yet individual experimentation and variation should be encouraged.

Piacenza is at the northern end of Emilia. This area was the birthplace of Christopher Columbus's mother. I wonder if, on his journey to the Americas, Columbus ate tortelli (or perhaps the ravioli popular with Genoese sailors) or if he had to eat Spanish food.

Tortelli alla Piacentina, often referred to in Emilia as tortelli di erbette, *is a popular summertime dish. I have reduced the quantities in Mr. Armani's recipe, but the balance and proportion are unchanged. Following the recipe are some of my own variations as well as recommendations for suitable wines.*

4–6 SERVINGS

Ripieno
1 pound fresh spinach
1¼ pounds fresh ricotta
1–2 eggs, depending upon size

1⅓ cups freshly grated
parmigiano or grana
Salt to taste

Sfoglia
3½ cups unbleached white flour
3–4 eggs

Cut off the stems of the spinach, wash the leaves carefully under cold running water, drain in a colander, and squeeze out the excess water. Finely chop the spinach and mix with the ricotta, eggs, grated cheese, and salt until the ingredients are thoroughly combined. Allow to rest in a cool place.

Make the *sfoglia* by combining the flour, eggs and, if necessary, enough tepid water to make a smooth dough that is neither dry nor too soft; otherwise it will be difficult to fold the tortelli into the right shape. Wrap the dough in a dishcloth until you are ready to roll it out. Using a rolling pin or, if you wish, a manual pasta machine, roll out the pasta and make the tortelli using either method in the instructions on page 69.

When ready, transfer each tortello to a floured cloth to prevent from sticking to one another. Boil the tortelli in a large pot of lightly salted water taking care not to break or damage them. As they rise to the top gently prod back into the water with a slotted ladle. Cook until just tender, approximately 12–15 minutes.

Drain thoroughly in a colander and gently transfer to a large casserole or bowl. Add several knobs of butter and some grated parmigiano or grana. Mix and stir slowly so that the tortelli are evenly coated with butter and cheese. To obtain good results, try holding the casserole by its handles or the bowl by its edges, turning back and forth in a circular fashion so that the butter and cheese are well distributed. Serve immediately.

VARIATIONS: You might want to add pepper and, perhaps, nutmeg to the *ripieno*. In other parts of Emilia the spinach is often lightly steamed before being chopped and blended with the ricotta. If you are adventurous, you may use other greens instead of, or in addition to, the spinach. I once chopped up cooked chicken and used it in place of the ricotta. You can also consider using a combination of chicken and ricotta.

❧ WINE: Gutturnio, Buttafuoco, Barbera, or Valpolicella.

Tortelli di Patate

Potato Tortelli

The best Tortelli di Patate I have tried all seem to come from the hilly regions not far from Reggio nell'Emilia. This area produces the finest grana cheese, known as parmigiano-reggiano or simply parmigiano. Wonderful fresh ricotta is also made there. Reggio itself was the birthplace of Ludovico Ariosto (1474–1533), whose Orlando Furioso *is the finest romantic epic produced in the Renaissance.*

6 SERVINGS

Ripieno
2 pounds potatoes	2 eggs
4 ounces fresh ricotta	Salt and pepper to taste
2 cups freshly grated grana	Pinch of nutmeg

Sfoglia
3½ cups unbleached flour
3–4 eggs

For the *ripieno*, wash the potatoes, and boil and peel them while still hot. Mash well. When cool, combine with the ricotta, grana, eggs, salt, pepper, and nutmeg.

Make a *sfoglia* and prepare the tortelli using either method according to the instructions on page 69.

Cook the tortelli carefully in a large pot of lightly salted boiling water. Drain and serve topped with more freshly grated grana and melted butter or Ragù Bolognese.

VARIATIONS: You may use *pasta verde* for the *sfoglia*. In Bologna I once had Tortelli di Patate with tiny bits of bacon in the *ripieno*. For this version, lightly sauté ¼ pound of bacon or prosciutto in 1 tablespoon of butter; finely chop before adding to the *ripieno*.

In Romagna I tried these with fresh watercress. For this, add 3 tablespoons of finely minced watercress to the *ripieno*. Add some slivers of prosciutto to the melted butter you serve on top of them.

Some Bolognesi like to add a ½ cup of Vecchia Romagna, the local brandy, to the *ripieno*. This is not to my liking, but many people enjoy it.

🍷 WINE: Buttafuoco, Barbera, Gutturnio, Sangiovese, or Valpolicella.

Caramelle di Verdi

I wonder if Giuseppe Verdi ever had a chance to try these luscious paste ripiene named in his honor. What music would he have been inspired to write as a result? These caramelle *(in Italian this means hard candy more than a chewy caramel) are prepared by Carlo Bergonzi, the tenor whose recipe for spinach gnocchi appears on page 184. They are shaped like pieces of wrapped candy. In most of Emilia they are called* tortelli con la coda *(tortelli with a tail), but I think that* caramelle *is more accurately descriptive and more appealing.*

For this dish you must prepare 3 sfoglie: a red one, a white one, and a green one. I recommend that you make this on special occasions and double the amounts, which means you will require 2 sheets of each kind of sfoglia. This preparation is complicated but well worth the fuss.

To make the pasta for these sfoglie, *see pages 52–58.*

6 SERVINGS

8 ounces roast veal	1 tablespoon freshly grated lemon peel
6 ounces braised beef (without gravy)	1 tablespoon finely minced fresh mint
4 ounces boiled ham or *mortadella*	1 tablespoon freshly grated orange peel
2 eggs	
½ cup freshly grated parmigiano	1 sheet egg pasta (white)
¼ teaspoon nutmeg	1 sheet spinach pasta (green)
Pinch of salt	1 sheet tomato pasta (red)
Pinch of freshly ground pepper	

Prepare the *ripieno*. Finely chop, mince, and grind the veal, beef, and ham or *mortadella* until thoroughly combined. Add the eggs, parmigiano, nutmeg, salt, and pepper, and blend well.

Divide the *ripieno* into 3 equal parts. Combine 1 part well with the lemon peel, 1 with the mint, and the third with the orange peel.

Set the 3 *ripieni* aside (perhaps in the refrigerator if you take a lot of time to make the *sfoglie*).

Make each *sfoglia* and roll out to between ⅛ and ¼ inch thick. Spread the sheet of white *sfoglia* on your working surface. Using Method 1 for making ravioli (page 65), put balls of the lemon-flavored *ripieno* the size of hard candy in a parallel row 1 inch from the edge of the *sfoglia*. The balls should be 3–3½ inches apart. Fold over the edge of the *sfoglia* to cover the balls of *ripieno*. Press firmly and then cut along this seam with a knife or ravioli wheel. Press down with your fingertips on the *sfoglia* between the *ripieni* to form individual tortelli. Cut them with the knife or ravioli wheel.

Lift the ends of each tortello with the fingertips of both hands. Turn your left hand toward you while turning your right hand away from you. In effect, you are wrapping the *ripieno* by twisting the *sfoglia* around it. The result should look exactly like a piece of wrapped candy. Repeat this process until you have wrapped all the pieces of lemon *ripieno*.

Follow the same procedure with green pasta and balls of mint sfoglia. Finally, wrap the red pasta around the orange ripieno.

Arrange the finished caramelle on your working surface so they do not touch one another. Cover with a dishtowel or cloth and let dry at cool room temperature for at least 24 hours. Cook in abundant boiling water until al dente (taste one to decide) and then serve with a rich tomato cream sauce (page 114).

Signor Bergonzi suggests melting butter (about 2 ounces, or ½ stick of butter) in a saucepan, adding a rather thick tomato sauce (page 109), salt, and pepper. Stir with a wooden spoon, then add heavy cream and continue stirring. The caramelle and sauce should be served with freshly grated parmigiano.

🍂 WINE: Signor Bergonzi serves excellent Lambrusco from Emilia. It is not likely that you can find Lambrusco this good in your area, so try something else. This dish calls for a great wine. I would recommend Barbaresco or a good Spanna.

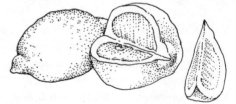

Tortellini alla Bolognese

This recipe includes the classic ingredients for tortellini as they are made in Bologna. Other versions of tortellini follow.

4–6 SERVINGS

Sfoglia

3½ cups unbleached flour
3–4 eggs
   or
3 cups unbleached flour

½ pound spinach, cooked, squeezed dry and minced
2–3 eggs

VERSION 1

Ripieno

2 ounces (½ stick) sweet butter
4 ounces loin of pork
4 ounces turkey breast
2 ounces beef marrow
4 ounces prosciutto
2 ounces *mortadella*

1¼ cups freshly grated parmigiano
2 eggs, beaten
Salt to taste
Freshly ground pepper to taste
Nutmeg to taste

Melt the butter in a pan and sauté the pork, turkey, and marrow for 8–10 minutes. Mince well, perhaps with a meat grinder, and then mince the meats again along with the prosciutto and *mortadella*. Put the ground meats in a mixing bowl and add the parmigiano, eggs, salt, pepper, and nutmeg. Combine the ingredients thoroughly to make a uniform paste.

Refrigerate the *ripieno*, covered, for several hours before making the tortellini. When you are ready to make the pasta, produce a *sfoglia* and prepare the tortellini as indicated on page 72.

After the tortellini have dried on a cloth for 30–45 minutes, cook in a good beef or chicken broth until al dente, 5–8 minutes. The classic way to serve tortellini is in a rich capon broth that has been skimmed.

Or bring a large pot of water to a boil, salt lightly, bring to a boil again and cook the tortellini in that until al dente. Serve with ragù (page 178), tomato and cream sauce (page 114), with a cream sauce (page 199), pistachio sauce (page 277), walnut sauce (page 172), herb sauce (page 115) or with melted butter topped with sautéed mushrooms or shaved truffle. The herb and nut sauces are not classic with this combination, but they have become increasingly popular. All the sauces may be served with grated parmigiano except the truffle and butter sauce.

VERSION 2
Ripieno

2 tablespoons sweet butter
8 ounces turkey or capon
   breast
4 ounces prosciutto
4 ounces boiled ham
2 ounces *mortadella*

¼ pound boiled calves brains
   (optional)
¾ cup freshly grated parmigiano
2 eggs, beaten
   Salt and pepper to taste
¼ teaspoon nutmeg

Melt the butter in a saucepan and sauté the turkey or capon until completely cooked. (As an alternative you may use leftover boiled or roast turkey or capon.) When the poultry is cooked, let cool slightly and then grind well in a meat grinder or by hand with the prosciutto, ham, *mortadella*, and brains. When you have a finely ground mixture, combine thoroughly with the cheese, eggs, and spices to form a uniform paste. Put the *ripieno* in the refrigerator, covered, for several hours. Prepare and cook the tortellini as indicated in version 1 and combine with one of the sauces indicated.

VERSION 3
Ripieno

2 ounces (½ stick) sweet butter
8 ounces mildly spicy sausage,
   without fennel seeds, skinned
8 ounces ground veal
8 ounces ground turkey,
   chicken, or capon breast

2 ounces *mortadella*
2 eggs, beaten
1 cup freshly grated parmigiano
   Salt and pepper to taste

Melt the butter in a saucepan. Crumble the sausage meat and cook for 5 minutes. Add the veal and poultry and continue cooking for about 6 minutes more until the meats are cooked. Turn off the flame and let the combination cool. Grind the 3 meats with the *mortadella*, add the eggs, cheese, salt, and pepper, and work the *ripieno* into a smooth paste. Put the *ripieno* in the refrigerator, covered, for several hours. Prepare and cook the tortellini as indicated in version 1 and combine with one of the sauces indicated.

WINE: A full-bodied red such as Sangiovese di Romagna, Barbera, Gutturnio, Amarone, Gattinara, or Sassella.

Salsa alla Panna per i Tortellini

Cream Sauce for Tortellini

This recipe will make enough sauce for the recipes for tortellini on pages 197–198.

4–6 SERVINGS

4 ounces (1 stick) sweet butter
¾ cup heavy cream

1 cup freshly grated parmigiano
Pinch of nutmeg

In a large pot of lightly salted boiling water cook the tortellini until just short of al dente. Melt a bit of butter in a large saucepan over a low flame. Add a little cream, some parmigiano and nutmeg. Add all of the drained tortellini. Gradually add more butter, cream, and some more parmigiano, stirring gently and allowing to form a velvety sauce that embraces the tortellini. Serve with additional parmigiano and, perhaps, some freshly ground pepper.

Cappelletti alla Romagnola

Cappelletti from Romagna

This classic pasta ripiena from Romagna is most frequently served in a rich beef broth into which a healthy amount of parmigiano is grated. You may also serve cappelletti with ragù or, perhaps, a tomato cream sauce.

6 SERVINGS

Ripieno
10 ounces fresh ricotta
1½ cups freshly grated parmigiano
1 egg, beaten
Pinch of nutmeg
Salt and pepper to taste (optional)

1 tablespoon minced parsley (optional)

4 quarts rich homemade beef broth

Sfoglia
3½ cups unbleached flour
3–4 eggs

Combine the ricotta, parmigiano, egg, nutmeg, and salt, pepper, and parsley in a bowl until thoroughly blended. If you think the *ripieno* is too loose, add a bit more parmigiano. Set aside.

Prepare the *sfoglia* for cappelletti as indicated on page 71. Cut the squares of *sfoglia*, filling and forming the cappelletti according to the directions, and set aside for 30 minutes or so. Cook in the broth until they al dente, about 5 minutes. Serve in the broth or skim out with a slotted spoon or ladle, and serve with ragù. If you are serving the cappelletti with ragù or another sauce, you may boil them in water, but they will not be quite as flavorful.

VARIATION: You may reduce the ricotta to 6 ounces and add 4 ounces of Bel Paese, Stracchino, Taleggio, or Fontina which has been cut into tiny bits.

❧ WINE: Sangiovese di Romagna or Barbera, Gutturnio, or Valpolicella.

Tortelloni della Vigilia

Christmas Eve Tortelloni

While it is traditional to eat meat-filled tortellini on Christmas Day in Bologna, cheese-filled tortelloni are usually consumed the night before.

4–6 SERVINGS

Ripieno

1 pound fresh ricotta	Pinch of nutmeg
1¾ cups freshly grated parmigiano	Salt and pepper to taste
1 egg, beaten	1 tablespoon finely minced parsley

Sfoglia

4 cups unbleached flour	2–3 eggs
2–3 eggs	8 ounces spinach, washed,
Milk, if necessary	cooked, squeezed, and
or	minced
3½ cups unbleached flour	

Combine all the ingredients for the *ripieno* in a mixing bowl until thoroughly blended.

Prepare the *sfoglia* and make the tortelloni according to the instructions on page 72. Set aside to dry for at least 30 minutes.

In a large pot of rapidly boiling lightly salted water cook the tortelloni until al dente, 6–8 minutes. Drain well and serve with either a ragù (page 178) or a rich tomato sauce (page 109), with lots of freshly grated parmigiano. These are also delicious with walnut sauce (page 172).

🍶 WINE: Sangiovese di Romagna, an excellent Lambrusco, Barbera, Gutturnio, or Valpolicella.

Tortelloni ai Quattro Formaggi

Four-Cheese Tortelloni

When a recipe is called ai quattro formaggi *it usually suggests pasta in a sauce of 4 cheeses. In this case, the 4 cheeses are inside the pasta, and it makes a delicious combination.*

4–6 SERVINGS

Ripieno
   8 ounces Emmenthal (Swiss) cheese, grated
   4 ounces Stracchino, cut in tiny bits
   4 ounces *mascarpone*

1¾ cups freshly grated parmigiano
   Freshly ground pepper (optional)
   Pinch of nutmeg

Sfoglia
   4 cups unbleached flour
2–3 eggs
   Milk, if necessary
   or
3½ cups unbleached flour

2–3 eggs
   ½ pound spinach, washed, cooked, squeezed and minced

Combine the ingredients for the *ripieno* until thoroughly blended. If you think the combination is too loose, add more parmigiano. If you think it is too solid (not likely), add a tiny amount of milk.

Set aside. Make a *sfoglia* of *pasta all'uovo* or *pasta verde* and prepare the tortelloni according to the instructions on page 72.

In a large pot of lightly salted boiling water cook the tortelloni until al dente. Drain well and serve with ragù (page 178), a rich tomato sauce (page 109), or walnut sauce (page 172). Grate on a lot of parmigiano.

🍶 WINE: Barbera, Gutturnio, Inferno, or Sangiovese di Romagna.

Balanzoni alla Delizia

Meat-filled Tortelloni

This dish is a specialty at the Ristorante da Carlo in Bologna. There, in the warm weather, you may dine outdoors under beautiful gothic porticos in the historic center of Emilia-Romagna's capital.

4–6 SERVINGS

Ripieno

- 2 ounces (½ stick) sweet butter
- 8 ounces ground veal
- 2 tablespoons minced onion (optional)
- ½ cup white wine
- 4 ounces *mortadella*, finely minced
- 4 ounces prosciutto, finely minced
- 1½ cups freshly grated parmigiano
- 2 eggs, beaten
  Salt and pepper to taste
  Pinch of nutmeg
- ⅛ teaspoon ground cloves (optional)

Sfoglia

- 4 cups unbleached flour
- 2–3 eggs
  Milk, if necessary

Sauce

- 1 ounce funghi porcini
- 6 ounces (1½ sticks) sweet butter
- 2 ounces prosciutto, cut into tiny cubes
  Freshly grated parmigiano

Melt the butter in a pan and sauté the veal and onion until halfway cooked. Pour on the wine and let evaporate. By now the meat should be cooked through. Drain off the liquid in the pan and combine the veal with the *mortadella* and prosciutto. Mince thoroughly or, preferably, run through a meat grinder using a medium blade. Combine the meat with the parmigiano, eggs, and spices until well blended. Cover the *ripieno*, and store in the refrigerator for 4–6 hours.

Two hours before you wish to serve the balanzoni, soak the funghi porcini.

When you are ready to make the pasta, prepare as you would tortelloni according to the instructions on page 72. Set aside for at least 30 minutes before cooking in a large pot of rapidly boiling salted water until al dente.

To make the sauce, drain the funghi porcini, pat in paper towels to remove all excess moisture; if they are large, slice. Melt the butter in a saucepan and add the funghi porcini and prosciutto. Stir gently and continuously until the balanzoni are ready. Drain well, make individual servings in warm bowls, top with the sauce, and grate on some fresh parmigiano.

🍷 WINE: Sangiovese di Romagna, an excellent Lambrusco, Gutturnio, or Barbera.

THE MARCHE (MARCHES) AND UMBRIA

Ragù di Castrato alla Marchigiana · Linguette Rustiche ·
Tagliolini Beniamino Gigli · Ravioli con Sogliola ·
Ragù di Maiale all'Umbra · Spaghetti con Asparagi e Pomodoro ·
Linguine al Morino · Agnolotti al Tartufo Nero ·
Lasagne di Gubbio

Ragù di Castrato alla Marchigiana

Mutton Sauce, Marches-Style

The word castrato *takes on a different meaning if you are dealing with an opera lover than it does if you are conversing with a fan of Italian cuisine. In opera, the castrato, also known as an* evirato *(an emasculated one), was a man who lacked certain things but made up for that by possessing remarkable vocal technique and often being able to sing in a 3-octave range. These men were frequently referred to as* voci bianche *(white voices) and were sought after throughout Europe not only for opera performances but also to be kept in courts by patrons who found them amusing, charming, pitiful, or desirable. The practice of creating castrati was outlawed toward the end of the eighteenth century. One of the last great castrati was Gaspare Pacchierotti (1740–1821) who was born in Fabriano. This beautiful little town in the Marches was also the birthplace of Gentile da Fabriano (1370–1427), one of the greatest artists of the early Renaissance. Fabriano has manufactured paper for centuries and has a population of friendly, hardworking people who enjoy good food. It was here that I first tasted mutton (castrato) sauce, though I have since eaten it throughout the Marches, the Abruzzi, and lower Umbria.*

2 ounces lard or 6 tablespoons olive oil	12 ounces ground lean mutton
1 onion, minced	1½ cups dry red wine (see wine note)
1 celery stalk, minced	8 ounces tomatoes, peeled, seeded, and pureed
1 carrot, minced	½ peperoncino, minced
1 clove garlic, crushed	Salt and pepper to taste
2 teaspoons rosemary	

Heat the lard or oil in a saucepan and sauté the onion, celery, carrot, and garlic for 1 minute. Add the rosemary and, 30 seconds later, the mutton. Brown briefly and then pour in the wine. When it evaporates, add the tomatoes, peperoncino, salt, and pepper. Cook the sauce over medium heat, partially covered, until rather condensed and thick. Serve with mezzani, penne, or maccheroni. I like to grate on Canestrato cheese, but pecorino is fine too.

🍂 WINE: Drink the wine you cook with. If possible, either a Rosso Conero or a Montepulciano d'Abruzzo would be an excellent choice.

Linguette Rustiche

This dish is served at the Ristorante da Silvano in Macerata, where it is prepared by Anna Maria Ferri, the chef. If possible, use very spicy sausage. Signorina Ferri uses the local wine in this sauce. If you want red, buy Rosso Conero; for white, buy Verdicchio.

6 SERVINGS

8 tablespoons olive oil	1 teaspoon oregano
2 tablespoons sweet butter	2 tablespoons finely chopped fresh basil or 1 teaspoon dried
1 small onion, chopped into medium-sized pieces	
1 peperoncino (red), minced	1 cup fresh peas (or frozen, if necessary)
1 pound sausage meat, removed from its casings	1 pound chopped tomatoes, peeled and, if canned, drained (reserve the juice)
1 cup wine	
½ teaspoon salt	1 pound linguette or tagliolini
2 teaspoons freshly grated pepper	

Heat the oil and butter in a heavy-bottomed pot. Sauté the onion and peperoncino until the onion is transparent. Add the sausage and cook for 5 minutes. Pour in the wine and, once some has evaporated, add the salt, pepper, oregano, and basil. Simmer for 5 minutes, then add the peas. After 5 more minutes, put the tomatoes in the pot. Cover the pot and simmer for 40 minutes, stirring occasionally with a wooden spoon. If you find the sauce is becoming too thick, add a bit of the reserved tomato liquid. Please note, however, that this sauce should be thick and flavorful, and the pasta should not swim in it.

In the meantime bring a large pot of water to a boil. Salt lightly and bring to a boil again. Start cooking the pasta about 5 minutes before the sauce is ready. Drain well and put in a large warm bowl or in individual plates. Top with the sauce. This dish should be served with grated grana or pecorino.

&. WINE: Rosso Conero or Verdicchio.

Tagliolini Beniamino Gigli

I sampled this dish in Porto Recanati, the birthplace of Beniamino Gigli (1890–1957), the legendary tenor. The velvety sweetness of Gigli's voice and his passionate phrasing made him immensely popular.

2–3 SERVINGS

1–2 small eggplants, about 8 ounces total	Pinch of salt
1 small peperoncino (red)	4 grindings of pepper
2–3 ounces pancetta	8 ounces tomatoes, peeled
2–3 ounces prosciutto	8 ounces tagliolini
4 tablespoons olive oil	1 tablespoon minced parsley

A good sharp knife is the key to this dish. Wash and peel the eggplants. Cut lengthwise into strips no thicker than a pencil. Wash the peperoncino and cut lengthwise into the skinniest strips possible. Cut the pancetta into thin strips and the prosciutto into tiny cubes.

Set a large pot of water to boil. Toss in a pinch of salt and bring to a boil again.

In a large saucepan heat the oil and then sauté the peperoncino and eggplant for 2 minutes. Add the pancetta, prosciutto, salt, and pepper, and continue cooking over a medium flame for 5 minutes, occasionally giving the pan a vigorous shake. Add the tomatoes, cover the pan, and simmer for 20 minutes.

About 5 minutes before the sauce is ready, cook the tagliolini in the boiling water. When al dente, drain well and add to the sauce along with the parsley. Toss quickly and thoroughly so that the eggplant strips curl up with the strands of pasta. Serve immediately with freshly grated grana.

🍷 WINE: Rosso Conero or Verdicchio.

Ravioli con Sogliola ·
Ravioli with Sole

Pesaro is a bustling provincial capital in the region of the Marches not too far south of Rimini on the Adriatic. In the summertime it is packed with northern Europeans who come for their holiday by the sea. Pesaro is also a major stop for opera lovers. This is the town that gave us Rossini (you can visit his house at Via Rossini 34) and soprano Renata Tebaldi. Its excellent music academy has produced generations of great musicians and composers, including Riccardo Zandonai, whose Francesca da Rimini *recently received an excellent production at the Metropolitan Opera. In August, Pesaro has a Rossini festival under the supervision of Maestro Alberto Zedda, a noted Rossini scholar, which should not be missed by anyone who loves this composer's brilliant music. Pesaro also has many good restaurants, including the Ristorante al Scudiero, not far from Rossini's house, where I found one of the finest pasta dishes I've ever tasted.*

6 SERVINGS

Sfoglia
- 4 eggs
- 1 pound flour
- Bit of salt

Ripieno
- 8 ounces fish (see Note)
- 12 ounces fresh unsalted ricotta
- 4 ounces freshly grated parmigiano
- 1 egg
- ¼ teaspoon nutmeg
- 1 tablespoon grated lemon peel

Sauce

2 tablespoons olive oil
2 slices pancetta, minced
  (optional)
½ small onion, minced
3 tablespoons minced fresh
  parsley
8 ounces sole fillets

½ cup Verdicchio or other dry
  white wine
8 ounces tomatoes (canned or
  fresh), crushed and peeled
1 tablespoon tomato paste
  Salt and pepper to taste

Prepare the pasta for the ravioli according to the instructions on page 52. In making this recipe, I have found that a few drops of oil or water in the flour are necessary. The success of this dish depends on its delicacy, so take care not to make the pasta layers too thick.

To make the filling: Poach the fish gently and briefly in water. Remove the fish from the water and drain well on paper towels. Mince well and put in a bowl with the other ingredients. Combine thoroughly.

Place little balls of the filling along 1 sheet of the pasta, as explained on page 65. Cover with the other sheet of the pasta, cut with a ravioli wheel or with a knife, and seal the ravioli with your fingertips. Set aside to dry slightly.

For the sauce: Put the oil and pancetta in a pan over medium heat. If you don't use the pancetta, add 2 additional tablespoons of oil. Add the onion and cook for 1 minute. Put in the parsley and sole. Sauté the fish until slightly cooked. Pour in the wine, raise the heat slightly, and let it evaporate. Add the tomatoes, tomato paste, salt, and pepper. Cook the mixture for 20 minutes, stirring occasionally. The sole will disintegrate, giving body to the sauce.

While the sauce is simmering, in a large pot of lightly salted boiling water cook the ravioli until done—7–9 minutes is average. Drain the ravioli and transfer to individual plates. Serve topped with the sauce. Do not serve grated cheese.

NOTE: I have used sole fillets. Any flaky white-fleshed fish will do.

🍂 WINE: Verdicchio from the slopes of the Marches, inland from Pesaro.

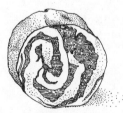

Ragù di Maiale all'Umbra

Umbrian Meat Sauce with Pork

I sampled this sauce in Perugia, a town where excellent pork is found. The great nineteenth-century contralto, Marietta Alboni, was born in nearby Città di Castello. She studied with Rossini, in whose operas she excelled. Alboni was famous throughout Europe for her portrayals in Il Barbiere di Siviglia, La Cenerentola, La Gazza Ladra *and* Semiramide. *Perugia was also the birthplace of Baldassare Ferri (1610–1680), perhaps the greatest castrato of his time. Serve Ragù di Maiale all'Umbra with penne, maccheroni, or tagliatelle.*

4 SERVINGS

½ cup olive oil
2 ounces pancetta, cubed
1 onion, minced
1 carrot, minced
1 stalk celery, minced
1 clove garlic, minced
1 tablespoon minced parsley

12 ounces ground lean pork
½ cup Orvieto or other dry
  white wine
  Salt and pepper to taste
8 ounces tomatoes, peeled,
  seeded, and pureed

Heat the oil in a saucepan and add the pancetta, onion, carrot, celery, garlic, and parsley. Sauté for a few moments and then add the pork. Cook for 2 minutes and pour in the Orvieto. When the wine evaporates, add a little salt and pepper and then the tomatoes. Cover and cook over medium heat for about 1 hour, stirring occasionally. The sauce should be thick, but if it needs a bit of liquid at any point, stir in a tablespoon of hot water. You may top this sauce with freshly grated parmigiano or pecorino.

VARIATION: Add a healthy pinch of ginger when you add the tomatoes.

🍷 WINE: Orvieto secco.

Spaghetti con Asparagi e Pomodoro

Spaghetti with Asparagus and Tomato

For those few precious weeks that asparagus are available I take every opportunity to eat them. Whenever you use asparagus for pasta sauces, be sure not to overcook. If anything, they should be underdone since they will receive further cooking in the sauce. I tasted this dish in Orvieto, birthplace of Luigi Mancinelli (1848– 1921), a conductor who was considered a direct predecessor of Toscanini. Mancinelli conducted at the world premieres of Verdi's Falstaff *and of* Tosca. *This recipe is popular in Umbria, though it is made throughout Italy. In Tuscany it is frequently served with penne instead of spaghetti.*

4 SERVINGS

8 ounces asparagus
½ cup olive oil
1 clove garlic
8 ounces tomatoes, peeled and seeded

Salt and pepper to taste.
1 pound spaghetti
Freshly grated pecorino or grana

Set a large pot of cold water to boil.

Scrape and cut away the tough ends of the asparagus. Steam or boil the tender stalks until barely al dente. Remove from the water and cut into small pieces. Heat the oil in a saucepan and add the garlic clove. Add the tomatoes, salt, and pepper, and simmer for 10 minutes. After the tomatoes have cooked, remove the garlic clove and add the asparagus. Continue to simmer. When the water is boiling, toss in a pinch of salt and start cooking the pasta. When al dente, drain well and transfer to a serving dish. Top with the sauce, sprinkle on freshly grated pecorino or grana, toss, and serve.

VARIATION: Before adding the sauce toss into the pasta a lightly beaten egg into which you have ground some pepper. If you have leftover chicken, cut it in bite-sized pieces and add to the tomato sauce along with the asparagus.

🍃 WINE: Chianti or Orvieto.

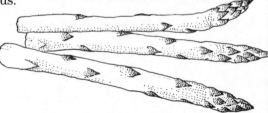

Linguine al Morino

This is the house sauce of the Ristorante Il Morino in Orvieto. It calls for ingredients more readily available in Umbria, yet with a bit of looking you can now locate them in the United States as well. Orvieto is a small town blessed with many riches: a great cathedral, a world-famous white wine, an Etruscan heritage, superb truffles, and friendly, if not overly demonstrative, citizens. Serve this pasta as a succulent first course before a meal of roast pork or veal.

4 SERVINGS

6 ounces (1½ sticks) sweet butter

3 tablespoons black truffle paste (see Note)

3 tablespoons olive paste (see Note)

3 tablespoons truffled mushroom paste (see Note)

10 ounces linguine

3 tablespoons freshly grated parmigiano

Set a large pot of water to boil. When boiling, toss in a pinch of salt and bring to a boil again.

In a casserole dish or heavy-bottomed pot, melt the butter, truffle paste, olive paste, and mushroom paste over a low flame for 10 minutes.

In the meantime, cook the pasta until al dente. Drain thoroughly and add to the sauce. Toss for 4 minutes over a low flame, adding the parmigiano just before serving.

NOTE: Truffle paste is available in many specialty food stores in major cities. If you have fresh truffles available to you, use a truffle shaved as thin as possible. Olive paste from Liguria is now sold in jars. If you cannot find it, take whatever black Italian olives you are partial to, remove the pits, and mash to a pulp in a mortar. Truffled mushroom paste, sold in tubes, has also appeared commercially in America, but you can make it yourself by sautéeing quality mushrooms in butter with a bit of garlic and a few shavings of truffles. This too can be mashed to create a smooth paste. To end up with 3 tablespoons of mushroom paste, you will need approximately 8 ounces of mushrooms to start.

❧ WINE: Orvieto secco.

Agnolotti al Tartufo Nero

This exquisite recipe comes from the Ristorante Morino in Orvieto.
The basis for its sauce is the wonderful black truffle of Umbria. The
ripieno *is different from some of those found further north in that*
it does not call for roast meats but for raw ground meat that cooks
inside the sfoglia. Also, notice the presence of tomato.

6 SERVINGS

Ripieno
- 8 ounces lean ground veal
- 4 ounces cooked chicken breast, chopped
- 4 ounces lean ground pork
- 2 ounces prosciutto, minced
- 2 ounces (½ stick) sweet butter, softened

- 12 ounces tomatoes, peeled and seeded
- Salt to taste
- ¼ teaspoon nutmeg

Sfoglia
- 1 pound flour
- 3–4 eggs

Sauce
- 1½ ounces fresh black truffle
- 4 ounces (1 stick) sweet butter
- 3 tablespoons fresh mascarpone
- ½ cup freshly grated parmigiano

Combine all the ingredients for the *ripieno* and work together until
a soft filling is formed. If it is too soft, add some bread crumbs or
grated cheese. Set aside.

Make the *sfoglia* as indicated on pages 52–58 and roll out 2 sheets
of equal size. Dot 1 sheet with neat rows of balls of *ripieno*, each
slightly more than 1 inch apart from one another. Carefully cover
with the other sheet of *sfoglia* (this is method 2 as indicated on page
66). Press down between each ball of *sfoglia* so that the agnolotti
will take shape. Then cut them into individual agnolotti using a knife
or ravioli wheel. Seal with your fingertips. Let the agnolotti rest for
a few minutes in a draft-free area before cooking in broth or rapidly
boiling salted water.

Put a large pot (about 6 quarts) of lightly salted water or light
broth to boil.

Carefully clean the truffle with a brush, making sure you do not crush or break it. Shave the truffle into a large, heavy-bottomed pot (preferably terracotta), add the butter and mascarpone, and let the mixture melt slowly over a low flame. After 2 minutes, add the parmigiano and let the mixture cook gently for 3 minutes. Remove from heat to a warm spot.

Cook the agnolotti in the broth or water for 5–6 minutes. Drain and transfer to the pot of sauce. Cook the pasta and sauce together for 3 minutes, gently stirring so that the agnolotti are bathed in the creamy sauce. Serve immediately on very warm plates.

& WINE: Orvieto secco.

Lasagne di Gubbio
Lasagne, Gubbio-Style

Even among the quiet, mystical towns of Umbria, Gubbio is special. There is an unusual stillness in the town that calls itself the "City of Silence." The favorite legend told is of the Wolf of Gubbio, who rampaged the countryside until St. Francis of Assisi showed him the error of his ways. The wolf gave his paw to St. Francis, seeking forgiveness, and then lived peacefully with the citizens of Gubbio. This scene is depicted in art and ceramics all over town. Gubbio suffered extensive damage in an earthquake in the spring of 1984. I sampled this dish in a small trattoria in Gubbio on All Saint's Day, 1974. I have never since experienced the sort of total silence I felt on that day.

4–6 SERVINGS

1 ounce dried funghi porcini, soaked
1 pound green or white lasagne, or a combination
12 ounces fresh mushrooms
1 teaspoon lemon juice
8 ounces prosciutto, cut in thin ½-inch strips

4 tablespoons olive oil
1 tablespoon sweet butter
1 clove garlic, minced
Pinch of marjoram
⅓ cup Orvieto or Vernaccia
1 cup grated parmigiano

Besciamella
2 cups milk
2 ounces (½ stick) sweet butter

4½ tablespoons flour
Pinch of nutmeg

Two hours before you start cooking, soak the funghi porcini. If you are making fresh lasagne, do that next, following the directions on pages 52–60.

When the lasagne are at hand, set a very large pot of water to boil. When boiling, toss in a pinch of salt and again bring to a boil.

Wipe the fresh mushrooms if necessary and slice as thin as possible. You might consider using a truffle shaver if you own one. When the fresh mushrooms are sliced, sprinkle the lemon juice over them and cut the prosciutto.

Drain the funghi porcini and reserve soaking liquid. Heat the oil and butter in a large pan and add the garlic, fresh mushrooms, and funghi porcini. Sauté for 30 seconds. Add the marjoram, prosciutto, and liquid from the funghi porcini. Cook for 1 minute and then douse with wine. Cover the pan and cook until the mushrooms are tender and most of the liquid is evaporated.

In the meantime, prepare the besciamella as explained on page 180. As the besciamella cooks, start boiling the sheets of lasagne, a few at a time, until about ¾ done. Drain and let cool slightly on a clean dishcloth or towel. Grease a lasagne pan or baking dish with butter. Cover the bottom with a layer of lasagne. Top with about ¼ of the besciamella, ¼ cup of parmigiano, and then about ⅓ of the mushroom-prosciutto mixture. Continue in the following sequence: lasagne, besciamella, parmigiano, mushrooms; lasagne, besciamella, parmigiano, mushrooms; and so forth. Drizzle any liquid left in the mushroom pan on top of the lasagne.

Bake in a preheated 375°F oven for 20 minutes, by which time the lasagne should be golden. Serve immediately with more grated parmigiano.

❧ WINE: I would prefer a red such as Sangiovese di Romagna, Rosso Conero, Chianti, or Inferno, but you may also drink the white wine used in cooking.

TOSCANA (TUSCANY)

**Pasta Corta alla Contadina ·
Maccheroni al Sugo di Coniglio della "Primetta" ·
Tagliatelle alla Panoc · Spaghetti coi Polipi alla Gigliese ·
Spaghetti coi Polipi all'Elbanese · Pappardelle all'Aretina ·
Pappardelle di Prato · Pappardelle al Cinghiale ·
Pappardelle alla Senese**

Pasta Corta alla Contadina

Short Pasta in the Style of a Tuscan Country Woman

Tuscan cuisine is direct, straightforward, and delicious. This recipe comes from Franco Paoletti, owner of the Trattoria da Franco of Strada in Chianti, in the province of Florence. The dish is easy to prepare and the portions indicated are not big, since this is the sort of pasta that would precede a second course of Bistecca alla Fiorentina or some other grilled meat. If you don't plan to eat much else, this recipe would make a substantial meal for 2 or even 3 persons.

4 SERVINGS

12 ounces pasta corta (that is, penne)	3 tablespoons tomato sauce
1 tablespoon sweet butter	3 tablespoons heavy cream
½ teaspoon minced fresh sage	Pinch of salt
½ teaspoon rosemary	2 grindings of fresh pepper

Set a large pot of water to boil. Toss in a pinch of salt. When it reaches a full boil again, add the pasta.

In the meantime, melt the butter in a saucepan with the sage and rosemary for 30 seconds. Add the tomato sauce, cream, salt, and pepper. When the pasta is al dente, drain well and add it to the sauce. Continue to stir the sauce with a wooden spoon until the pasta is completely coated and the combination has lost all "soupiness." Serve with grated parmigiano.

❧ WINE: Perfect with a young Chianti.

Maccheroni al Sugo di Coniglio Della "Primetta"
Maccheroni with Rabbit Sauce

This is genuine Tuscan cooking. This dish is served at the Ristorante Petroio at Radda in Chianti, between Florence and Siena. On the Petroio estate are 15 hectares of vineyards and 3 hectares of olive groves. Much of the food served in the restaurant benefits from the availability of wonderful wine and oil. Try to use the freshest, youngest rabbit you can find.

4 SERVINGS

4 pieces (about 1 pound) rabbit (legs, ribs, thighs)
Rabbit heart and liver
1½ cups extra-virgin olive oil
½ red onion, coarsely chopped
2 tablespoons chopped fresh parsley
1 stalk celery, coarsely chopped
2 cloves garlic, minced
Salt and pepper to taste
1 tablespoon tomato paste
1 pound maccheroni

Clean the rabbit meat, heart, and liver, and put in an earthenware pot with ½ cup of olive oil and 4 tablespoons of water. Cover and gently cook for 1 hour.

About 10 minutes before the rabbit is ready, heat 1 cup of olive oil in an aluminum pan over a very low flame. Add the onion, parsley, celery, garlic, salt, and pepper, and fry only until the onion starts to darken. When the rabbit is done, bone it and chop the meat into chunks. Add the meat to the aluminum pan, stir in the tomato paste, and cook 15 minutes.

About 7 minutes before the sauce is done, cook the maccheroni in rapidly boiling salted water until al dente. Drain well and top with the sauce. You may sprinkle on some grated parmigiano if you wish.

🍷 WINE: Chianti Classico.

Tagliatelle alla Panoc
Tagliatelle with Cognac

This is a tasty pasta to serve as a first course before a meal of fowl, game, or grilled beef. It is prepared at the Trattoria da Franco of Strada in Chianti, Tuscany.

4 SERVINGS

12 ounces fresh tagliatelle (page 58), or store-bought
1 tablespoon sweet butter
4 heaping tablespoons heavy cream
2 walnuts, shelled and finely chopped
4 ounces cognac
Pinch of salt
2 grindings of pepper

In a large pot of water that has been brought to a boil, lightly salted, and again brought to a boil, cook the pasta until al dente.

In the meantime, melt the butter in a pan large enough to hold the pasta.

Drain the pasta and add it to the butter. Toss and immediately add the cream; continue tossing over a low flame. Add the walnuts and, finally, the cognac, salt, and pepper. Give the pan a few good shakes to combine the ingredients and serve immediately. Grated parmigiano is optional.

🍷 WINE: Serve with a good Chianti.

Spaghetti coi Polipi alla Gigliese
Spaghetti with Baby Octopus, Giglio-Style

The seas that wash onto the Italian peninsula offer a dazzling selection of fish and seafood. One of my favorites is octopus. In addition to the large octopus we are familiar with, baby octopi of varying sizes also appear frequently in fish stews and pasta sauces. The most common term for a baby octopus is polipo. In Emilia-

Romagna they are called fragoline di mare *(sea strawberries) when they are pinkish in color. Although baby octopus is not readily available, I include this recipe and Spaghetti coi Polipi all'Elbanese for those people fortunate enough to find them.*

Giglio is one of my favorite spots in all of Italy. This little island off the coast of Tuscany in the province of Grosseto was popular in Roman times as a vacation spot and so it is today. Stendhal called it the Island of Sirens, though I have yet to sight a mermaid in its sapphire-colored waters.

2 SERVINGS

10 ounces baby octopus	½ teaspoon salt
3 tablespoons olive oil	8 ounces spaghetti
1 clove garlic, minced	2 tablespoons minced fresh
8 ounces tomatoes, peeled	parsley

Carefully clean the octopus with cold water. Heat the oil in a saucepan for 30 seconds, add the garlic, then the tomatoes, then the salt, and finally the octopus. Cover and cook over medium heat for 35–45 minutes, stirring occasionally.

When the sauce is nearly done, cook the spaghetti in a large pot of water that has been brought to a boil, lightly salted and again brought to a boil, until the pasta is al dente. Drain thoroughly and transfer to individual bowls. Top with the sauce and sprinkle on fresh parsley.

❧ WINE: Bianco di Toscana or Vernaccia di San Gimignano.

Spaghetti coi Polipi all'Elbanese

Spaghetti with Baby Octopus, Elba-Style

Elba is the largest island in the Tuscan archipelago. Though it has been important since Etruscan times as a source of copper and iron, its place in history was secured by Napoleon, who lived there in exile from May 3, 1814, to February 26, 1815. The man who once ruled much of Europe must have been restless on this little island. He spent his days developing the mining industry, build-

*ing roads, and gazing west to his native Corsica. Nowadays, Elba
has the most famous nudist beaches in Italy. If Napoleon were alive
today, one could say "the Emperor has no clothes" without worry
—he wouldn't need them. I sampled this dish in Portoferraio (Iron
Port), Elba's capital.*

2 SERVINGS

10 ounces baby octopus
4 tablespoons olive oil
1 clove garlic, minced
2 teaspoons capers
1½ ounces pitted black olives

Salt and pepper to taste
8 ounces spaghetti
2 tablespoons fresh parsley,
   minced

Carefully clean the octopus with cold water. Heat the oil in a saucepan for 30 seconds. Add the garlic, capers, olives, octopus, pepper,
and salt. Cover and cook over medium heat for 30–40 minutes, stirring occasionally. If you don't think there is enough liquid—remember that the octopus will give off some water—add a bit more oil or
a few drops of white wine.

When the sauce is almost ready, cook the spaghetti in a large pot
of water that has been brought to a boil, lightly salted and again
brought to a boil, until al dente. Drain thoroughly and transfer to
individual bowls. Top with the sauce and sprinkle on some fresh
parsley.

& WINE: Moscato di Elba is ideal if you can locate it. Other good
choices are Bianco di Custoza, Bianco di Toscana, or Verdicchio.

Pappardelle all'Aretina

Pappardelle, Arezzo-Style

*The hills and valleys of Arezzo's province in Tuscany are bordered
by the Arno River to the west and the Tiber River to the east. Italy's
famous Chianina beef, along with excellent chickens, ducks, geese,
wheat, walnuts, chestnuts, and cherries, are all grown near Arezzo.
This area has also produced many brilliant men. Guido d'Arezzo,
who died in 1050, was the Benedictine monk who invented the
musical scale. Artists such as Masaccio, Michelangelo, Piero della
Francesca, and Paolo Uccello were all from Arezzo or nearby, as
were the writers Pietro Aretino and Petrarch. Giorgio Vasari*

(1511–1574), an architect, painter, and historian from Arezzo, wrote Le Vite de' piu eccellenti architetti, pittori e scultori italiani *(The Lives of the Most Eminent Italian Architects, Painters and Sculptors), known as* Lives of the Artists. *This book, written in 1550 and revised in 1568, is one of the greatest primary sources on the artists profiled as well as on life in the Renaissance. With such a rich patrimony as this town of Etruscan origin has, it should not surprise you that Arezzo is one of the leading antique markets in Europe. You may make Pappardelle all'Aretina with either domestic duck, wild duck, or goose.*

4–6 SERVINGS

1 pound pappardelle (3½ cups flour, 4 eggs)
4 tablespoons sweet butter
4 tablespoons olive oil
2 ounces prosciutto, diced or slivered
1 onion, finely chopped
1 carrot, minced
1 stalk celery, minced
Pinch of sage (optional)

1 young duck, mallard, or goose, cleaned
1 cup white wine
1 pound tomatoes, peeled, seeded, and pureed
Pinch of nutmeg
⅛ teaspoon cloves
Salt and pepper to taste
1 cup hot beef or chicken broth
1 cup freshly grated grana

If you are making fresh pappardelle, prepare as indicated on pages 52–59, using the amounts of flour and eggs listed above. Once the pappardelle are in hand, start making the sauce.

In a large casserole, gently melt 1 tablespoon of butter in the olive oil. Add the prosciutto, onion, carrot, and celery, and sauté for a few seconds. If you are using sage, add that now. Once these ingredients have browned slightly, add the duck, which has been meticulously cleaned and trimmed of extra fat. Reserve the duck liver and, if you have them, the spleen and heart. Cook the duck, turning it occasionally so that all sides are browned. Try to skim the extra fat that might collect at the bottom of the pan. Add the wine, tomatoes, nutmeg, cloves, salt, and pepper, and cook 45–60 minutes over a low flame. Check the sauce every so often to make sure it does not become too dry. If so, add a bit of hot broth. Remember, though, that you want a thick, rich sauce, so do not dilute too much.

Five minutes before the sauce is done, mince the duck liver, heart, and spleen, and stir into the sauce. At the same time, drop the pappardelle into a large pot of water that has been brought to a boil, lightly salted and again brought to a boil. When al dente, drain well. At this point you have 2 choices to make: Do you want to bake the pappardelle or serve them immediately with sauce (see Note)? Do you want the duck in the sauce or will you eat it as a second course? No matter what choices you make, you should first remove the duck from the sauce and place it on a platter. If you plan to bake the pappardelle, butter a baking dish, put in a layer of pasta, a coating of sauce, and a sprinkling of grated cheese. Repeat this process until all ingredients are used, finishing with cheese. Dot with butter and bake in a preheated 375°F oven for a few minutes. In making the layers for this dish, you may add duck meat along with the sauce. If you do not want to bake the pappardelle, transfer to a warm bowl after draining, dot with 3 tablespoons of butter, add some sauce, sprinkle on some grated cheese, toss well, and serve with more cheese if available. If you are adding duck to the sauce, slice it into small pieces and toss on the meat along with the sauce, before adding the grated cheese. If you are eating the duck as a second course, serve it with cooked greens such as escarole or spinach, to which a bit of oil and garlic has been added.

NOTE: if you plan to bake the pappardelle, do not boil as long as you normally would, since they will receive further cooking in the baking dish.

&❧ WINE: Drink the white wine you use for cooking. In Arezzo they often use Val di Chiana, but you will have equal success with Vernaccia di San Gimignano. If you want red, drink a good Chianti Classico.

Pappardelle di Prato

Prato (population 150,000) is where many of the stunning fabrics that go into Italian high fashion are made. It is also the birthplace of Fra Filippo Lippi (1406–1469), one of the great artists of the Renaissance. I passed Prato once a week for a year commuting from Bologna to Florence. From the train one can see Prato's cathedral, including a beautiful and peculiar outdoor pulpit designed in 1439 by Michelozzo and Donatello. Frescoes by Lippi are inside the church. When I finally got off the train once to explore Prato, one of my pleasant discoveries was this dish. According to the pratesi, the best meat to use for this sauce is from an ewe that has never become a mother.

4–6 SERVINGS

1 pound pappardelle
8 tablespoons olive oil
8 ounces very lean lamb, cut in cubes
8 ounces very lean lamb, ground
2 carrots, cut in small pieces

1 small onion, minced
1 stalk celery, minced
1 cup Chianti or Galestro
1 pound tomatoes, peeled
Salt and pepper to taste
Grated pecorino

Prepare the pappardelle as indicated on page 59.

Heat the oil in a large pot. Sauté the lamb until lightly browned. Add the carrots, onion, and celery, and cook for 3–4 minutes. Pour in the wine and continue to cook slowly. As soon as the alcohol from the wine has evaporated, add the tomatoes. (If you are cooking with canned tomatoes, do not use the liquid in the can.) Add salt and pepper to taste, cover the pot, and cook slowly for 30 minutes. The sauce should become quite thick. If you want to thin it a little, add a few drops of hot water. Remember, though, that this is a sauce and not a soup, so it should not be watery.

Cook the pappardelle in water that has been brought to a boil, lightly salted and again brought to a boil, until al dente. Drain well and transfer to a platter or to individual bowls. Add a bit of butter and serve with grated pecorino.

VARIATIONS: I have added fresh peas and mushrooms to this sauce at the same time I put in the tomatoes. Though it certainly is not necessary, it is a nice touch.

🍷 WINE: If you prefer red, drink Chianti Classico. If you want white, I recommend Galestro.

Pappardelle al Cinghiale
Pappardelle with Wild Boar Sauce

San Gimignano is one of the leading tourist destinations in Tuscany. The town's most distinguishing features are the many medieval towers that have earned San Gimignano the nickname of

"The Manhattan of Italy." Perhaps then it is fitting that the native of San Gimignano who provided me with this recipe should be a relative of a famous New Yorker. Assunta Cuomo, who operates the Ristorante La Mangiatoia, told me that she is a distant cousin of the Governor of New York. Incidentally, Signora Cuomo serves an excellent example of Vernaccia di San Gimignano, the town's famous white wine. This is easily located in the United States. You may have more difficulty finding wild boar, whose tasty meat is popular in Tuscany. If you find it, however, meat from the loin is recommended.

4 SERVINGS

2½ tablespoons olive oil
2 cloves garlic, minced
1 pound loin of wild boar, cut into small pieces
Healthy pinch of *fresh* rosemary or 1 tablespoon dried rosemary
1 cup Vernaccia or a similar white wine such as Orvieto Secco

1 tablespoon tomato paste
½ cup pitted fresh black olives (Gaeta olives work well here)
1 pound fresh pappardelle
Freshly grated grana or pecorino (optional)

To make the sauce, heat the oil in a pan. Add the garlic, boar, and rosemary. Gently cook for 10 minutes, stirring occasionally with a wooden spoon. Then bathe the sauce with the Vernaccia, continuing to stir until the alcohol in the wine has evaporated. Add the tomato paste, which has been diluted in a bit of water (or better still, add 3 or 4 fresh plum tomatoes that have been peeled). Let the sauce cook, partially covered, for 5 minutes. Add the olives and cook gently another 15 minutes, uncovered, stirring occasionally.

Cook the pappardelle as directed on pages 80–82. Put the pasta on warm plates and add enough sauce to flavor the pasta without smothering it. Serve immediately. Cheese is optional, but for those who choose it, pecorino or grana work equally well.

❧ WINE: Vernaccia di San Gimignano, of course.

Pappardelle alla Senese

Pappardelle with Squab

This dish is a specialty of Siena. The natives of this town in central Tuscany are proud of their independent traditions, the pureness of the Italian they speak, of their age-old rivalry with Florence, of superb red wines, and of the excellent local cuisine. Siena was the birthplace of Ettore Bastianini (1922–1967), a fine Verdi baritone.

4 SERVINGS

Pasta
3½ cups flour
 4 eggs

Sauces
 3 tablespoons olive oil
 6 tablespoons sweet butter
 1 stalk celery, minced
 1 medium onion, minced
 1 medium carrot, minced
 4 ounces prosciutto, minced
 ½ teaspoon fresh sage

 2 squabs (1–1½ pounds each, approximately) cleaned and quartered
 1 cup Chianti or other red wine
 1 pound canned tomatoes, peeled and pureed
 Salt and pepper to taste

Make the pappardelle as indicated on page 59. Set aside.

In a large, deep pan heat the oil and butter and then add the celery, onion, carrot, prosciutto, and sage. After 3–5 minutes add the pieces of squab and cook 5 minutes, moving the pieces about so they cook evenly. Pour in the Chianti and, when it is nearly evaporated, add the tomato puree. Add salt and pepper and cook another 45–60 minutes, covered. If you find that the sauce is condensing too much, add a bit of hot broth or a little more tomato puree.

When the sauce is almost done, cook the pappardelle in a large pot of water that has been brought to a boil, lightly salted and again brought to a rapid boil. When the pasta is al dente, drain thoroughly and transfer to a warm bowl. Top with the sauce, keeping the squab aside to serve as a second course. Serve with grated parmigiano, though it should be used sparingly.

VARIATION: When the sauce is nearly done, remove the squab and add ¼ cup of broth to the pan. Cut the meat into small pieces and combine with the sauce.

୬ WINE: Chianti.

LAZIO (LATIUM)

Spaghetti al Cacio e Pepe ·
Spaghetti alla Carbonara di Luciano Pavarotti ·
Penne all'Arrabbiata ·
Bucatini all'Amatriciana ·
Rigatoni all'Amatriciana di Renata Scotto ·
Fettuccine Alfredo · **Fettuccine al Radicchio** ·
Fettuccine alla Papalina · **Fettuccine di Trastevere**

Spaghetti al Cacio e Pepe

Spaghetti with Pecorino and Pepper

This dish is probably the easiest to prepare of any in this book, yet it is delicious. This is a specialty of Rome, whose citizens are justifiably proud of their excellent pecorino romano. It is widely available in the United States.

1 SERVING

4 ounces spaghetti
½ cup freshly and coarsely grated pecorino

1 tablespoon olive oil
Freshly ground black pepper

Set a large pot of water to boil. When it reaches a boil, toss in a pinch of salt, bring to a boil again and start cooking the spaghetti. In the meantime, grate the cheese. When the pasta is al dente, drain, leaving a few drops of water clinging to the spaghetti. Transfer the pasta to a bowl, spoon on the oil, sprinkle on the cheese, grind on abundant fresh pepper, toss well, and enjoy. In making this dish follow your own tastes by adding as much pecorino and pepper as you like.

🍃 WINE: Frascati or Bianco dei Castelli Romani.

Spaghetti alla Carbonara di Luciano Pavarotti

Luciano Pavarotti's Spaghetti, Charcoal Burner-Style

Luciano Pavarotti is the world's most famous opera singer. When speaking of the tenor from Modena it is difficult not to use superlatives. He has brought more people to opera than ever before thanks to his beautiful voice and engaging personality. Signor Pavarotti has kindly given me his version of a classic Roman dish that is popular throughout Italy. The only difference between this recipe and the way it is prepared in Rome is that Signor Pavarotti uses the wonderful parmigiano of his native region while a Roman might use pecorino. You may use either or a combination. The proportions in this recipe are the correct ones. In North America the sauce is usually too liquidy and frequently has cream added. This is wrong. The sauce should coat and flavor the pasta without giving it a bath. Romans often eat Spaghetti alla Carbonara late at night after drinking a lot of wine.

6 SERVINGS

1 to 1¼ pounds spaghetti (do not use thin spaghetti), or bucatini	5 eggs Pinch of salt Pinch of freshly ground black pepper
2 tablespoons olive oil	¾ cup grated parmigiano (or pecorino)
6 tablespoons butter	
8 ounces pancetta (or bacon), cut in cubes	

Set a large pot of cold water to boil. When it reaches a rolling boil, toss in a pinch of salt. Start cooking the spaghetti.

In the meantime, heat the oil and gently melt the butter in a pan and add the pancetta. Sauté until it turns a dark pink or light red. However, it should remain soft rather than turn crisp.

While the bacon is cooking, beat the eggs, salt, pepper, and 2 tablespoons of grated cheese in the dish you will use as a serving bowl. When the spaghetti are al dente, drain thoroughly and add to the egg mixture. Toss quickly and well, top with the pancetta (and, if you wish, some of the pan liquid), and toss again. Serve right away with additional grated cheese.

VARIATION: This is one of my favorite dishes, and I eat it frequently. My taste, and that of some Romans, is to use as much freshly ground black pepper as I can take. I grind a lot into the eggs and then add more on top of the spaghetti when served.

NOTE: This is a great dish for 1 person. The proportions are: 4 ounces spaghetti, 1 egg, salt, lots of pepper to taste, 2 ounces pancetta, 4 tablespoon grated cheese, 1 tablespoon butter, and 2 teaspoons olive oil.

&❧ WINE: Frascati, Bianco dei Castelli Romani or Bianco dei Colli Albani.

Penne all'Arrabbiata

"Enraged" Penne

If any soprano had trouble getting into character before going on-stage to sing a mad scene, a bowlful of Penne all'Arrabbiata would put the requisite fire in her belly. This is real hot stuff, as only the Romans could make it. How angry a sauce you make depends on your own taste, so vary the amount of peperoncino accordingly. Nowadays, cooks often add ham, mushrooms, peas, and even cheese to this sauce, but I recommend the classic preparation. Use pepper flakes only if absolutely necessary.

4–6 SERVINGS

3–4 cloves garlic
  1 peperoncino or dried chili
     pepper flakes
  4 tablespoons olive oil
  1 pound tomatoes, peeled,
     seeded, and perhaps pureed

  1 pound penne or spaghetti
1½ tablespoons chopped fresh
     parsley.

In thinking about this dish, you must make one decision: Do you want to eat the garlic and peperoncino or only have them lend their flavors to the sauce? If you decide to leave these seasonings in, mince them. If you plan to remove them, cut the garlic cloves in half and cut the peperoncino in thirds.

Heat the oil in a saucepan and add the garlic and peperoncino. Cook for about 3 minutes or until the garlic starts to turn brown, whichever comes first—do not let the garlic brown. If you plan to remove the garlic and peperoncino, now is the time. Add the tomatoes and stir to combine with the oil. Simmer, stirring frequently, until the sauce thickens as the liquid evaporates. Bring a large pot of water to a boil, toss in a pinch of salt, bring to a boil again and cook the penne until al dente. Drain thoroughly, transfer to individual bowls, spoon on some sauce, and sprinkle on some parsley.

🍷 WINE: Frascati or Bianco dei Castelli Romani.

Bucatini all'Amatriciana

This is one of the most popular pasta dishes in Italy. It originated in the town of Amatrice, northeast of Rome, in the hilly region where Latium borders on Umbria, the Abruzzi, and the Marches. Any cook can produce a version of Bucatini all'Amatriciana, though most demonstrate either ignorance or laziness about the fine points that make Amatriciana sauce a classic. Foremost among these points: The bacon must be very lean, and only the flesh, not the juice, of the tomatoes is used.

1 SERVING

2 ounces lean bacon or, preferably, pancetta (known in Latium as *guanciale*)	2 plum tomatoes
	1 tablespoon olive oil
½ small onion	Salt and pepper to taste
Small piece of a piquant peperoncino	4 ounces bucatini or spaghetti
	Grated sharp pecorino cheese

Set a large pot of water to boil. When boiling, add a pinch of salt and again bring to a boil.

Cut the pancetta into cubes. Slice the onion and peperoncino into tiny pieces. Cut the tomatoes crosswise and squeeze gently to drain all of the liquid. Scoop out the flesh with a spoon. Discard the skin. Mash the tomato flesh in a bowl with the spoon.

Heat the oil in a large saucepan over moderate heat. Add the pancetta and sauté until a rosy color but not crisp. Remove the pancetta with a slotted spoon and fry the onion and peperoncino in the pan juices. When the onion becomes transparent, add the tomato, salt, and at least 5 grindings of fresh pepper.

Put the bucatini into the boiling water.

Cook the sauce for 6 minutes, then add the pancetta.

Drain the bucatini, which should be al dente. Add the pasta to the sauce and toss continuously while cooking for another 2–3 minutes. Serve with lots of sharp pecorino cheese.

🍂 WINE: Est! Est!! Est!!! or Orvieto Secco or a white from the Castelli Romani.

Rigatoni all'Amatriciana di Renata Scotto

This is a faster, easier, and good version of the classic dish from Latium. It was created by Renata Scotto, the soprano from Savona who is one of the foremost singing actresses in opera. She is widely known to television audiences in North America through her many appearances on the "Live from the Met" series of telecasts. She played Mimi in La Bohème *opposite Luciano Pavarotti in the Met's first telecast on March 15, 1977. Since that time she has created vivid portrayals in* Otello, Luisa Miller, Don Carlo, Manon Lescaut, *as the three heroines in Puccini's* Il Trittico, *again in* La Bohème *(as Musetta), and as* Francesca da Rimini. *Miss Scotto recommends de Cecco brand pasta.*

4 SERVINGS

1 medium onion, chopped	Pepper or paprika
5 tablespoons olive oil	1 large can crushed tomatoes
6 bacon slices, finely chopped	1 pound rigatoni
Salt	Freshly grated pecorino

Lightly brown the onion in the olive oil. Add the bacon to the pan. Add salt and a generous portion of freshly ground pepper or paprika. Cook over a low flame for 5 minutes. Add the entire contents of the tomato can and cook 6 minutes or until some of the water begins to evaporate.

While the sauce is simmering, bring a large pot of water to a boil, toss in a pinch of salt, bring to a boil again and cook the rigatoni until al dente. Drain well and put in individual bowls. Top with some sauce and serve with the pecorino.

🍂 WINE: Same as for Bucatini all'Amatriciana.

Fettuccine Alfredo

Fettuccine with Butter and Parmigiano

This recipe is the classic unadulterated version of a dish that has been corrupted in America by cooks who seek to be fancy rather than authentic. This dish requires only three ingredients: wonderful fresh fettuccine, superb sweet butter, and first-class parmigiano. Here, chefs make such unnecessary additions as ham, peas, cream, nutmeg, red pepper, black pepper, and garlic.

Fettuccine Alfredo is from Rome, though you won't find too many Romans eating it. Two restaurants, each named Alfredo, claim to have originated the recipe. Both are near the Italian parliament and the offices of major Italian publications. Their clientele is a boisterous mix of politicians, roving reporters, noisy tourists, and movie starlets eager to be noticed. The walls are filled with photographs of American and Italian stars of Rome's La Dolce Vita *days —long before anyone cared about cholesterol—when Fettuccine Alfredo, served with gold forks, was the only dish anyone who was anyone would eat.*

1 SERVING

    4 ounces fresh fettuccine (page 59), or store-bought
    2 ounces (½ stick) sweet butter
       At least 3 ounces freshly grated parmigiano

Set a large pot of water to boil. When boiling, toss in a pinch of salt. Start cooking the fettuccine when the water again reaches a full boil.

Place half the butter in a warm dish. When the pasta is ready, drain thoroughly and put in the dish. Add the cheese and the rest of the butter, toss well, and serve immediately!

VARIATIONS: I do not advise adding other ingredients to this classic preparation. The only changes you might make would be in the amounts of butter and cheese used. The full name of this dish is Fettuccine Maestose al Triplo Burro (Majestic Fettuccine with Triple Butter). Indeed, the fettuccine *are* majestic with tons of butter, but some people find it too rich. I tend to use more than 3 ounces of cheese, but that is up to you. To prepare this dish for several people, simply multiply the quantities of ingredients by the number of guests you have.

&. WINE: Rome's Frascati is ideally suited to Fettuccine Alfredo. A good red wine would be Montepulciano d'Abruzzo.

Fettuccine al Radicchio
Fettuccine with Radicchio

This is an unusual dish because the sauce has a dark pink color and a bitterness that is unexpected. If you put aside your precon- ceptions about what you expect Fettuccine al Radicchio to be, I think you will be intrigued. Though radicchio is the local vegetable of Treviso, north of Venice, this recipe was created at the Ristorante Aquilanti in Viterbo, a provincial capital north of Rome.

I went to Viterbo on September 4, 1983, specifically to sample this dish. At the time I was walking with a cane while recovering from a broken foot. The day turned out to be the 750th birthday of Saint Rose, the saint of Viterbo who is supposed to bring health to the handicapped. The town was overflowing with nuns on pilgrimages from Rome and with many disabled people from all over Italy. There were bustling crowds swept up in the emotion of the day, screaming, crying, and praying. People were handing food and money to the handicapped, myself included. I, in turn, gave all of this to others. The piety and humanity, generosity and humility, all undercurrents in the Italian character, welled up in one spon- taneous mass outburst on that day in Viterbo, and its impact on me remains vivid and haunting. The distinctive taste of this dish is indelibly connected to the experience.

4–6 SERVINGS

1 pound radicchio	1 pint heavy cream
4 ounces (1 stick) sweet butter	½ cup milk
2 teaspoons freshly ground pepper	1 pound fettuccine

Wash the radicchio well and chop into small pieces. Melt the butter in a large casserole and add the radicchio and pepper. After 10 seconds add the heavy cream. Stir well so that the ingredients are combined. Cook over low to medium heat for at least 2 hours, stirring occasionally. The sauce may boil gently, but make sure it does not stick to the pot. If you think the sauce is becoming too condensed, add some milk. When finished, the sauce should be rich and creamy, brownish-pink in color, and have a bitter peppery flavor.

When the sauce is nearly done, set a large pot of cold water to boil. When it reaches a boil, toss in a pinch of salt, bring again to a boil and cook the fettuccine. When al dente, drain well and transfer to a warm serving dish. Top the pasta with the sauce, toss well, and serve. You might want to sprinkle on some freshly grated parmigiano, but it is not necessary.

🍷 WINE: Est! Est!! Est!!! from nearby Montefiascone or white wine from the Colli Albani.

Fettuccine alla Papalina

Papal Fettuccine

I don't know if the Pope eats Fettuccine alla Papalina, but everyone else in Rome does. This dish benefits from the wonderful sweet peas available in the Roman countryside. You may also use this sauce on cappelletti, as Romans do.

2 SERVINGS

2 tablespoons sweet butter	8 ounces fettuccine or cappelletti
¼ small onion, sliced	
⅓ cup fresh peas	1 egg
2–3 ounces boiled ham (or prosciutto cotto), diced	1 tablespoon freshly grated parmigiano
Salt and pepper	

Set a large pot of lightly salted water to boil. In the meantime, melt the butter in a saucepan, add the onion and then the peas. When the peas are nearly cooked, add the ham, salt, and pepper.

Start boiling the pasta.

Beat the egg in a bowl with the parmigiano.

When the pasta is al dente, drain thoroughly and add to the egg. Toss until the egg coats the fettuccine, then add the ham and peas. Top with another tablespoon of sweet butter, more parmigiano, and some freshly ground pepper.

VARIATION: To make this sauce even richer, add an extra egg yolk.

&❧ WINE: Frascati or Bianco dei Castelli Romani.

Fettuccine di Trastevere

Trastevere is a very special quarter on the quiet side of Rome's Tiber River. Its name comes from its location: Tras (across) Tevere (Tiber). Romans say Trastevere is the most Roman of all neighborhoods in the Eternal City. Recently, Trastevere became somewhat chic and, in attempting to lure tourists and outside business to the area, has lost some of its charm. But not too much. It is still a pleasure to sit at a table in a small outdoor trattoria, drink a carafe of the delightful white wine from the hills, and eat delicious and authentic Roman cooking. This is a generous portion, but then Romans are healthy eaters. If you are dining with someone else, this recipe can be shared if you plan to follow with another dish or a large salad or fruit and cheese. Of course, keep drinking that wine, which makes anything it accompanies seem graceful.

1 SERVING

½ small onion
1 tablespoon sweet butter
4 ounces boiled ham, cut in julienne strips
4 ounces chicken giblets, cut into small pieces
¼ cup dry white wine

1 squeeze of tomato paste (see note on tomato paste on page 293)
Pepper to taste
1 sage leaf, chopped
4 ounces fresh fettuccine
Grated pecorino

For cooking the pasta, bring a large pot (at least 6 quarts) of water to a boil. Salt lightly and bring to a boil again. In a saucepan, sauté the onion in the butter, then add the ham and giblets. Pour in the wine, add the tomato paste, and stir. Add the pepper and sage. Drop the fettuccine into the boiling water, cook until al dente, drain well, and then put the pasta in a bowl. Pour on the sauce, toss, and eat. Serve with grated pecorino.

🐌 WINE: Rome's Frascati wine is ideal with this dish.

THE SOUTH:
Campania, the Abruzzo (Abruzzi), Puglia (Apulia), Basilicata, and Calabria

---

**Spaghetti al Filetto · Vermicelli alla Puttanesca ·
Tagliolini Enrico Caruso · Maccheroni Calabresi alla Cipolla ·
Farfalle alla Zafferano · Orecchiette alla Cicolella ·
Vermicelli a Surchio · Spaghetti con le Cozze ·
Spaghetti alla Tarantina · Timballo di Mezzani all'Albanese ·
Ravioli di Melanzane · Sagne Chine**

Spaghetti al Filetto
Spaghetti with "Fillets" of Tomato

In this sauce the tomatoes do not disintegrate. You are cooking with rather firm "fillets" of tomato, and the result should be a bit chunky.

1 SERVING

2 tablespoons olive oil
1 clove garlic
4 ounces fresh or canned tomatoes, peeled, seeded, and cut in half

3–4 fresh basil leaves or a pinch of oregano
4 ounces spaghetti or vermicelli

Set a large pot of cold water to boil. In the meantime, heat the oil in a saucepan. Add the garlic and let it turn golden brown as slowly as possible. Add the tomatoes and basil or oregano, and cook over medium heat for 10 minutes. Occasionally give the tomatoes a nudge with a wooden spoon so that they do not stick to the bottom.

Toss a pinch of salt into the pot of boiling water, return to boil and add the spaghetti. Cook until al dente and then drain well. Transfer to a warm bowl. Remove the garlic clove from the tomato sauce and add the sauce to the pasta. Toss briefly and serve. You may add grated cheese if you wish.

❧ WINE: Valpolicella.

Vermicelli alla Puttanesca
Vermicelli, Whore's Style

If chicken soup is Jewish penicillin, is this Italian penicillin? This dish is eaten throughout Italy, but its origin seems to be somewhere between Naples and Rome. There are many stories about how puttanesca sauce got its name. The most frequently cited reason is that this dish can be made very quickly so that a prostitute can have a nourishing meal between appointments. Other people, especially romantics and hypochondriacs, say the name of the sauce has to do with the special properties of garlic. When you drive down the old Via Appia Antica outside Rome, you see prostitutes parading up and down near bonfires they have set. Romans tell me they do that to attract attention and to keep warm, but I prefer to believe that they are waiting for the pasta to become al dente. In any case, this is a great favorite, made in Naples with vermicelli, in Rome with spaghetti.

1 SERVING

1 tablespoon olive oil
1 clove garlic, cut in slivers
1 anchovy fillet, minced (optional)
4 ounces tomatoes, peeled, seeded, and perhaps pureed
¼ teaspoon capers

2 ounces black Gaeta olives, pitted and perhaps sliced
Pinch of oregano
Salt and pepper to taste
Tip of a peperoncino
4 ounces vermicelli or spaghetti

Set a large pot of cold water to boil. When it reaches a full boil, toss in a pinch of salt and bring to a boil again.

In the meantime, heat the oil in a saucepan and add the garlic and anchovy. When the garlic turns golden in color, add the tomatoes and cook for 5 minutes, stirring occasionally. Add the capers, olives, oregano, salt, pepper, and peperoncino.

Start cooking the pasta and let the sauce simmer, stirring occasionally. When the pasta is al dente, drain well, top with the sauce, toss, and serve.

WINE: Any fresh young white wine such as Frascati, Bianco Toscano, or Soave.

Tagliolini Enrico Caruso

Tagliolini with Chicken Livers and Fresh Tomatoes

The great tenor Enrico Caruso (1873–1921) was probably this century's most legendary singer (his only challenger to that claim would be Maria Callas). His sensual singing of opera and the music of his native Naples still grips us even if he sounds remote on scratchy old 78 rpm records. After making his debut in Cavalleria Rusticana *at the Teatro Nuovo in Naples in 1895, he quickly rose to international fame and first appeared at the Metropolitan in 1903. He remained in New York until 1920. Caruso was a man who usually knew what he liked, and he was quite fond of chicken livers. Today, dishes named Caruso usually feature chicken livers.*

2 SERVINGS

3 tablespoons olive oil	1 tablespoon tomato puree (optional)
1 tablespoon sweet butter	
¼ teaspoon fresh rosemary	8 ounces fresh tomatoes, unpeeled, chopped, and seeded
¼ onion, minced	
6 ounces chicken livers, finely chopped	
	Salt and pepper to taste
3–4 tablespoons broth, warm water, or wine	8 ounces tagliolini, fresh or dried

Set a large pot of water to boil.

In a saucepan, gently heat the oil and butter. Add the rosemary and onion, and cook until the onion turns golden. Add the chicken livers, broth, and tomato puree. Heat for 1 minute and add the tomatoes, salt, and pepper. Keep the sauce at a simmer, half-covered. It should thicken somewhat as it cooks. In the meantime, when the water comes to a boil, add a pinch of salt, bring to a boil again, and boil the tagliolini until al dente, drain well, and transfer to a warm dish. Dot with butter and top with the sauce. Toss well and serve. Have grated grana or pecorino available for those who want it.

🍂 WINE: A wine from Caruso's native Campania would be logical: a red Aglianico or a white Lacryma Christi. Also possible would be reds or whites from Capri, Ischia, Sorrento, or Ravello. If you cannot find these, try a medium-bodied Chianti or Orvieto secco.

Maccheroni Calabresi alla Cipolla
Calabrese Maccheroni with Onions

During my student days in Bologna, I had a friend from Reggio di Calabria who frequently made this easy and tasty dish. It is typical of its region of origin in its use of peperoncino rosso, as well as in employing simple, inexpensive, and readily available ingredients. A perfect dish for students on a budget or for anyone who has to make a meal when there are only oil and onions in the pantry. Incidentally, Calabria is the native region of Francesco Cilea (1866–1950), a leading composer of the verismo school whose most enduring work, Adriana Lecouvreur, *has been an excellent vehicle for sopranos such as Renata Tebaldi, Renata Scotto, and Joan Sutherland.*

1 SERVING

1 small onion, thinly sliced	A few small pieces of
3–4 tablespoons olive oil	peperoncino rosso or a pinch
4 ounces maccheroni	of red pepper flakes

Soak the onion slices in the olive oil in a small bowl or glass for at least 2 hours.

Set a large pot of cold water to boil. When it reaches a boil, toss in a pinch of salt, bring to a rolling boil and start cooking the maccheroni.

When the pasta is al dente, drain, leaving a few drops of water attached to the maccheroni, and transfer to a serving dish. Pour on the onions and oil, add the peperoncino, toss well, and serve.

VARIATION: This is the recipe as I learned it. I have also prepared it by soaking the onion and the peperoncino rosso in the oil. The result is different in that the individual flavors are less distinct, but the combined taste is quite intriguing.

❧ WINE: Cirò rosso or Cirò bianco.

Farfalle allo Zafferano
Saffron Butterflies

An exotic name for a pleasing dish. This is popular in the Abruzzi, which produces most of Italy's saffron, and Milan, which consumes most of it.

1 SERVING

4 ounces farfalle, butterfly-shaped pasta (page 60), or commercially prepared
1 tablespoon sweet butter
¼ cup heavy cream

1 teaspoon saffron or ½ teaspoon dried saffron powder
1 ounce grated grana

Set a large pot of water to boil. Toss in a pinch of salt. When the water again reaches a full boil, start cooking the farfalle.

Melt the butter in a saucepan, add the cream, and crumble in the strands of saffron. Continue to stir the sauce over a low flame, making sure it heats but does not boil.

Drain the farfalle when al dente and put in the saucepan. Add the cheese. Stir until the pasta is completely coated with the sauce. Transfer to a dish and serve immediately. Be sparing with any additional cheese since the key flavor in the sauce is the delicate saffron.

NOTE: If possible, use strands of saffron. If you cannot find strands of saffron, powder is acceptable.

❧ WINE: Either red or white goes well with this dish. I particularly recommend any wine from the Oltrepò Pavese, the wine-producing region south of Pavia where the Po and Ticino rivers meet. A Montepulciano d'Abruzzo is another good choice.

Orecchiette alla Cicolella

This simple and tasty dish is the specialty of the restaurant in the Hotel Cicolella in Foggia. I have found that recipes I gathered in Apulia are geared to large appetites and this is no exception. The Cicolella chef says this serves four persons, but I would make it a first course for six.

4–6 SERVINGS

1 pound orecchiette	8 ounces (2 sticks) sweet butter
8 ounces proscuitto	2 cups tomato sauce
9 ounces fresh mozzarella, approximately	1¾ cups freshly grated parmigiano

You may use dried orecchiette—many fine pasta companies in the Abruzzi and Apulia export it to the United States—or make fresh orecchiette according to the instructions on page 62.

Set a large pot of water to boil. When boiling, add a pinch of salt and bring again to a boil. Mince the prosciutto into tiny bits. Cut the mozzarella into cubes the size of dice.

Start cooking the pasta in the boiling water.

Melt the butter in a pan with the prosciutto and then add the tomato sauce.

When the orecchiette are done (about 10 minutes), drain well and transfer to a warm dish. Top with the mozzarella, parmigiano, and sauce; toss so that the mozzarella melts in the hot tomato sauce. Serve immediately.

🦐 WINE: A medium-bodied to slightly robust red is indicated, such as Montepulciano d'Abruzzo.

Vermicelli a Surchio

Remember when your parents admonished you about slurping your spaghetti? Here is a dish in which you are invited to inhale your pasta with the abandon of a happy child. Surchio is Barese dialect: probably the best translation in English would be "sucka-ble." The pasta and sauce should be served very hot so that the eater quickly sucks the long strands of vermicelli into his mouth. This is an easy recipe whose success comes with the use of the best ingredients available. It is prepared at the Ristorante Vecchia Bari in the center of Bari. The owners, Anna and Giuseppe Lagrasta, emphasize traditional Apulian cooking, insisting on using "the simple ingredients and excellent extra-virgin olive oil that are gifts to us from our beautiful Apulia."

4 SERVINGS

4 salted anchovy fillets
3 tablespoons capers
3 tablespoons extra-virgin olive oil
1 clove garlic

1 pound vermicelli
8 ounces fresh or canned tomatoes, peeled (if canned, drain the liquid)
Pepper

Set a large pot of water to boil. When boiling, toss in pinch of salt and again bring to a boil.

Rinse the anchovies and mince along with the capers. Heat the oil in a pan and add the garlic. When the garlic takes on a bit of color, remove and add the anchovy and caper mixture.

At the same moment start cooking the vermicelli in the boiling water.

Two minutes later put the tomatoes in the pan and cook for 5 minutes, stirring gently with a wooden spoon. If you choose to, you can break up the tomatoes with the spoon.

In the meantime, drain the vermicelli which should be al dente, leaving a bit of the cooking water with the pasta. Add the vermicelli, along with the water to the pan holding the sauce and toss well for 2 minutes. Grind a little fresh pepper over the pasta and serve. According to Signor Lagrasta, it is *forbidden* to top with grated cheese.

🍷 WINE: Any fresh wine, red or white, from southern Italy will do: Lacryma Christi, Cafaro, Castel del Monte, and Salentino are good choices.

Spaghetti con le Cozze
Spaghetti with Mussels

If you live near the seashore or have access to fresh mussels, this may be your dish. In addition to being tasty, mussels are very inexpensive. Since Italy is a peninsula, it has an unusually long shoreline for a country of its size. Therefore, mussels appear in many of the different Italian regional cuisines. The mussels of Portovenere in Liguria are known as datteri di mare *(sea dates) and are highly prized. Taranto, in the foot of the Italian boot, is also known for its mussels; they are referred to as* mitili. *Taranto has also given us the tarantula and the tarantella.*

1 SERVING

12 mussels
2 tablespoons olive oil
1 clove garlic, crushed
1 tablespoon chopped parsley

8 ounces ripe tomatoes, peeled, chopped, and seeded
Pepper to taste
4 ounces spaghetti

Bring 2–3 cups of water to a boil. Thoroughly scrub the mussels and remove their beards, then cook them in the water. As their shells open, remove the mussels from the pot. Discard any that don't open and reserve the liquid. Remove the mussels from the shells and discard the shells.

For cooking the pasta, bring a large pot (at least 6 quarts) of water to a boil, including the liquid reserved from cooking the mussels. When boiling, add a pinch of salt and again bring to a boil.

In a saucepan, heat the olive oil and briefly sauté the garlic. Add the parsley, tomatoes, and pepper. Simmer partially covered for 15 minutes.

Add the mussels to the warm tomato mixture.

Time the spaghetti (thick spaghetti take longer than spaghettini, which are thinner) so that they are ready when your sauce is. When cooked, drain well and transfer to a bowl. Pour the sauce over the spaghetti, toss lightly, and serve.

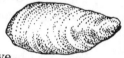

NOTE: Do not use grated cheese on this dish.

🦐 WINE: A very dry white such as Verdicchio or Soave.

Spaghetti alla Tarantina

Spaghetti, Taranto-Style

Taranto is the birthplace of Giovanni Paisiello (1740–1816). The port city, in the heel of the Italian boot, is blessed with a remarkable array of shellfish in its local water. In particular there is a great variety of clams and mussels. You can adapt this recipe to the seafood available to you. A Long Islander or a New Englander might use a lot of clams while a resident of Washington, D.C., would favor oysters from nearby Chesapeake Bay. I like to mix clams, mussels, and oysters. Minced shrimp, crab, and lobster also work in this recipe, but only in small quantities in addition to the clams and mussels.

4–6 SERVINGS

2 pounds shellfish (see above for possible combinations)	2 cloves garlic
1 pound spaghetti	Juice of ½ lemon
½ cup olive oil	¼ cup minced parsley
	Fresh black pepper

Wash the shellfish carefully and remove the beards from the mussels. Put the shellfish in a steamer or large covered pot and steam only until they open. Remove from the heat and carefully remove the meat from the shells. Set aside. Into a separate dish strain the liquid through a cheesecloth to get rid of sand and other particles.

Set a large pot of water to boil. When boiling, add a pinch of salt and again bring to a boil.

Mince any other shellfish (cooked and shelled) to be added to the sauce.

Start cooking the spaghetti.

Heat the oil in a pan and add the garlic. When the garlic turns light brown, remove the cloves and add all the shellfish and the strained liquid. Squeeze in the lemon juice. Cook over a medium flame for 3–5 minutes.

When the pasta is al dente, drain and add to the sauce. Throw in the parsley and grind on a healthy amount of pepper. Toss over the flame until the pasta and sauce are well mixed. Serve immediately.

VARIATION: I once had this dish with ditalini, short hollow pasta, and I much preferred it this way.

🦪 WINE: Any dry white wine is suitable. Soave or Verdicchio are widely available and go well with this dish.

Timballo di Mezzani all'Albanese
Licia Albanese's Baked Mezzani

Most opera fans agree that Licia Albanese is one of this century's foremost Italian sopranos. Her lovely voice, beautiful phrasing, and vibrant personality have made Madame Albanese particularly suited to the heroines of the great operas of Puccini and Verdi. Most Albanese admirers have their favorite portrayal. Mine is Violetta in La Traviata. *Madame Albanese is originally from Bari in Apulia. Her recipe is a classic that is especially well prepared in her native region.*

4–6 SERVINGS

1½ cups tomato sauce, perhaps with fresh basil (page 109)
1 pound ground lean beef or veal
1½ cups freshly grated parmigiano or pecorino
1 egg
1 tablespoon lemon juice
2 tablespoons finely minced parsley
Salt and pepper to taste
1 clove garlic, minced (optional)
Olive oil
1 pound mezzani or 1½-inch-long maccheroni
1 medium-sized ripe tomato, thinly sliced
1 cup bread crumbs

Once you have made the tomato sauce, set it aside and prepare tiny, fingertip-sized meatballs. Put the meat, ½ cup of grated cheese, egg, lemon juice, parsley, salt, pepper, and garlic in a bowl, and combine until thoroughly mixed. Do not work the mixture more than you need to. Form the meatballs and fry in approximately 3 tablespoons of olive oil until well browned. Let the meatballs drain on absorbent paper.

Cook the mezzani in a large pot of lightly salted boiling water until nearly but not quite al dente. Drain the pasta well. Grease an earthenware casserole with olive oil and put in a layer of mezzani. Alternate casually between tomato sauce, meatballs, grated cheese, and more mezzani until you have used all the ingredients. Top the casserole with slices of fresh tomato. Drizzle on a little more olive oil and top the whole thing with bread crumbs. Bake in a preheated 350°F oven for 30 minutes and then let the timballo cool for 15 minutes before serving.

WINE: Any good medium-bodied red.

Ravioli di Melanzane

Eggplant Ravioli

This recipe is popular in Sicily, although I tasted it in Tropea, a stunning seaport in Calabria. I particularly like the pepper in the sfoglia, an uncommon touch that works wonderfully well here.

4 SERVINGS

Ripieno
- 1 pound eggplant, preferably several small ones
- ¼ cup olive oil
- 6 ounces fresh ricotta
- ¼ cup grated pecorino
- 1 egg

- 3 tablespoons chopped fresh basil
- 2 tablespoons minced fresh parsley
- Salt and pepper to taste

Sauce
- 2 cups tomato sauce (page 109)

Sfoglia
- 1 pound flour
- 1 tablespoon freshly grated pepper

- 1 large or 2 small eggs
- 1 tablespoon oil
- 1 cup warm water

Wash and peel the eggplants and cut either lengthwise or in discs. Sprinkle with salt and set aside on a dishcloth or paper toweling to drain off excess liquid and bitterness. If you are making fresh tomato sauce, now is the time to do it.

After the eggplant has sat for 30–40 minutes, cut into small cubes. Heat the oil in a pan and add the eggplant. Fry until the cubes turn a deep golden brown but are not yet crisp. Drain on paper toweling. In a bowl, combine the eggplant, ricotta, pecorino, egg, basil, parsley, salt, and pepper. Blend the mixture until you form a uniform paste. Set aside.

Prepare the *sfoglia*. Combine the flour and pepper before adding the egg(s) and liquids as indicated on pages 52–58. Work the dough until smooth.

Roll out 2 sheets of *sfoglia* and make the ravioli as indicated on pages 65–68. These ravioli should be 1–1½ inches square. Allow to rest for 20–30 minutes in a draft-free area. In the meantime, in a large pot, bring water to a boil. Toss in a pinch of salt and again bring to a boil. Cook the ravioli in the rapidly boiling water. Serve with a good tomato sauce, perhaps one that is laced with a healthy amount of garlic, and lots of freshly grated pecorino.

NOTE: Read about eggs on page 282 and about making dough for pasta *ripiena* on page 62.

🍷 WINE: Cirò red or white.

Sagne Chine

This is lasagne as prepared in southern Italy. In Calabria it is called Sagne Chine; in Campania it is known as Sagna Chiena. *There is much room for variation in making this version of lasagne, though little meatballs, artichokes, hardboiled eggs, tomato sauce, and a melting cheese are constant. I will give you the Calabrian recipe and encourage you to try the variations listed as well as some of your own.*

6 SERVINGS

2 ounces dried or 8 ounces fresh mushrooms, sliced	Bread crumbs, if necessary
12 ounces ground pork	1 small onion, minced
1 clove garlic, minced	1 carrot, minced
Olive oil	1 stalk celery, minced
1 egg	4 artichoke hearts, sliced
1½ cups freshly grated pecorino	1 pound lasagne
1 tablespoon minced fresh parsley	1 cup tomato sauce with basil
Salt and pepper to taste	3 hard-boiled eggs, sliced
	8 ounces fresh mozzarella or scamorza, sliced

If you are using dried mushrooms, soak them in advance.

When you are ready to start cooking, begin by making little meatballs. Sauté the pork and garlic in 2 tablespoons of olive oil. When the pork is browned, remove from the pan with a slotted spoon. Set aside the pan and remaining cooking fat. Combine with the raw egg, ½ cup of pecorino, parsley, salt, and pepper. (If the mixture is too loose, add some bread crumbs.) Form meatballs the size of cherries and fry in the reserved pan, adding oil as needed until browned.

While the meatballs are cooking, heat ½ cup of olive oil in another pan and add the onion, carrot, and celery, and sauté until the onion is transparent. Add the mushrooms and gently cook for 10 minutes. Remove from the heat and set aside. When the meatballs are ready, drain on paper towels and set aside.

Prepare the artichoke hearts. If using fresh artichokes, cut out the hearts, slice them, and drop into a bowl of cool water to which lemon juice has been added. If you are using artichoke hearts that have been soaked in oil and lemon juice, drain well and slice. Heat ½ cup of olive oil in a pan and cook the artichoke hearts for 10 minutes, or until barely tender, adding ½ cup of water after 5 minutes. Remove the artichoke hearts with a slotted spoon and set aside.

Once all the ingredients for the filling are prepared, boil the lasagne a few at a time in a large pot of water which has been brought to a boil, lightly salted and again brought to a boil. The lasagne should be cooked until slightly more than al dente. Drain and let dry briefly on a cloth. Grease well with olive oil a lasagna pan or a large, deep baking dish. Spoon in enough tomato sauce to just cover the bottom of the pan. Cover with a layer of lasagne and spread with 1 or 2 tablespoons of tomato sauce. Place on a few meatballs, a little bit of the mushroom mixture, some egg and cheese slices, and a few pieces of artichoke. These ingredients should be arranged so that they form 1 relatively thin layer. In other words, they should be adjacent rather than on top of one another. Sprinkle a generous amount of pecorino on top of this layer. Continue making layers until all the ingredients are exhausted. The top layer should have only lasagne, tomato sauce, and pecorino. Bake in a 375°F oven for 25–35 minutes, until the surface is golden and the cheese is melted.

VARIATIONS: You may use veal instead of pork. Or, since this dish is often associated with Easter, try lamb. If you use lamb, try fresh mint instead of parsley.

Another nice touch is 8 ounces of fresh or frozen peas added with the water while cooking the artichokes. If using peas cook the artichoke-pea mixture together for 10 minutes instead of the additional 5 called for in the basic recipe.

Green, red, or yellow peppers may be cooked with the onion-mushroom mixture.

Instead of basil, try some ginger in the tomato sauce. This is typical of Calabria, where ginger is often added to tomato sauces served with maccheroni.

Instead of tomato sauce, you might want to use a good meat gravy.

Although olive oil is the traditional cooking fat of the south, you might want to try butter instead.

🍷 WINE: Taurasi, a good aged red from Campania, or Cirò Rosso from Calabria.

THE ISLANDS
Sicilia (Sicily) and Sardegna (Sardinia)

**Chiama Vinu · Spaghetti Fraddiavolo ·
Spaghetti Orlando e Rinaldo ·
Linguine con le Zucchine o le Melanzane Fritte ·
Maccheroni alla Siciliana · Pasta alla Norma · Bucatini all'Alioto ·
Cannelloni con Provolone · Lasagne alla Trapanese ·
Ragù di Agnello alla Sarda · Malloreddus · Culurzones**

Chiama Vinu
The Wine Call

*The name of this dish comes from the dialect of Catania, Sicily. It
is a variation on a dish that is prepared throughout old Magna
Graecia—what we know as southern Italy and Sicily. On the mainland it is often called Pasta con la Mollica (Pasta with Bread
Crumbs). Chiama Vinu does just what it promises: It is so thirst-
provoking that it calls for a lot of robust local wine to satisfy the
eater.*

1 SERVING

1 salted anchovy fillet
4 ounces pasta corta (penne,
  maccheroncini, or any short
  pasta)
4 tablespoons olive oil

4 tablespoons bread crumbs
  (made from stale bread rather
  than store-bought)
  Freshly ground black pepper

Set a large pot of water to boil. When boiling, salt lightly and bring to a boil again.

Rinse the anchovy and chop into tiny pieces.

Start cooking the pasta.

In a saucepan heat the oil over a low flame and then add the bread crumbs, which should become toasty but not burned, the anchovy, and a good deal of pepper. When the pasta is al dente, drain well, transfer it to a dish, add the sauce, toss thoroughly, and serve immediately.

VARIATIONS: In Naples this dish is made with vermicelli. Neapolitans often use 2 saucepans to make this; the oil is divided equally, and the anchovy cooks in one pan while the bread crumbs toast in the other. This results in a sauce in which the 2 major elements are joined at the last moment—an interesting idea but probably unnecessarily fussy. In Apulia orecchiette (little ears) are the pasta of choice. Each bit of pasta gets an earful of sauce, and the result is quite nice. In Bari, I am told, finely chopped almonds are sprinkled over the orecchiette after they have been tossed. Throughout Magna Graecia it is not uncommon for a clove of garlic to be placed in the oil as it heats. Make sure not to burn the garlic and remove it before adding the bread crumbs.

❧ WINE: In Catania you would be served wine from the slopes of nearby Mount Etna. Though there is fish in the recipe, red wine (Etna Rosso) is actually preferable. Cirò Rosso, produced in Calabria, is another suitable choice. In Apulia the wine would be Castel del Monte Rosso.

Spaghetti Fraddiavolo

This easy and tasty Sicilian sauce comes from Giuseppa Priulla, owner, and Salvatore Cascino, chef, of the Ristorante La Botte in Monreale, near Palermo. The same restaurant also provided the recipe for Spaghetti Orlando e Rinaldo on page 250. This dish is a fine example of how to create a good sauce using only readily available materials.

6 SERVINGS

8 ounces canned or fresh
  tomatoes, peeled
1½ pounds spaghetti
3 tablespoons olive oil
3 cloves garlic, minced
1 small peperoncino, finely
  chopped
10 mint leaves, minced

10 basil leaves, minced or,
  preferably, torn into bits
1 bunch parsley, minced
  Pinch of oregano
4 ounces grated piquant cheese
  (that is, pecorino,
  caciocavallo, or canestrato)

Set a large pot of water to boil. When boiling, lightly salt and again bring to a boil.

Cook the tomatoes in a small pot until the liquid is reduced and you are left with a pulpy sauce. Set aside.

Start cooking the spaghetti in the boiling water.

Heat the oil in a pan. Add the garlic and, 30 seconds later, the peperoncino. Sauté for 1 minute and then add the tomato sauce, mint, basil, parsley, and oregano. Stir.

When the spaghetti are al dente, drain well and place in a large serving dish. Top with the sauce and cheese. Serve with additional cheese if available.

🍷 WINE: Corvo bianco.

Spaghetti Orlando e Rinaldo

I wonder if the creator of this recipe, Salvatore Cascino, is a fan of the operas of George Frideric Handel. Signor Cascino, who cooks at the Ristorante La Botte in Monreale, Sicily, has named his dish after 2 of Handel's great operas. Rinaldo received its first performance on February 24, 1711 (the composer's twenty-sixth birthday) at the Queen's Theatre in London. Rinaldo was played by Niccolo Grimaldi, one of the leading castrati of that era. It first appeared at the Metropolitan Opera on January 19, 1984, with the superb Marilyn Horne in the title role. (I am told that no castrati appeared to try out for the part.) Orlando was written in 1733 and is filled with marvelous music. I have no idea which Orlando and Rinaldo this dish is named for, but whoever they are, they have been done a great honor.

6 SERVINGS

4 ounces (1 stick) sweet butter
1 clove garlic, minced
1 small onion, finely chopped
6 tablespoons capers
½ cup pitted black olives
½ cup pitted "white" olives
  (fresh or lightly cured green
  olives)

2 pounds tomatoes, peeled
Pinch of oregano
4 tablespoons minced parsley
Pepper to taste
6 tablespoons olive oil
10 anchovy fillets, drained of oil
1½ pounds spaghetti
⅞ cup freshly grated parmigiano

In a medium-sized pot, melt the butter and sauté the garlic and onion for 1 minute. Add the capers and olives, and cook over moderate heat for 2 minutes more. Add the tomatoes, oregano, parsley, and pepper, cover, and simmer for 15 minutes, stirring occasionally.

Set a large pot of water to boil. In a small pan heat the oil slowly. Add the anchovies and dissolve gradually in the oil. When the water in the large pot reaches a boil, add a pinch of salt, bring again to a boil and start cooking the spaghetti. By this time the sauce will have been somewhat reduced. Add to it the anchovy-and-oil mixture. Stir until thoroughly combined. When the spaghetti is al dente, drain well and put in a warm bowl. Add some sauce and parmigiano, and toss well. Top the pasta with more sauce and cheese, toss again lightly at the table, and serve.

❤ WINE: Corvo red or white are excellent choices.

Linguine con le Zucchine o le Melanzane Fritte

Linguine with Fried Zucchini or Eggplant

This dish comes from Signora Francesca Santonocito, an excellent Sicilian cook whose recipes I have come to know through her daughter Luciana. It is quite easy to prepare and very tasty. As usual, the success of this dish depends on timing and on the high quality of ingredients you use.

2 SERVINGS

1 medium-sized zucchini or 2
  baby eggplants
Olive oil

8 ounces linguine
Grated pecorino or
parmigiano

Set a large pot of cold water to boil. When it reaches a full boil, toss in a pinch of salt and bring to a boil again. In the meantime, wash the zucchini or eggplant well, chop off the ends, and slice into the thinnest discs possible. Take a large frying pan and pour in just enough olive oil to coat the bottom.

At this point, start cooking the linguine in the water.

Heat the oil over a relatively high flame—do not let it smoke—and then add the zucchini or eggplant. The important thing is that the discs have room to fry; do not pile them on top of one another. Fry the discs until golden but not brown. Quickly flip them over, fry briefly on the other side, and then remove from the pan to drain on paper toweling.

When the pasta is al dente, drain well and transfer to a serving dish. Pour the oil from the frying pan over the pasta and place the zucchini or eggplant on top. Serve with abundant grated pecorino or parmigiano. You may also grind on some fresh black pepper if it appeals to you.

🍂 WINE: Corvo or Etna, red or white.

Maccheroni alla Siciliana

Good recipes have a way of getting around. They also have a tendency to be corrupted or compromised in transit. For that reason, it is wise to learn the origins of a dish and understand the dynamics that make it work. This recipe benefits from the wonderful crunchiness of fried eggplant, the richness of melted mozzarella, and the tang of an excellent fresh tomato sauce. All of these are standard ingredients, especially in southern Italian kitchens. It is their juxtaposition that makes Maccheroni alla Siciliana special. This recipe was given to me by Laura Cozzi, a friend from Lombardy who knows a lot about the subtleties of cooking food from all parts of Italy.

4 SERVINGS

Tomato sauce (see recipe for Pummarola, page 110)
1 large eggplant, peeled and cut in 1-inch cubes
11 ounces mozzarella, cut in 1-inch cubes
Olive oil

Salt
1 pound maccheroni or tortiglioni
2 tablespoons sweet butter
Pepper to taste
¾ cup freshly grated parmigiano

While the sauce is simmering, cut the cubes of eggplant and mozzarella and grate the parmigiano. Set a large pot of cold water to boil. When the sauce is done, set aside.

Take a large frying pan and pour in just enough olive oil to completely cover the bottom. Heat the oil. When it is quite hot but not smoky, add the cubes of eggplant and fry until slightly crunchy but not brown. Remove the cubes from the pan and let drain on paper toweling. Salt liberally. Toss a pinch of salt into the boiling water, bring again to a boil and cook the pasta. When the maccheroni are not quite al dente, drain well and transfer to a buttered baking dish. Add the eggplant, grind on some fresh pepper, then add the mozzarella, the parmigiano and finally the tomato sauce. Toss the ingredients until thoroughly combined. Bake in a preheated 400°F oven for 10 minutes. Serve piping hot.

VARIATIONS: Instead of Pummarola try Sugo di Pomodoro e Menta. Instead of mozzarella, try scamorza cheese. Instead of parmigiano, try pecorino or caciocavallo.

❧ WINE: Any red with body. Cirò Rosso, Cabernet del Friuli, Montepulciano d'Abruzzo, and Spanna are all good choices.

Pasta alla Norma

I cannot think of a more operatic recipe. This dish is a classic from Catania, Sicily, birthplace of Vincenzo Bellini (1801–1835). Norma, his greatest work and the favorite opera of many people, was performed for the first time on December 26, 1831, at La Scala. The title character was sung by Giuditta Pasta (1797–1865), one of the great divas of all time whose particular vocal style Bellini called "sublimely tragic." If I could have gone to the major artists of the past in search of their favorite recipes, this is the singer I would have pursued most. Imagine, if you can, Pasta alla Pasta. By the way, the premiere of Norma was, according to Bellini, a "fiasco." The second performance was considerably more successful, and Norma gained its place in the forefront of the operatic repertory.

4 SERVINGS

3 medium or 2 large eggplants	Salt and pepper to taste
½ cup plus 3 tablespoons olive oil	12 ounces spaghetti
2 cloves garlic, minced	1 cup grated ricotta salata or pecorino dolce
12 ounces tomatoes, peeled and seeded	
½ cup fresh basil, torn into small pieces, or 1 tablespoon dried	

Two hours before you plan to serve the dish, wash and dry the eggplants (cut off the ends) and cut them into ½-inch slices. Salt the eggplant generously and put in a colander for 1 hour. This will allow the eggplant to drain off excess water. If necessary, rinse the eggplant gently to get rid of some salt, dry the slices with paper toweling, and set aside.

Heat 3 tablespoons of olive oil in a saucepan and sauté the garlic until golden. Add the tomatoes, basil, salt, and pepper, cover, and simmer for 20 mintues.

Set a large pot of water to boil. When boiling, salt lightly and bring to a boil again.

Gently heat ½ cup of olive oil in a pan and fry the eggplant slices a few at a time. Let the slices drain on paper toweling. Try to time your cooking so that the eggplant and spaghetti will be ready at the same time. Cook the spaghetti in the boiling water until al dente and then drain thoroughly. Transfer the pasta to a warm serving dish and top with half the grated cheese. Add the tomato sauce, eggplant and, finally, the rest of the cheese. Toss well and serve.

&❧ WINE: Etna rosso or bianco.

Bucatini all'Alioto

Bucatini with Clam Sauce

This delicious dish has been served for over 20 years at the Ristorante Costa Azzurra in Catania, Sicily. Its owner, Cavaliere Francesco Alioto, has kindly shared his recipe.

6 SERVINGS

1 pound clams	1½ pounds bucatini
2 peppers, preferably 1 green and 1 either yellow or red	4 ounces (1 stick) sweet butter
	½ cup tomato sauce

1 teaspoon minced peperoncino or ½ teaspoon dried red pepper flakes	Large pinch of fresh basil or parsley

Wash the clams and steam until open. Remove from their shells and, if you wish, conserve the liquid for some other use.

Roast the peppers over a flame on top of the stove or under a good hot broiler. Remove the skins and cut into strips, discarding the stems and seeds.

Start cooking the bucatini in a large pot of boiling water, lightly salted.

In another large pot or casserole, melt the butter. Add the clams, tomato sauce, peperoncino, and basil or parsley. Combine well.

When the bucatini are cooked al dente, drain thoroughly and add to the sauce. Toss the pasta and sauce briefly until combined. Transfer to a warm serving dish, top with pepper strips, toss thoroughly, and serve.

ᓀ WINE: Etna bianco or white Corvo or Segesta.

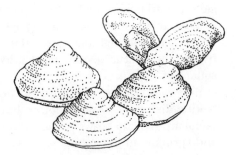

Cannelloni con Provolone

This dish is served at the Ristorante Il Pescatore in Taormina, Sicily. Taormina is one of those magnificent places that one somehow finds with startling regularity in Italy. It sits 675 feet above the Mediterranean and faces Mount Etna.

The town has been a popular resort since Hellenic times. In the third century B.C. the Greeks built an outdoor theater that is still in use. Every year Taormina hosts the awards ceremony for the Davide di Donatello, the Italian equivalent of the American motion picture industry's Oscar.

In preparing this dish, use authentic Italian provolone. There are 2 types: dolce (sweet) and piccante (sharp). I prefer the latter. Provolone is often smoked; if you like it that way, the particular flavor will make your cannelloni even more unusual.

4 SERVINGS

Sfoglia
2¼ cups unbleached flour
2–3 eggs

Besciamella
  2 cups whole milk
  6 tablespoons sweet butter

  6 tablespoons flour
    Pinch of salt

Ripieno
  1 pound provolone, grated or shredded
  8 ounces boiled ham, diced
  1 cup freshly grated grana
    Pinch of nutmeg

    Fresh pepper (optional)

  2 cups tomato sauce (page 109)
  1 cup freshly grated grana

Make the *sfoglia* and cut into 8 squares 4½–5 inches, as indicated on pages 52–58. After they have dried on a cloth for about 30 minutes, cook 2 or 3 at a time in a large pot of boiling water, lightly salted, until half done. Drain on a towel.

Make the besciamella sauce (page 180) and let cool.

Combine the ingredients for the *ripieno* in a bowl and then distribute the mixture evenly in lengthwise strips in the center of each square of *sfoglia.*

Roll each square to form cannelloni. Arrange them in a buttered baking dish next to one another but not touching. Pour the besciamella around and between the cannelloni. Top with the tomato sauce and sprinkle on the grana.

Bake in a 375°F oven for about 20 minutes.

VARIATIONS: Try making the *ripieno* with 8 ounces of steamed and minced fresh spinach, 12 ounces of grated provolone, 8 ounces of diced boiled ham, and a pinch of nutmeg. Or make the regular *ripieno* but use spinach pasta (page 60). I have also made this (with and without spinach) using boiled tongue instead of ham, a wonderful alternative.

🍷 WINE: Etna rosso or red Segesta, Cirò or Corvo.

Lasagne alla Trapanese

Lasagne, Trapani-Style

Trapani, at the western tip of Sicily, is the focal point of a region that derives a great bounty of food from both land and sea. The waters of the Mediterranean provide tuna and lobster. Nearby Segesta and Marsala produce famous wines. Corn, citrus, and other foods are grown locally, as is cotton. This recipe is an example of lasagne used as a pasta to be sauced and served rather than to be baked.

2 SERVINGS

Pasta
1¾ cups flour
   2 eggs *or*
   8 ounces lasagne

Sauce
   4 ounces blanched almonds
   2 cloves garlic
   4 tablespoons olive oil
   1 small bunch basil, torn into
      leaves

   1 teaspoon freshly ground
      pepper
2–3 tomatoes, peeled, seeded,
      and pureed

If you are making fresh lasagne, follow the instructions on pages 52–60. If you are using commercially prepared pasta, set a very large pot of water to boil while you prepare the sauce. When water boils, toss in a pinch of salt and again bring to a boil.

Use a mortar to crush the almonds and garlic in oil. When you have made a paste, add the basil and pepper. Continue to pound with the pestle until well combined. Fold in the tomato puree and mix thoroughly. (As an alternative to all this, you may combine all the ingredients in a blender, which you should operate at high speed for about 1 minute. If you use a blender, you do not need to puree the tomatoes in advance.)

In either case, once the sauce is ready, boil the lasagne until al dente, drain carefully, and transfer to a warm dish. Top with the sauce, toss with care, and serve.

NOTE: If you double this recipe, boil the pasta in 2 pots so that they have room to cook.

ख़ WINE: Segesta rosso or bianco.

Ragù di Agnello alla Sarda

Sardinian Lamb Sauce

This sauce requires some extra work, but the reward for the effort is something delicious. This ragù is a specialty of shepherds in the Sardinian highlands.

4–6 SERVINGS

 2 cloves garlic
 2 teaspoons rosemary
    Pinch of saffron (optional)
1½ pound leg of lamb, cut in
    small cubes
 ⅓ cup olive oil
 ¾ cup white wine such as
    Vernaccia
 1 small onion, minced
    Salt and pepper to taste
 6 ounces tomato puree

Crush the garlic in a small bowl and add the rosemary and saffron. Once you have a uniform paste, cut slits in the cubes of lamb. Put a little paste into each slit. Once this is accomplished, place the cubes of lamb in a pot over a medium flame. Pour on the oil and sauté for 2 minutes. Add the wine and let it evaporate. Add the onion, salt, pepper, and tomato puree. Cover and cook over a very low flame for 2 hours. When finished, the sauce should be quite thick. If during the course of the cooking you feel the sauce is becoming too thick, add a little boiling water.

This sauce goes well with culurzones (page 260), gnocchi, maccheroni, or the typical Sardinian pasta, Malloreddus (next page).

☙ WINE: Sardinian reds such as Cannonau, Alghero, Oliena, and Barbera Sarda. Otherwise try Chianti Classico, Gattinara, or Inferno. If you prefer white, try a Vernaccia or a full-bodied Chardonnay.

Malloreddus

Sardinian Gnocchi

These gnocchi are traditional in Sardinia, in whose dialect the word means "baby bulls." I do not know the origin of this appellation, but I can speculate that they might have been named in the city of Alghero which became a possession of the Catalans in 1345. Today, its citizens still speak the Catalan language as it was spoken 630 years ago, and Alghero has the nickname Little Barcelona. My theory might seem even more plausible when you note that malloreddus are made with saffron, a spice on which Iberians are quite bullish.

Traditionally, the indentations in malloreddus are made by pressing them against a ribbed straw basket called a ciuliri, *but you may use the tines of a fork. Malloreddus are usually left to dry for 6–8 hours before cooking. Purists insist that they dry for 24 hours. They can also be purchased commercially. Serve with Ragù di Agnello alla Sarda (opposite page), fresh tomato sauce, or simply with melted butter, grated pecorino sardo, and lots of freshly ground pepper.*

4 SERVINGS

Pinch of saffron	3½ cups semolina flour
¾ cup warm water	Pinch of salt

Soak the saffron in the water for 30 minutes. Sift the flour and salt together into a mound on your working surface and form a well in the center. Add some of the saffron-soaking water and start combining it with the flour. Add more water and keep blending until you form a soft, homogenous dough. If you still need more liquid after using up the saffron water, use tepid water. Once the dough is made, form gnocchetti as indicated on pages 73–74. The malloreddus should be the size of your thumbnail. Press with the tines of a fork to create the traditional indented lines, if desired. Remember to let the malloreddus dry for at least 6 hours before cooking.

⋟ WINE: Sardinia's Alghero rosso or another sturdy red from the mainland such as Chianti or Carema.

Culurzones

These are agnolotti brought by the Piedmontese to Sardinia, where they acquired their local name. The key to this dish, a specialty of Sassari, is the availability of soft, milky pecorino cheese, preferably from Sardinia. It is similar in consistency to cottage cheese and fresh ricotta but derives its particular flavor from sheep's milk. The only possible alternative I could suggest would be a fresh goat's milk cheese. This recipe also requires aged pecorino for grating. Pecorino sardo is preferable, but pecorino romano and pecorino siciliano are also acceptable.

4–6 SERVINGS

Ripieno
10 ounces fresh spinach
2 ounces (½ stick) sweet butter
1 pound fresh pecorino sardo
1 cup aged pecorino sardo,
  grated

Salt and pepper to taste
2 eggs

Sfoglia
3½ cups flour
2–3 eggs

Wash the spinach well and steam it, using only the water left on the leaves. When cooked, squeeze the leaves dry and chop well. Melt the butter and sauté the spinach until well flavored with the butter. Transfer the spinach to a mixing bowl, add the 2 types of pecorino, salt, pepper, and eggs. Combine the ingredients thoroughly. Set aside.

Prepare the *sfoglia* as indicated on pages 52–58. Roll out 2 fairly thin sheets of sfoglia. Prepare the culurzones using either method 1 or method 2 for ravioli as explained on pages 65–67. Each culurzon should be 2–2½ inches square. Remember to seal them with your fingertips before letting them rest for 30 minutes.

Boil in abundant salted water until al dente. Serve with Ragù di Agnello alla Sarda (page 258), topped with freshly grated aged pecorino sardo.

ᕙ WINE: There are several good Sardinian reds, among them Cannonau, Alghero, Oliena, and Barbera Sarda. If you cannot find these, try a Chianti Classico or Inferno.

Vari Capricci

Spaghetti Mare e Monti · Vermicelli "Don Giovanni" ·
Spaghetti with Green Prawns · Fettuccine Antonia e Arabella ·
Pasta al Tricolore · Pasta ai Tre Formaggi Americani ·
Capelli di Angelo Primavera alla Fred · Conchiglie al Dragoncello ·
Pasta con Avanzi di Pollo ·
Rigatoni con Prosciutto Cotto e Cavalfiore · Penne agli 8 "P" ·
Tagliatelle Ernani · Gnocchi Divino · Ravioli ai Ciliegi ·
Salsa di Pistacchi

Spaghetti Mare e Monti

Spaghetti with Scallops and Wild Mushrooms

A phenomenon I discovered in Italy which I never considered in the United States is the very distinct preference people have for either the mountains or the sea. Many Italians I've met come to very fast judgments about a person based on whether he prefers life down by the shore or up in the still of some alpine forest. It also occurred to me that characters in Ibsen plays are either pious loners who go off to the hills or free spirits who derive great inspiration from maritime depths they know exist but cannot see. Some of these characteristics are evident in Italy as well. Imagine, for example, the films of Federico Fellini without the presence of the sea. Think of the many Italian religious figures who have retreated to the mountains to feel small in the presence of God and Nature. I will not divulge which place I prefer, but in my effort to reconcile my feelings about the mountains and the sea I created a dish to appeal to pasta eaters in both locales. Geography aside, scallops and mushrooms are delightfully compatible.

2 SERVINGS

1　ounce funghi porcini or other dried wild mushrooms
6–8　ounces spaghetti
3　tablespoons sweet butter
1　clove garlic, minced

4　ounces bay scallops
Pinch of minced fresh parsley
Freshly grated pepper

If the mushrooms you are using are dried, rinse them gently but quickly in cold water and then let them soak in a bowl of cold water until firm and ready to use—about 30 minutes.

Set a large pot of water to boil. When it reaches a rolling boil, add a pinch of salt, bring again to a boil and add the spaghetti.

In a saucepan, melt the butter slowly, add the garlic and sauté for 10 seconds, stirring with a wooden spoon. Add the scallops and cook for 30 seconds; next, add the mushrooms. Sauté carefully until the scallops are done—about 2 minutes. Add the parsley and pepper. By now the spaghetti should be al dente. Drain quickly and place in a warm dish. Cover the pasta with the sauce, toss the mixture thoroughly, and serve immediately.

🍴 WINE: This marriage of bosky mushrooms from the mountains and fresh scallops from the sea requires a wine to honor and cherish both partners. A hearty Chardonnay from the Veneto or a Gavi from Piedmont would fill the bill handsomely.

Vermicelli "Don Giovanni"

In creating this recipe, my prime inspiration was Byron, not Mozart.

> *While Venus fills the heart (without heart really*
> *Love, though good always, is not quite so good),*
> *Ceres presents a plate of vermicelli—*
> *For love must be sustained like flesh and blood—*
> *While Bacchus pours out wine, or hands a jelly:*
> *Eggs, oysters, too, are amatory food;*
> *But who is their purveyor from above*
> *Heaven knows—it may be Neptune, Pan, or Jove.*
> Don Juan, *canto II, verse 170*

Ceres, by the way, was a goddess from Campania who had a temple in Rome, so Byron knew well enough to have her serve the pasta of her native region. This recipe is, of course, for 2 persons.

If you are the Don Giovanni making this dish for your Donna Anna, Donna Elvira, Zerlina, or any of 2,065 other women, you might suggest eating it from the same bowl. For less romantic meals, serve in individual bowls.

2 SERVINGS

1–1½ pounds fresh oysters
   8 ounces vermicelli
   2 egg yolks
   1 tablespoon minced fresh
      parsley

Salt and pepper to taste
1 tablespoon sweet butter

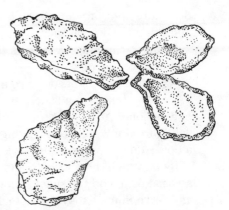

Set a large pot of water to boil. When boiling, lightly salt and bring to a boil again.

Rinse the oysters well and shuck them over a large bowl to catch the liquid as it trickles out of the shells. Put the fruit—as Italians refer to the meat of shellfish —in a separate bowl and pour any additional oyster juice from the large bowl on top of the oysters.

At this point you should start cooking the vermicelli. Be careful not to overcook them—they must be served al dente.

In a metal bowl, beat briefly with a wire whisk the egg yolks, parsley, salt, and pepper. Combine mixture with the oysters and their juice in a saucepan over a moderate flame for no more than 10 seconds. Remove pan from the stove, add the butter, and stir briefly.

Drain the pasta thoroughly and transfer to a warm dish. Add the sauce, toss well, and serve.

🍷 WINE: Champagne or a Spumante secco.

Spaghetti with Green Prawns

Kiri Te Kanawa is a magnificent singer who is also one of the dearest people I know. There is nobody I would rather hear sing

Mozart, and she does honor to many other composers as well. You might recall that it was she who sang Handel's "Let the Bright Seraphim" at the wedding of Prince Charles and Lady Diana Spencer. Though Kiri is the only opera singer in this book who is not Italian (she was born in Gisborne, New Zealand), she knows a good deal about pasta and has created a wonderful recipe.

6 SERVINGS

1–1¼ pounds green prawns, approximately, cleaned and shelled
  1 pound spaghetti

  8 ounces (2 sticks) butter
  Juice of 6 lemons
3–4 cloves garlic, pressed
  3 bay leaves

Set a large pot of water to boil. When boiling, toss in a pinch of salt and bring to a boil again.

In the meantime, clean and shell the prawns. Halve the lemons and remove any pits.

When the water reaches a rolling boil, add the spaghetti.

Melt the butter in a saucepan. Squeeze in the juice of the lemons, one by one. Add the garlic and bay leaves. Heat the ingredients gently for a few minutes, making sure the mixture does not come to a boil. Add the prawns and cook only until they turn pink.

By this time the spaghetti should be al dente. Drain, transfer it to a warm dish, add the sauce, remove the bay leaves, toss thoroughly, and serve immediately. Do not add grated cheese.

NOTE: Green prawns may be hard to come by, but the large shrimp available in American markets is eminently acceptable for this dish. Of course, it is highly preferable that the shrimp be fresh rather than frozen.

꒰ WINE: Gavi or Lacryma Christi.

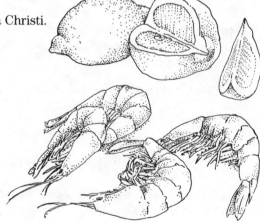

Fettuccine Antonia e Arabella

Certain dishes are named not for the ingredients that go into them but for the personalities surrounding them. This recipe was created and prepared by Antonia von Hirschberg for her friend Kiri Te Kanawa in March 1984. Miss Te Kanawa was appearing at the Metropolitan in her wonderful characterization of Richard Strauss' Arabella.

I was very impressed with this dish and am pleased to include it in this book. Although smoked meat is seldom seen in Italy outside of the Trentino-Alto Adige, the smoky flavor of the Canadian bacon does special things to the sauce of scallops and shallots.

4 SERVINGS

4 ounces Canadian bacon, diced
4 shallots, diced
Butter
1 pound bay scallops (if sea scallops, cut up)

3 level tablespoons flour
Milk
3 tablespoons white wine
Salt and pepper to taste

Sauté the diced bacon and shallots in 1 tablespoon of butter until brown. Add the scallops and quickly cook until tender, only 2–3 minutes. Remove scallops, bacon, and shallots from the pan and keep in a warm spot. Reserve any liquid remaining in the pot.

Melt 1 tablespoon of butter in the same pan used to cook the scallops. Add flour and make a roux. Cook a few minutes but do not burn. Remove from the heat. Add enough milk to the reserved liquid to make up 1½ cups. Pour slowly into the roux, stirring constantly to prevent lumps from forming. Return to the heat and continue stirring until the sauce thickens. Add the wine and continue cooking gently for 10 minutes. The sauce should be a thin consistency. Add the bacon, shallots, and scallops to the sauce and mix well. In the meantime, fill a large pot with water and bring to a boil. When the water boils add the fettuccine. Cook until tender, 3–5 minutes. Drain, rinse, and keep warm. Place the fettuccine in a large shallow serving dish and add the scallops mixture to it. Toss gently until the fettuccine and scallops are mixed well. Season to taste.

℘ WINE: A Pinot Grigio or Chardonnay from the Friuli or Trentino-Alto Adige regions.

Pasta al Tricolore

Pasta of the Italian Flag

One of the more unusual declarations of love I have ever heard is sung by Maurizio to the title character in Cilea's Adriana Lecouvreur: *"Bella tu sei, come la mia bandiera delle pugne fiammanti entro i vapor," which can be translated as, "You are as beautiful as my flag in the smoke and flame of battle." I wonder if Adriana takes that as a compliment. Though I devised this recipe, cooks in Italy have combined these ingredients for centuries. The inspiration, of course, is the red, white, and green Italian flag.*

4 SERVINGS

6 ounces fresh spinach, meticulously cleaned
1 tablespoon sweet butter
⅓ cup heavy cream
Pinch of nutmeg
8 ounces tomato fettuccine or tagliolini
Freshly grated grana

Set a large pot of cold water to boil. When it boils, toss in a pinch of salt.

In the meantime, wash the spinach well and steam in a pan using only the water still clinging to the leaves. When the spinach is cooked, drain well and squeeze out all the liquid. (You may save this liquid to use for making soup or, as I do, add the liquid to the boiling water for the pasta to give a bit more flavor.) Chop the spinach into tiny bits and set aside.

In a saucepan melt the butter and, when it becomes foamy, add the cream and the nutmeg. Stir continuously over a low flame for 10 seconds. Add the spinach.

Put the pasta in the pot of boiling water. Keep stirring the sauce —do not let it boil. When the pasta is al dente, drain well and transfer to a warm dish. Pour the sauce over the pasta, toss well, and serve. Grate on some grana to taste.

🐌 WINE: When people think of spinach in Italian cooking, they think of Florence. This is correct, though spinach is probably second in importance to beans in the Tuscan garden, not to mention tomatoes and olives. A good Chianti marries well with this spinach-based sauce.

Pasta ai Tre Formaggi Americani
Pasta with Three American Cheeses

I created this dish while attending the University of Wisconsin. Italian cheeses were not available so I used local products. Incidentally, the caraway seeds in the Wisconsin cheddar are very nice in the sauce. I must admit that in adapting this recipe for publication I have bent to a preference for cheddar from New York, my home state. I really do think it is better, though sharp Wisconsin cheddar is very good. Now when I make this dish I use only Italian grana, since it is, without question, much superior to its American cousin.

1 SERVING

4 ounces pasta (rigatoni, fresh fettuccine, or tagliolini)
¼ cup light cream
⅙ cup grated *sharp* New York (or Vermont) cheddar
⅙ cup finely sliced Monterey Jack cheese
⅙ cup finely sliced mild Wisconsin cheddar with caraway seeds
¼ cup freshly grated grana
Freshly ground pepper to taste

For cooking the pasta, bring a large pot (at least 6 quarts) of cold water to a boil. Lighly salt and bring to a boil again.

In the meantime pour the cream into a saucepan (or, if you prefer, a double boiler) and gradually add the cheeses, reserving half the grana for later use. Simmer gently over a very low flame, stirring with a wooden spoon. Once the mixture is smooth, add the pepper.

When the pasta is ready, drain well and add to the cheese sauce. Mix quickly until the pasta is well coated. Transfer to a bowl, top with the remaining grana, and serve.

⦿ WINE: Any full-bodied red, perhaps a Pinot Noir or Zinfandel from California.

Capelli di Angelo Primavera alla Fred

For everything there is a season, and for this dish the season is spring. Pasta alla primavera *always makes me think of Botticelli and the Tuscan countryside. The delicate sauce goes well with an equally delicate pasta. Ideally, you should use* capelli di angelo *(angel's hair), the thinnest of all pastas. This particular recipe is my own version of a dish that has become quite chic in recent years. Many of the tonier new restaurants in New York now offer* pasta alla primavera, *but what you wind up eating is usually heavy and/or mushy. When it is well prepared, though, the classic version of this dish can be wonderful. My recipe, however, should appeal to the calorie-conscious since it leaves out the heavy cream usually found in others. It is important, in cooking this dish, to make sure the vegetables remain crisp.*

1 SERVING

3 stalks asparagus, peeled and cut in 1-inch pieces
½ cup fresh broccoli florets, cut in 1-inch pieces
1 very small zucchini, quartered lengthwise and cut in 1-inch pieces
6 string beans, cut in half
4 mushrooms, thinly sliced
1 tablespoon butter
1 tablespoon olive oil
1 clove garlic, crushed

1 teaspoon chopped fresh parsley
1 tablespoon chopped fresh basil (if not available, use ½ teaspoon dried basil)
1 teaspoon pinoli
Pepper to taste
4 ounces capelli di angelo (linguini and spaghettini are also acceptable)
Grana (optional)

Bring a large pot (at least 6 quarts) of cold water to a boil. Lightly salt and bring to a boil again.

Wash and prepare the vegetables, then put all except the mushrooms in a large metal colander or strainer. Put the colander into the boiling water for 20–30 seconds. Remove and set aside.

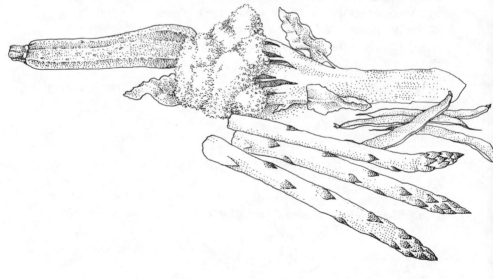

Heat the butter and oil gently in a medium-sized skillet. Do not let the butter burn. Add the garlic and mushrooms, and sauté very gently, using a wooden spoon. Add the other vegetables, parsley, basil, pinoli, and pepper.

Immediately put the pasta in the boiling water. Capelli di angelo need only 30–45 seconds to cook; in the meantime, continue to sauté the vegetables.

Once the pasta is ready, drain and put in a bowl. Pour the vegetables and their juices on the pasta, toss lightly, and serve. Grate on grana if you wish, but I recommend that you try the dish before you add cheese. The grana is tasty, but it might make the fine strands of pasta stick together.

VARIATION: I once added some boiled baby shrimp to the sauce at the same time as the vegetables and pinoli, and the result was delectable.

๖ WINE: Delicacy remains the word here. If you want a white, a Pinot Grigio from the Veneto might do. So would Vernaccia di San Gimignano, Orvieto Secco, or a good Frascati. If you prefer red wine, I would try Bardolino or Merlot from the Friuli or a very young Chianti. Each of these reds, when accompanying this dish, benefits from a slight chilling.

Conchiglie al Dragoncello

Shells with Tarragon

The inspiration for this dish was a gift of some wonderful fresh tarragon. You can use any hollowed-out pasta such as lumache, maccheroncini, margherite, ditali, orecchiette, or conchiglie.

2 SERVINGS

8 ounces pasta	1 teaspoon minced fresh
1 tablespoon sweet butter	tarragon
2 ounces prosciutto, cut in bits	⅓ cup heavy cream
4 ounces chicken breast, cut in	1 teaspoon grated grana
very small strips	¼ teaspoon tomato paste

Set a large pot of water to boil. When boiling, toss in a pinch of salt. Bring to a boil again. Start cooking the pasta.

In a saucepan, melt the butter over a low flame. Add the prosciutto, then the chicken. Cook gently for 1 minute. Add the tarragon, cook for 15 seconds, then add the cream, grana, and tomato paste. Continue to cook, stirring frequently. Do not let the sauce boil.

When the pasta is al dente, drain well and combine in a warm dish with the sauce. Serve immediately with more grated grana.

ॐ WINE: Bianco dei Castelli Romani, Frascati, or Orvieto.

Pasta con Avanzi di Pollo

Pasta with Leftover Chicken

This dish requires a pasta shape such as ziti, rigatoni, or mezzani. It is easy, fast, and tasty.

1 SERVING

¼ ounce dried funghi porcini or 3 ounces fresh mushrooms, sliced
4 ounces pasta
1 tablespoon sweet butter

3 ounces cooked chicken, diced
1 tablespoon Marsala
2 ounces heavy cream
1 tablespoon grated parmigiano
Salt and pepper to taste

If you are using dried mushrooms, soak them in advance.

When you are ready to cook, set a large pot of fresh water to boil. When it is rapidly boiling, toss in a bit of salt, bring to a boil again and start cooking the pasta.

In a saucepan, melt the butter and add the drained or fresh mushrooms. Sauté for a few seconds, then add the chicken, salt, and pepper. Once the chicken has taken on a bit of color, add the Marsala and turn up the flame until the alcohol has evaporated. Turn down the flame and add the cream and parmigiano. When the pasta is al dente, drain thoroughly and add to the sauce. Combine well and serve with grated parmigiano if available.

VARIATIONS: If you have any leftover asparagus tips, add them as you pour in the cream. If you have leftover turkey, it is a fine substitute for chicken.

ॐ WINE: Any medium-bodied red.

Rigatoni con Prosciutto Cotto e Cavalfiore

Rigatoni with Boiled Ham and Cauliflower

Here is another example of successfully creating a dish (in this case, to feed a hungry friend who popped in unexpectedly) using only ingredients immediately available. Sometimes this sort of experimentation does not succeed, but then one can also learn from one's mistakes. As it turned out, I was pleased with the dish I concocted.

2 SERVINGS

6–8 ounces cauliflower florets	2–3 ounces heavy cream
8 ounces rigatoni	1 grating of fresh pepper
1 tablespoon butter	Freshly grated nutmeg
5–6 ounces boiled ham, diced or sliced	Grana

For cooking the pasta, bring a large pot (at least 6 quarts) of cold water to a boil. Lighly salt and again bring to a boil. Put the cauliflower florets in a colander or strainer and steam over the boiling water until hot but still crisp. Remove the cauliflower and set aside.

Begin to cook the rigatoni; dry pasta should require quite a few minutes of cooking until al dente.

In the meantime, heat the butter in a saucepan and gently sauté the ham to heat it, making sure not to let it brown. Soon after you start cooking the ham, add the cauliflower florets so they pick up the flavor of the ham. Then add the cream, pepper, and as much nutmeg as you like (I am generous with this spice; other people are more stinting). Let the mixture cook for a minute to warm through but do not boil. Drain the pasta, put in a warm bowl, and add the sauce. Toss, grate on grana to taste, and eat.

VARIATION: I once tried *broccoli* instead of cauliflower. I left out the nutmeg and added a bit of garlic when I sautéed the vegetables with the ham. My guest liked the dish, but I yearned for the more delicate cauliflower preparation. You might try mixing cauliflower and broccoli florets, leaving out the garlic. It will certainly be esthetically pleasing and will probably taste pretty good too.

❧ WINE: Any medium-bodied red.

Penne agli 8 "P"

This theme and variation in the key of P is actually a combination of 2 dishes I sampled—one in the Valtellina near Switzerland, the other in Lucca. I have dropped a P (parsley), since it does not quite fit now that the recipes are combined. Porcini, panna (heavy cream), and pepper were in the alpine recipe while penne, piselli(peas), pasta di tartufo (truffle paste), and pomodoro (tomato) are derived from the Tuscan dish. Parmigiano and prosciutto are used in both.

4 SERVINGS

1 ounce dried porcini mushrooms
12 ounces penne
2 ounces (½ stick) sweet butter
4 ounces prosciutto, cut in bits
5 ounces peas, preferably fresh
1 teaspoon tomato puree or ¼ teaspoon tomato paste

¼ teaspoon salt
1 teaspoon truffle paste
1 cup heavy cream
  Freshly grated pepper
1 cup freshly grated parmigiano

Carefully wash the mushrooms and soak for a few hours before you make this dish.

When you are ready to cook, set a large pot of water to boil for the penne. Drain the mushrooms, but reserve their soaking liquid. Slice them into medium-sized pieces. Strain the mushroom liquid.

Start boiling the pasta. Melt the butter in another large pot, preferably earthenware, and add the prosciutto and peas. After 1 minute add the mushrooms, tomato puree, and salt. Cook 1 minute more and then turn off the flame. Spoon in the truffle paste and stir.

When the penne are almost al dente, drain well and add to the pot with the sauce. Turn the flame on very low and stir so the pasta is flavored by the sauce. Add the cream and, while stirring, add parmigiano a little at a time until you have used ½ cup. Keep the rest for later. When the mixture is creamy, serve into individual warm bowls. Top each serving with a bit of freshly ground pepper and pass more parmigiano.

NOTE: You may want to add a bit of the strained mushroom liquid to the sauce along with the cream or perhaps use it in the water in which you boil the pasta.

🦋 WINE: Inferno, Grumello, or Chianti Classico.

Tagliatelle Ernani

Tagliatelle with Artichokes and Peas

Ernani, Verdi's fifth opera, premiered at the Teatro La Fenice in Venice on March 9, 1844. Based on a highly controversial play by Victor Hugo, the opera brought Verdi international fame. It was the first of 9 operas by the composer to use a libretto by Francesco Maria Piave, who was a director at La Fenice before moving to La Scala in 1859. The opera has remained popular since its debut and in recent years has received new productions at La Scala (with Placido Domingo and Mirella Freni) and at the Metropolitan (with Luciano Pavarotti and Leona Mitchell). This exquisite recipe is the favorite of Francesco Ernani, the secretary general of La Scala, who kindly gave it to me.

In act one of Ernani, *Elvira says, "Every heart harbors a mystery." In this recipe, the mystery of its special flavor goes straight to the heart—of the artichoke, that is.*

4 SERVINGS

Pasta
2½ cups semolina flour
3 eggs
1 tablespoon olive oil
Pinch of salt

or

14 ounces fresh store-bought tagliatelle

Sauce
4 artichokes
½ lemon
1½ pounds fresh peas in their pods
7 tablespoons sweet butter
8 tablespoons extra-virgin olive oil

½ onion, minced
1 clove garlic, minced
1 tablespoon minced parsley
½ cup dry white wine
Salt and pepper to taste
1 cup water
Grated parmigiano (optional)

If you are making fresh pasta, use the quantities indicated and follow the instructions for making tagliatelle on page 58.

Prepare the sauce: Pull away the tough outer leaves of the artichokes and cut off their stems. Carefully cut away the chokes. Slice the artichoke hearts relatively thin and place in a large bowl of cool water to which 3 tablespoons of lemon juice or a few lemon slices have been added.

Remove the peas from their pods.

Heat the butter and oil in a saucepan and sauté the onion. Drain the artichokes and add to the sauce along with the peas, garlic, and parsley. Cook for 4 minutes over a low flame, stirring every now and then with a wooden spoon. Add the wine and let it evaporate. Add the salt, pepper, and water, cover the saucepan, and cook over a very low flame for 1 hour. Though this sauce should not be liquidy, you may add a little more water during the cooking process if you think it is getting too thick.

While the sauce is cooking, set a large pot of water to boil. When boiling, lightly salt and bring to a boil again.

When the sauce is almost done, boil the tagliatelle al dente, drain well, and transfer to a warm serving dish. Pour over the sauce, toss, and serve. If you want grated parmigiano, use it sparingly with this delicate dish.

&. WINE: Lugana from Lake Garda, Riesling dell'Oltrepo Pavese, or a Valtellina white.

Gnocchi Divino

In November 1980 I was one of the organizers of "Commedia all' Italiana," a festival of Italian film comedies held in New York City. One of my jobs was to serve as an interpreter for Giancarlo Giannini and other Italian film people who attended the festival. Figuring that the Italians would seek out good food while visiting the city, I asked Giannini where they were eating in New York. He mentioned Divino Ristorante at 1556 Second Avenue, and one evening a group of us went there. The food was indeed delicious, and I became especially fond of Gnocchi Divino, the recipe for which the restaurant Divino was kind enough to give me. Since the preparation is a bit complicated, I recommend this as a dish for guests rather than for eating alone. Read about gnocchi (small potato dumplings) on page 73.

6 SERVINGS

Gnocchi
- 6 medium-sized potatoes, preferably russet
- 2 cups flour
- 4 egg yolks

Sauce
- 4 ounces prosciutto, thinly sliced and cut into small strips
- 1 cup heavy cream
- 6 tablespoons softened sweet butter
- 8 ounces asparagus tips, cut into small pieces
- 4 tablespoons grated parmigiano

Peel the potatoes and boil in salted water until well cooked. Puree through a sieve or use a potato masher. Place the pureed potatoes on a wooden board or a marble-top table. Mix, adding a little flour. As the mixture gets dry, add 1 egg yolk at a time. With your fingertips, mix the flour and potatoes, working rapidly and not kneading more than necessary. The mixture should be dry and firm enough to handle but not hard. (You will have about ½ cup of flour left over. Reserve for later use.)

Roll the dough with your hands to form several sausage-like rolls about the thickness of your thumb. With a small knife, cut into pieces about 1 inch long. You can use them as they are or, if you wish to complicate your life and be more traditional, take a dinner fork, prong side up, and roll each little dumpling rapidly over the prongs. The result will be slightly curved dumplings decorated with small grooves. Roll lightly in remaining flour.

In a large kettle, bring at least 6 quarts of cold water to a boil. Lightly salt. When water again comes to a rolling boil, drop in about 10 or 12 dumplings at a time; when they come to the surface, remove with a slotted spoon.

While the gnocchi are cooking, place the prosciutto in a medium-sized saucepan and sauté, in its own fat, for a few minutes until golden brown. Add the rest of the ingredients for the sauce and heat for 5 minutes. Add the gnocchi and cook until the sauce thickens. Add the parmigiano and serve right away.

🍷 WINE: Amarone (as a red) or Chardonnay del Friuli (as a white).

Ravioli ai Ciliegi
Ravioli with Cherries

*According to an old piece of wisdom in pasta cookery it is wise to
eschew the sweet for the salty, spicy, or sour. In spite of this, sweetness does appear, especially with good cream and cheese or ripe
tomatoes and peppers. Bearing this in mind, I created the following
dish. In Italy there are wonderful sour cherries (especially near
Verona, Modena, and Arezzo) that are preferable for the* ripieno.
*However, sweet cherries are fine. Note that the amount indicated
for the cherries is after they have been pitted.*

4 SERVINGS

Ripieno
12 ounces fresh cherries
3 tablespoons lemon juice
8 ounces fresh ricotta

¼ teaspoon cloves
½ teaspoon nutmeg

Sfoglia
3½ cups unbleached flour
3 eggs

Pit and halve the cherries, and macerate in lemon juice in a covered
dish for about 4 hours. If desired, chop the cherries into smaller bits
for a well combined *ripieno*. Add the cherries and accumulated juice
to the ricotta along with the cloves and nutmeg. Blend well and set
aside.

Prepare the *sfoglia* as indicated on pages 52–58 and then make
the ravioli using 1 of the 3 methods suggested on pages 65–68. Set
the ravioli aside for a few minutes before cooking in a large pot of
lightly salted boiling water. When the ravioli "flower" drain carefully
using a slotted spoon and transfer to warm serving dishes. Serve
with Salsa di Pistacchi (page 277).

❧ WINE: Dry Spumante is my choice. You may also drink Bardolino
or Est! Est!! Est!!!

Salsa di Pistacchi

Pistachio Sauce

This sauce is a subtle change from the equally delicious yet alarm-
ingly chic Salsa di Noci (walnut sauce). Though I do enjoy Salsa
di Noci, this Ligurian sauce turns up too often in stylish New York
restaurants adorning the wrong types of food. It is best suited to
Pansôti (page 176) and certain other paste ripiene. *Try Salsa di*
Pistacchi on tortellini or on Ravioli ai Ciliegi. If possible, use
undyed, unsalted pistachio nuts.

4 SERVINGS

4 ounces pistachio nuts
2 ounces (½ stick) sweet butter
¼ cup heavy cream

2 tablespoons freshly grated
grana
Pinch of nutmeg

Crush the pistachio nuts by hand, with a blender, or in a food processor. I favor using a mortar and pestle, yielding something akin to
pistachio paste. This paste will make a silkily rich sauce. Melt the
butter in a saucepan, add the cream and pistachio paste, and heat
gently, stirring with a wooden spoon. Bring the sauce almost to a
boil, add the grana and nutmeg, and continue to heat the sauce until
it has condensed to a thickness you find desirable.

VARIATION: I once added a tablespoon of kirsch after cooking the
butter, cream, and pistachio nuts for 2 minutes. When the alcohol
had evaporated, the sauce was left with a subtle fruity flavor that
married well with the delicate pistachios.

❧ WINE: This depends what you serve the sauce on. Bardolino is a
good choice for tortellini or other meat-filled pasta. It also works
well with cheese-filled pasta. Frascati or Est! Est!! Est!!! are excellent selections if you want white wine. For Ravioli ai Ciliegi, serve a
dry spumante.

The Pasta Cook's Pantry

INGREDIENTS FOR PASTA COOKING AND SAUCING

AMARETTI: These little macaroons are produced in Lombardy. They are light, crunchy, and slightly bitter. Though traditionally consumed after a meal with espresso or liqueur, amaretti may also be crushed and added to the filling for tortelli and other stuffed pasta. Several brands of amaretti are available in North America, the most famous being Lazzaroni.

ANCHOVIES: These little fish are found in great abundance in the Mediterranean, and they flavor a great many Italian dishes, especially those of Sicily. A netful of anchovies is a dazzling sight—they are silver-colored with sky-blue markings. When you buy fillets in cans or jars, they are brownish and salty. You might want to soak them in cool water to reduce the saltiness, especially those that are packed in salt rather than oil. A modern convenience is anchovy paste, sold in tubes, which essentially is composed of pureed anchovies, perhaps with a little olive oil and salt added. If you buy anchovy paste, keep it refrigerated.

ASIAGO: A delicious hard sheep's milk cheese for grating, produced in the province of Vicenza in the Veneto. This area also gave us Palladio (1508–1580), one of history's great architects. Asiago has about 110 calories per ounce.

BASIL: This herb, which has always been a basic ingredient in Italy, has recently come into great favor in North American kitchens. It grows very easily so you can have it all the time by cultivating some on your windowsill, as they do in Genoa. In the spring and summer it is available in such abundance that you should have it around to flavor all manner of dishes. In Genoa they wipe basil carefully with a cloth rather than wash it, which they say robs the herb of its spe-

cial flavor and perfume. Tear basil leaves rather than cut them. The flavor of basil tends to intensify when the leaves are subjected to prolonged heating. Add them to fresh sauces that are almost finished cooking so that their flavors will be enlivened rather than over-powered.

BAY LEAVES: When Tiberius lounged around his villa on rainy days on Capri, he wore a wreath of bay laurel leaves, thinking that it would save him from being struck by lightning. This dated back to a belief held by the Greeks who so cherished the plant that they placed crowns of the leaves on the heads of heroes, making them laureates. Use this herb sparingly in cooking. The leaves impart a very assertive flavor and should be removed before serving, since they are not fun to eat. Bay leaves are grown in all the Mediterranean countries.

BEL PAESE: A soft neutral cheese created in 1906 by Egidio Galbani, who built one of Italy's leading cheese factories. You can always distinguish this cheese by its wrapper which depicts in green a map of Italy, the "Bel Paese." The flavor is less distinctive than others, yet it serves as a good foil in a pasta dish when combined with other, more assertive ingredients. It has about 89 calories per ounce.

BITTO: Comes from the Bitto valley in the Valtellina area of Lombardy. It is a smooth hard cheese made primarily of cow's milk with some goat's milk added. It may be eaten as a young fresh cheese or, when aged, used in pasta dishes such as *pizzoccheri* and *sciatt.* Bitto has about 100 calories per ounce.

BREAD CRUMBS: The best bread crumbs are those you make yourself from stale bread. You may also lightly toast sliced bread and then grate it. It is perfectly acceptable to buy commercially prepared bread crumbs, of course; however, you should purchase only plain bread crumbs. If you want additional flavorings (herbs or grated cheese), add fresh ingredients as you prepare your dish.

BROTH: This is an essential ingredient in pasta cookery. Broth made of chicken, capon, beef, or veal lends richness of flavor to a sauce without adding bulk. In addition, many stuffed pastas are cooked and served in broth. In Bologna, for example, many natives will eat tortellini only in a rich capon broth rather than tossing the little belly button-shaped pastas in a cream, meat, or tomato sauce.

Italian broth should not have a powerful flavor—this would cause it to overshadow any other foods it shares a bowl with. Rather, it should be a flavorful liquid with a particular perfume. The broth I use most frequently is made of a well cleaned capon, 1 small onion, 1 carrot, 1 stalk of celery, salt and pepper to taste, and perhaps some fresh parsley. Put the ingredients in a pot and add enough cold water so that the ingredients are covered by a couple of inches. Bring the water to a boil and then simmer for 3 to 4 hours, skimming off the fat every so often. Strain the liquid, reserving the other ingredients for use elsewhere, and let cool before refrigerating it. Skim off all the fat before using the broth, which may be frozen in smaller quantities for future use. Beef, veal, or chicken (or maybe even a combination of these) may be used instead of capon.

In Italy it has now become very popular to use bouillon cubes. Obviously, they save a lot of time and effort, but they can never replace real broth. Some Italian cooks add a half or whole cube directly to sauces instead of cooking them in water first. This gives a rather direct, unsubtle flavor. And bouillon cubes contain a great deal of extra salt. So use them only as a convenience if you do not have the time or ingredients to make real broth, and, if possible, cut back or eliminate the salt in the recipe.

BUTTER: Whenever this ingredient is called for in this book, use *sweet* butter. Please don't think that it is acceptable to use salted butter—it would impede your efforts to make authentic Italian sauces. This is especially true when butter combined with sage *is* your sauce. Make sure not to burn the butter; if it turns brown, do not use it. Butter is the traditional cooking fat of Lombardy and parts of Emilia. It has about 220 calories per ounce, compared to approximately 260 calories for the same amount of olive oil.

CACIOCAVALLO: A general name for a family of cheeses popular throughout southern Italy. There are variations of caciocavallo ranging from sweet and soft to piquant and hard. When you buy it, try to find out if it is from Campania, Calabria, Lucania, Apulia, or Sicily. You will probably develop preferences and, if you want to be authentic, you can match regional cheeses and recipes. The young soft cheese is for eating as is; the older caciocavallo is grainy and wonderful when grated on delicious southern Italian pasta dishes. Caciocavallo is made of cow's milk and in its mature form has about 115 calories per ounce. Some caciocavallo is made with partially skimmed milk.

CANESTRATO: A flavorful sheep's milk cheese from Sicily. For pasta cookery one uses the aged version to grate on Sicilian specialties. The name comes from the word *canestro*, basket. Traditionally, canestrato is pressed into wicker baskets, which produces a characteristic crisscross design on the crust of the finished cheese. As *incanestrato pepato*, the cheese has black peppercorns embedded in it, which makes it excitingly piquant when grated. You may substitute it for pecorino in the recipe for Spaghetti al Cacio e Pepe.

CHEESE: One of the world's oldest foods. The most famous story about its origins is of the Arab who put milk in a sack made of a sheep's stomach before embarking on a desert journey. The heat of the desert and the rennin in the sack turned the milk into a rudimentary form of cheese. Then there is the saying that cheese is milk's leap to immortality. Nowadays the most popular milk for cheese comes from cows. In Roman times cows were used for work and as a source of meat. For making cheese, the Romans preferred milk from sheep and goats as well as water buffaloes, which were introduced to the Italian peninsula during the fourth century B.C.

Cheese is composed primarily of minerals, protein, fat, and water, a good nutritional match for the carbohydrates in pasta. You may read more about individual Italian cheeses under their own headings in this chapter, many of which are now available in North America in fine food stores and by mail order. For cheeses requiring grating, do not grate them until you need them. Otherwise they will dry out and lose their distinctive flavor and aroma.

EGGS: In Italy eggs tend to be smaller than those in North America. To make fresh pasta, use the number of eggs indicated in the recipe. If you find you need extra flour for a proper dough, next time use smaller eggs. When you find an egg size that is right for your pasta dough, stay with it. Large eggs were used in the recipes in this book.

EMMENTHAL: The generic name for cow's milk cheese known more frequently as Swiss Cheese. It is produced in Switzerland, where the name of the country is stamped on the rind of the cheese, as well as in Italy, France, Austria, West Germany, Finland, Sweden, Norway, and the United States. Each country produces an Emmenthal that is distinctive in taste, though all are characterized by the gaping holes in the cheese. The Swiss article is authentic and very fine, of course, but some of those produced in other countries are good too. I am especially fond of French Emmenthal in cooking, where its slightly sharp taste enhances many dishes. Emmenthal averages 110 calories per ounce.

FONTINA: The classic cheese from the Valle d'Aosta. It is produced elsewhere in Italy and in Scandinavia, but you should use only the genuine article, which has a reddish-brown crust. The cheese itself is straw-colored and sweet, and occasionally reveals a mild mushroom flavor. Fontina has wonderful melting properties and is the basis for *fonduta* (fondue). You may also melt Fontina (120 calories per ounce) to serve with gnocchi or fresh tagliatelle.

FUNGHI PORCINI: A term referring to wild mushrooms also known as *Boletus edulis.* They are grown in many parts of Italy but especially in the mountainous area north of Bergamo and in the Valtellina. Funghi porcini from Italy are widely available in North America in dried form. Soak them in warm water for at least an hour and be sure to use the flavorful strained liquid in cooking. When you purchase the transparent little packages, check that the mushrooms look fleshy and full and that they have not crumbled. Since imported funghi porcini can be expensive, even though one needs very little, I sometimes combine them and the water they soaked in with 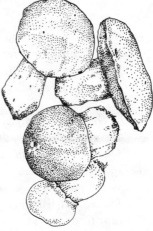 fresh cultivated mushrooms. Remember, though, that store-bought cultivated mushrooms tend to be bland, lacking the special characteristics and fragrance of those from the forest. Though *Boletus edulis* are Italian wild mushrooms, and this is an Italian cookbook, if you only have access to other wild mushrooms *and* if you know which are not poisonous, experiment with them. There are now wild mushrooms available from France, Germany, Poland, and other places. Remember to cook wild mushrooms very slowly.

GARLIC: When people who are not familiar with Italian cuisine are asked to describe it, they usually refer to it as "garlicky." This is seldom meant to be favorable. In fact, garlic is used carefully and wisely in Italy, whose cooks appreciate its sweetness and fragrance. Do not use garlic salt or powder in cooking—in no way does it approximate the effect of fresh garlic. Buy plump heads of garlic with healthy-looking cloves. I do not recommend a garlic press for cooking. Pressing garlic will give you intense juice that will overpower your delicate dishes. Rather, use full or half cloves to impart flavor, or garlic slivers if you plan to eat it.

GORGONZOLA: A wonderfully creamy blue-veined cow's milk cheese produced in Lombardy. *Gorgonzola dolce* comes straw-colored with a sweet buttery flavor, while *Gorgonzola piccante* is white

and much sharper. I prefer the latter for making sauce for pasta, though either is fine. The crust, incidentally, is not edible. Most Gorgonzola is now industrially made, though 10 percent is still produced by hand in small farms and factories. It averages 92 calories per ounce.

GRANA: A generic name for a delicious cow's milk cheese used for grating, of which Parmigiano-Reggiano is the most famous. The flavor of grana can alternately be nutty, salty, and sweet. It is grated over the marvelous pasta dishes of Emilia-Romagna, which along with Lombardy, produces most of Italy's grana. Famous grana comes from Lodi, Brescia, Mantua, Piacenza, Alessandria (in Piedmont), and from communities along the Po River, where it is called *grana padano*. The king of grana is, of course, the one that is made in Parma and Reggio Emilia. Grate the cheese only as you need it and keep it in the refrigerator wrapped tightly in 2 or 3 layers of aluminum foil.

GRUYÈRE: A sweet, delicate cow's milk cheese produced in Switzerland, often confused with Emmenthal. It has tiny holes and good melting ability, which makes it ideal for Pasta ai Quattro Formaggi. In Italian the cheese is called *groviera*, and it has about 109 calories per ounce.

LEMON: These were imported by the Romans and were first grown in Italy in the seventh century. In the symbolism of the Catholic Church, the lemon often appears to represent fidelity. The juice of this fruit, omnipresent in Italian cooking, especially that of the south, gives wonderful flavor and life to the dishes it is added to. Lemons are so abundant in Sicily (which produces 90 percent of Italy's total) that one could paraphrase the cliche about coals to Newcastle, substituting lemons and Palermo. Use lemon juice to prevent cut fruits and vegetables such as apples and artichokes from discoloring. Lemon peel, washed and perhaps air-dried, is delicious when judiciously grated into certain sauces and fillings for stuffed pasta.

MARSALA: This fortified Sicilian wine is listed apart from other wines because of its special role in cooking. The name is of Arabic origin, meaning "the port of God," but it is actually produced in the western tip of Sicily, in Marsala, a town in the province of Trapani. The wine was born by accident: An Englishman named John Woodhouse was in Trapani around 1770. He wanted to bring some local wine back to England, so he put some in a red wooden cask and added more alcohol to fortify it for the trip. This process is not unlike that used by English wine merchants in importing Madeira, port, and sherry from Iberia. As methods of cultivation, distillation, and fortification were refined, Sicily's most famous wine came into being. British merchants traded heavily in Trapani and were greatly alarmed when Garibaldi and his army of a thousand men landed there to start the march through Sicily and up the Italian peninsula to campaign for Italian unity. The British were greatly relieved when their Marsala was left untouched. There is now a type of Marsala Superiore labeled "G.D." (Garibaldi Dolce). The finest is probably Marsala Vergine, which is aged at least 5 years and is the original wine without anything added to it. You may use Vergine, Fine, or Superiore for cooking.

MASCARPONE (OR MASCHERPONE): Originally a cheese produced at Abbiategrasso, near Milan, this rich cheese is now produced in other areas of Lombardy as well as Piedmont and Emilia. Mascarpone is made from the cream of cow's milk and is produced only in cold weather months, since it spoils easily. It is a cheese often served as a dessert, mixed with brandy, coffee, or cocoa. In pasta dishes, mascarpone adds richness to anything it touches. Its color ranges from pure white to light gold; it is like rich butter in consistency and has about 127 calories per ounce.

MINT: The fresh perfume of this aromatic herb is a particular favorite of Roman cooks. Although there are over 20 species and many subspecies of mint, the one used most often in Italian cooking is spearmint. One may use mint in combination with cheese to fill cannelloni or ravioli or add a few torn leaves to a fresh tomato sauce. Use only fresh mint in cooking.

MORTADELLA: This luscious sausage is a specialty of Bologna which, in a drastically diminished version, appears in our markets as bologna. Do not confuse the two. *Mortadella* is an exquisitely delicate but rich combination of pork, spices, whole peppercorns and, on occasion, pistachios. When thinly sliced or cubed it makes a great appetizer. It is also part of the traditional filling for tortellini. Sophia

Loren tried to smuggle a large mortadella into the United States in the 1972 film *Lady L,* but if you try this you will run into problems. Ham, salami, and sausage may not be imported to the U.S., so we can only use domestic *mortadella.* It is a reasonable substitute, though not the real thing.

MOZZARELLA: The famous cheese from the Naples region of Campania. A particularly esteemed example comes from Battipaglia. Once it was only made from the curds of milk from water buffaloes, but now it is produced in combination with, or totally of, cow's milk curds. The ideal mozzarella should be soft, moist, and creamy. It usually comes in ovals that weigh approximately 1 pound and are stored in cool water until they are sold. Commercially prepared mozzarella in North America is often too salty and gummy, lacking the requisite freshness. There are now stores and cheese companies that produce good, fresh mozzarella—you should seek them out. Mozzarella is a good food for weight watchers. Its fat content (22 percent) is lower than that in most cheeses and, at 76 calories per ounce, it goes well with a lean pasta sauce such as Salsa Cruda (page 113).

NUTMEG: This spice is a particular favorite in the kitchens of Modena, where it may be found in pasta stuffings, cream sauces, meat dishes, and desserts. Used in moderation, fragrant nutmeg is a key ingredient in pasta cookery. Many gourmet shops sell whole nutmegs from Italy, packaged with a little grater. These make nice gifts for authentic pasta cooks, since freshly grated nutmeg is superior to commercially packaged ground nutmeg.

OLIVE OIL: This is the basic cooking fat of Mediterranean countries, including Italy. It is produced in many parts of the country; Sicily, Apulia, Campania, Umbria, and Liguria make excellent olive oils, but it is generally agreed that the finest come from Tuscany. Many of these are now available in North America. If the oil is in any way considered virginal *(extravergine, sopraffino vergine, fino vergine,* or simply *vergine)* you are on the right track. This is the purest liquid derived from pressing excellent olives. The virginal terminology refers to acidity which, by law, may not exceed 4 percent. To my taste the most flavorful is the jade-colored *olio extravergine di oliva.* This is the most basic, least processed olive oil, whose innocence is the source of its goodness. Oil that is more processed (more pressed or occasionally blended) is usually gold in color. You are also likely to find olive oil mixed with other oils. It is less expensive but not nearly as good. Try to buy good Italian olive oils for cooking. Though fine olive oil is produced in California, it is not quite as good as the top Italian oils. I prefer bottled oil, but when I buy it canned I transfer it to dark glass jars and store it in a cool spot. Though olive oil is fattening (1 tablespoon of olive oil has 124 calories while 1 tablespoon of butter has 100), it is also very good for your skin, hair, and digestion.

OLIVES: Along with wheat and grapes, olives form the historic trinity of Mediterranean agriculture. The tomato is a relative newcomer and does not partake of the symbolism the other 3 foods are endowed with. We break bread, extend an olive branch, find truth in wine. Try to imagine Italy without bread (or pasta) and wine. Think of the Tuscan countryside depicted in Renaissance painting, and you see neat rows of vines and olive groves. The Apulian plain produces great quantities of wheat as well as many tons of olives and grapes for oil and wine.

Olives have long been a food of the poor. The olive tree is cheaper to raise than a pig or cow, so olive oil is a more accessible cooking fat than lard or butter. Olives, which are fruit, are green or black. Green olives are picked before they are fully ripe. They are particularly popular in Tuscany, Apulia, and Sicily. Romans, especially Jews, like to eat young green olives that have been soaked in lightly salted water. Black olives are more mature. They are washed well, briefly soaked in salt water, dried in the sun, and preserved in olive oil and herbs. I use black olives in cooking unless the recipe calls for green ones. My basic cooking and eating olives come from Gaeta, between Naples and Rome. These are widely available in delicatessens and specialty food shops. Avoid olives sold in cans, cocktail olives, and any others that seem as though they have passed through too many processes since leaving the grove.

ONION: Sweet fragrant onions give character and substance to a whole range of dishes. They are vital as starting ingredients for meat sauces and in some fillings for stuffed pastas such as agnolotti and tortellini. In the case of one dish from Calabria (page 238), onions *are* the sauce. When sautéeing onions in butter, melt the butter gently until it is foamy but has not turned color. Add the onions and cook until they reach a golden translucence. To sauté them in oil, heat the oil until it is hot but not very hot or smoky. Add the onions and cook them slowly enough so that they do not burn or fry. For most uses, small- to medium-sized yellow onions are preferable.

OREGANO: This herb is most closely associated with Naples, where volatile lovers of flavorful food respond passionately to oregano's call to be noticed. Add oregano, fresh, if possible, to sauces or on top of melted cheese when cooking is nearly completed. Though oregano dries more successfully than most herbs, it too can become old and musty. Rub a pinch between your fingers and sniff before using the dried oregano. This herb is also called wild marjoram. Its sweet cousin is simply called marjoram and can usually be interchanged with oregano.

PANCETTA: This is bacon, Italian-style. The major difference between *pancetta* and our bacon is that *pancetta* is cured rather than smoked. It is often shaped into a round or oval form that is then sliced. If a recipe calls for cubes, buy a thick slice of *pancettta* and dice it. You may freeze thick slices of *pancetta*, but use it as soon as it has defrosted. Our smoked bacon in classic preparations such as Spaghetti alla Carbonara does not do these dishes justice. However, if you absolutely cannot find *pancetta* or unsmoked bacon, boil smoked bacon for 2 minutes in a large pot of water to remove some of the smokiness. In Rome, by the way, the popular local version of *pancetta* is called *guanciale*.

PARMIGIANO-REGGIANO: "A man who has been three years biting his nails on a desert island, Jim, can't expect to appear as sane as you or me. It doesn't lie in human nature. Was it cheese you said he had a fancy for?"

"Yes, sir, cheese," I answered.

"Well, Jim," says he, "just see the good that comes of being dainty in your food. You've seen my snuffbox, haven't you? But you never saw me take snuff, did you? The reason being that in my snuffbox I carry a piece of Parmesan cheese—a cheese which is made in Italy, very nutritious."

It may not be true, as Dr. Livesey suggests in *Treasure Island*, that a bit of parmigiano is the key to sanity. Yet it is definitely a food I would bring along with me if I were to be confined on a desert island.

This magnificent cheese, whose full name is Parmigiano-Reggiano (from Parma and Reggio Emilia) is commonly known as parmigiano. In English it is Parmesan, but for our purposes the Italian name is used.

This is a type of grana cheese (page 284), yet it has achieved greater acclaim than its cousins in Piacenza, Lodi, and elsewhere. The cheese originated in Reggio, but somehow Parma got the fame, probably because Reggio was once part of the duchy of Parma. It is made only with milk produced between April and November, and then is aged until it becomes the rich nutty cheese we know well. Parmigiano should be grated only when you need it. Store it as you would all grana cheeses. Genuine Parmigiano-Reggiano has its name engraved on the crust. In cutting the cheese, always include a piece of the crust.

PARSLEY: This herb is sadly dismissed in most kitchens as pretty green decoration for important dishes. Yet it probably furnishes more vitamin C than any other food, and it has a freshness that livens food and tames such bossy flavors as garlic. Parsley with flat leaves is often called Italian parsley, and it is the preferred type for the recipes in this book. In its absence, though, feel free to use the curly parsley you are used to.

PAZIENZA: The word *pazienza* is frequently uttered in Italy, often with a slight shrug of the shoulders. Patience is a great virtue, one characteristic of many Italians. It helps them endure hardships born of bureaucracy as well as the daily dramas of lives lived passionately. For cooks, patience will permit you to carefully knead, roll out, and cut or fold dough for pasta. You may patiently dice and slice ingredients for sauces using fantasy and creativity. By not heating a meat sauce too quickly, you will be rewarded with a delicious ragù in which all the elements have successfully blended to create a magnificent total.

PECORINO: This is a generic term in Italy for any cheese made of sheep's milk. There are many regional varieties, from the many eating cheeses in Tuscany and Liguria to the soft, fresh, young Fiore Sardo of Sardinia to the grating cheeses produced in Sicily, Sardinia, the Friuli, and especially Latium, which gives us the famous pecorino romano. Specifically, whenever pecorino is called for in this book, I am referring to pecorino romano unless otherwise indicated. This cheese is readily available throughout North America in stores and by mail order. It has been imported to the New World since the beginning of this century to meet the demands of immigrants from southern Italy. Traditionally it has a smoky black seal on the crust. Pecorino romano has a pleasing piquant taste and is the grating cheese of choice for most pasta dishes from southern Italian kitchens. It is not indicated for dishes from the north, except for pesto. Pecorino romano has about 120 calories per ounce. Grate it only as needed.

PEPERONCINO: This is the Italian word for spicy red pepper or chili pepper. There is also a green variety that is slightly less sharp. Peperoncino is a key ingredient in pasta sauces in central and southern Italy, especially in Calabria. Whenever it is available, make a point of using fresh peperoncino in quantities you enjoy. Beware: It is very spicy.

PEPPER (BLACK): Invest in a pepper mill. It does not have to be fancy—the pretentious ones you see in restaurants are no better than those you can use at home. Grind pepper only as you need it by milling the peppercorns over the pot or dish. Few foods are more delicious than a bowl of Spaghetti alla Carbonara with lots of freshly ground pepper. In general I recommend black pepper unless you are making a delicate, light sauce, in which case white pepper will do.

PEPPERS (GREEN, RED AND YELLOW): Italy has a wonderful bounty of *peperoni* which give color and flavor to a great many dishes. Green peppers have a fresh, young taste. As they mature on the vine they often turn red or yellow, acquiring a more distinctive flavor. When red or yellow peppers are available, use them to improvise sauces made with foods of other colors and textures.

PINOLI: This is the Italian plural apellation for what we refer to in English as pignoli. Ours seems a strange name since a *pignolo* in Italian is a picky, fussy person. I prefer the Italian spelling when speaking of the buttery-flavored pine seeds. Pinoli are popular in desserts and should be included in any authentic pesto. Buy them in small amounts since pinoli turn rancid very quickly and a few will go a long way in cooking.

PROSCIUTTO COTTO: This is what we call boiled ham. Do not confuse it with prosciutto crudo, which is discussed below. In general it is less fattening than prosciutto crudo, since much of the fat has cooked off. When it is made of pork shoulder, it is called *spalla cotta.* When eaten alone it is usually very thinly sliced, so that it melts succulently in your mouth. In cooking with prosciutto cotto, use slivers or cubes cut from a whole piece.

PROSCIUTTO CRUDO: In North America when we speak of prosciutto we are thinking of the salted, air-cured ham taken from a pig's thigh that Italians call prosciutto crudo. Parma is famous for its prosciutto, but there are also excellent prosciutti made in the rest of Emilia and in the Friuli. Unfortunately, they are not available in the United States. We must content ourselves with domestic brands, some of which are pretty decent. Prosciutto crudo is rich in flavor and quite fattening. For our purposes it is usually employed as an ingredient to lend a special flavor to sauces. For cooking, rather than for eating with melon, it should be quite thinly sliced. Occasionally recipe instructions call for diced prosciutto, which should be cut from a whole piece.

PROVOLONE: When you think of old photos of Italian-American delicatessens, hanging next to the salamis are the pear- and cone-shaped cheeses known as provolone. This is one of the most popular cheeses in southern Italy, where it is produced either *dolce* (sweet) or *piccante* (sharp). Sometimes provolone cheese is smoked. Provolone is made of cow's milk and is often salted and aged. It averages 135 calories an ounce.

RAGÙ: Though this word is a variation on the French term meaning stew, in Italian it suggests a meat sauce served with pasta. The most famous example is the wonderful Ragù Bolognese, made of beef, but there are also sauces of lamb, pork, mutton, and so forth. Two pastas particularly indicated for ragù are tagliatelle and rigatoni.

RICOTTA: Generic name for a cheese produced throughout Italy from milk whey that is cooked again (*ricotta* in Italian means cooked again) after being separated from the curds. The most famous and appreciated ricotta is from Rome. It is smooth, milky, and soft, and is wonderful when stuffed into cannelloni. Originally it was made of sheep's milk, but now it is often produced from the combined milk of sheep and cows. There are also ricottas from goat and water buffalo milk. Cooks in North America often substitute cottage cheese for ricotta. I do not recommend this practice; try instead to locate ricotta. There are commercially made ricottas available that are adequate for cooking even if they do not approach the special taste of ricotta romana. If you live in an area where fresh ricotta is made, try some. It averages 110 calories an ounce.

In Italy there is also ricotta salata, salted, aged, drier, and compact. It is good when grated over rich tomato sauces.

RIPIENO: The Italian word for the filling used to stuff pasta. This may be made of meats, vegetables, cheeses, or herbs, alone or in combination.

ROSEMARY: In the Roman spring the citizens of Italy's capital eat *abbacchio* (lamb) flavored with fresh rosemary. This herb is indispensable in cooking with lamb and, indeed, is popular with other foods in Italy as well. A couple of sprigs of fresh rosemary are sufficient. Use less of the herb when it is dried.

SAGE: The Italian word for this wonderful herb is *salvia*, from the Latin *salvere*, to save. In Roman times sage was thought to relieve many ailments. Fresh sage is popular in Rome in a dish known as *saltimbocca*, in which it is combined with veal and prosciutto. In Tuscany and further north, sage is often added to sauces and main courses made of chicken livers or game. Try to use fresh or newly dried sage. When dried sage is kept for a while it can take on an unpleasant flavor.

SALT: As I mentioned in the preceding chapter, salt has been an important commodity in Italy for over 3,000 years. Until very recently it was produced and packaged by a government monopoly and was available only in tobacco shops. In the past decade, as people in North America have cut down on salt consumption, there has been a marked difference in the saltiness of Italian and American food. It is for this reason that most of the recipes in this book suggest that you add salt according to your own taste.

One special note: You should always cook pasta in lightly salted boiling water (see page 79 for the method of cooking pasta). This will give some saltiness to your dish. The sauce itself might also include some salt, especially if you have added anchovies or meats such as prosciutto, salami, mortadella, or sausage. The cheese you grate on will probably add more saltiness, particularly if it is pecorino romano or ricotta salata. *Never* sprinkle salt on your pasta once it is cooked and topped with sauce.

SAUSAGE: Our sausage, even what is called Italian sausage, seldom matches the subtlety of flavoring and the quality found in Italy. My suggestion is that you look around for the best local market or pork butcher and see what he has. His products often contain flavorings you may not want. Be especially alert for the distinctive taste of fennel. It is delicious but not necessarily suitable for what you plan to cook. If you find a good version of *luganega* (page 44), go with it. This mild sausage will enhance your sauces without unbalancing them. If you cannot locate an Italian-style sausage to your liking, then and only then should you use another type of sausage as a substitute.

SCAMORZA: A briefly aged cheese produced near Naples either of water buffalo's or cow's milk. Scamorza is more commonly used as an appellation for smoked mozzarella. When thinly sliced it gives a special taste to baked pasta.

SEMOLINA: In Italian it is called *semolino.* This is the hard durum wheat often used in gnocchi and in the pasta-making of southern Italy. Oddly enough, the people of the northern city of Ferrara often claim to produce the best semolina, but if you find *semolino* from Apulia or somewhere else in Italy, you may purchase it with confidence. Only if you cannot locate the Italian article should you use hard durum grown in North America.

SFOGLIA: This is the general Italian term for pasta dough once it has been rolled out. One often speaks of *sfoglia* when discussing *pasta ripiena* (stuffed pasta), that is, ravioli, tortellini, anolini, and so forth.

TALEGGIO: A creamy cow's milk cheese from Lombardy, originally from the area around Bergamo. This soft, buttery cheese is usually sweet and fragrant. It is a good substitute if you cannot find Bitto cheese.

TOMATOES: A crucial ingredient in pasta cookery. For a more complete discussion of these *pomi d'oro* (golden apples), see page 106.

TOMATO PASTE: In the town of Fidenza, 14 miles west of Parma, tomato lovers in the last century put tomato sauce out in the sun. When it dried, this concentrate was kept to impart tomato flavor to food during the winter months. Today, *concentrato di pomodoro* is sold in tubes in Italy. Once you open the tube, store it in the refrigerator. Use the tomato paste very sparingly—even a dot of it will lend color and flavor to a sauce or to tomato pasta. As flavorful as *concentrato* is, *doppio* (double) and *triplo* (triple) are even richer.

TRUFFLES: The sad but true association that most people first make when they think of truffles is not flavor or fragrance but money. Indeed, truffles are expensive (currently about $25 an ounce in New York) and can only be consumed at special times. Yet on those occasions there are few foods as capable as the truffle in turning an important moment into a memorable one. Part of the reason for their cost is that demand far outstrips supply. Truffles cannot be mass-produced: The French have synthesized truffles, but the real thing is far superior. Truffles are tubers that grow underground, attached to the roots of trees such as oaks, poplars, and chestnuts. In Italy black truffles are found near Spoleto and Norcia in Umbria, and white or lavender truffles grow near Alba in Piedmont. Sensitive dogs or pigs are employed to sniff for truffles. There is a school for truffle hounds in Piedmont in the town of Rodi. If you are going to spend money to buy a truffle (which is often stored in rice that you should later cook and eat), invest a few extra dollars to purchase a proper truffle shaver. These may be found in specialty shops or ordered by mail. Nowadays it is also possible to buy Umbrian truffle paste in tubes. It is expensive, of course, but is logical if you want to spread truffle flavor around.

WATER: The gifts from the earth and air and the power of fire would all be useless to a cook who has no water. This crucial element is too often ignored by those who discuss food preparation. Water is the primary component in many foods. It is essential for washing ingredients; cooking food in boiling water is one of the most ancient of all methods. To speak of the social and economic development of Italy is to speak of the availability of water. The Po valley is so rich because the land is so fertile. Parts of southern Italy are extremely impoverished because so little can be grown. Intensely regional Italians even differ on who has the best water. Neapolitans explain why they are considered to make the nation's best cup of coffee by stating that they have the best water. They also say that their water combined with flour produces Italy's finest pasta. The natives of the mountains in the Abruzzi make the same claim. I have been to many restaurants in the province of Parma where owners proudly serve fresh local water instead of bottled mineral water. People in the Alpine regions, north of Venice, Verona, Milan, and Turin, all say their water is the best. People throughout Italy all tend to drink a lot of bottled mineral water, which comes either *con gas* (carbonated) or *senza gas* (flat). The labels on these bottles feature detailed chemical analyses along with a statement by a professor from the local university describing the properties this particular water has for curing specific ailments. Many Italians "take the cure" once a year. That is, they vacation in spas such as Montecatini and Chiancino Terme to drink water.

For the purposes of this book, your everyday water is fine.

To make pasta, water is often a key ingredient. Some pasta made in northern Italy uses only eggs and flour, which might be softened with a little milk or water. In southern Italy, though, only water and flour (usually semolina) are employed.

To cook pasta, fill a very large pot with cold, fresh water. Bring the water to a boil and then toss in a pinch of salt. When the water returns to a boil, add the pasta.

Water is often called for in preparing pasta sauces. You might be tempted to use a more flavorful liquid such as wine or broth. This is not wise. It may be the very neutrality of water that makes it the most desirable liquid for a particular sauce. Pay close attention to recipe instructions. If, for example, you are told to leave a bit of water clinging to spinach or to spaghetti, this may well be the key step that determines the success of your dish.

WINE

Italy and France regularly vie for the title of world's leading wine producer. They also lead everyone else in wine consumption. France has a justly earned reputation for producing extraordinary wines. Though they are less well known, the great Italian reds such as Barolo, Chianti Classico, Brunello di Montalcino, and Amarone are among the best wines produced anywhere, and they usually cost less than their French cousins. More importantly, perhaps, Italy produces dozens of inexpensive yet wonderful wines for daily consumption. Many of these are available to wine lovers in North America. It is great fun to sample these wines and select your *vino da tavola* for regular drinking. My daily red comes from the Valtellina; my white is usually Orvieto or Vernaccia di San Gimignano. Pick your own. Most of the recipes in this book include suggestions for suitable wines to accompany them. As a rule, try to drink a wine native to the region where the dish originates. For example, a Roman eating Spaghetti alla Carbonara would drink his local Frascati or Marino white rather than a Piedmontese Gavi, a Tuscan Galestro, or a Sicilian Corvo. You should do the same. What follows is a regional listing of wines you might try. Most of them are available in better wine stores.

Region	Reds	Whites
VALLE D'AOSTA	Donnaz	
	Enfer d'Arvier	
PIEDMONT	Barbaresco	Asti Spumante**
	Barbera	Cortese dell'Alto
	Barolo	Monferrato
	Carema	Cortese di Gavi
	Dolcetto	Erbaluce di Caluso
	Freisa	
	Gattinara	
	Ghemme	
	Grignolino	
	Nebbiolo	
	Spanna	

LIGURIA	*Dolceacqua* *Dolcetto Ligure* *Rossese*	*Cinqueterre* *Vermentino*
LOMBARDY	*Buttafuoco* *Cellatica* *Chiaretto del Garda** *Franciacorta* *Frecciarossa* *Grumello* *Inferno* *Sassella* *Sfursat* *Valgella* *Valtellina Superiore*	*Bianco della* *Valtellina* *Franciacorta* *Frecciarossa* *Lugana* *Moscato*** *Riesling dell'Oltrepò*
TRENTINO-ALTO ADIGE	*Lagrein* *Pinot Noir* *Santa Maddalena* *Terlaner*	*Moscato Atesino*** *Muller-Thurgau* *Riesling* *Sylvaner* *Traminer*
FRIULI	*Cabernet* *Merlot* *Refosco*	*Pinot Bianco* *Pinot Grigio* *Tocai*
VENETO	*Amarone* *Bardolino* *Cabernet* *Clinton* *Merlot* *Recioto* *Rubino del Piave* *Valpolicella*	*Bianco di Custoza* *Chardonnay* *Colli Euganei* *Lugana* *Pinot Grigio* *Prosecco*** *Soave* *Tocai di Lison*
EMILIA-ROMAGNA	*Barbera* *Gutturnio* *Lambrusco di* *Sorbara**** *Sangiovese* *Vien Tosc Rosso*	*Albana* *Trebbiano*
MARCHES	*Rosso Conero* *Rosso Piceno*	*Verdicchio*

TUSCANY	*Brunello di*
	   Montalcino
	 Chianti (there are
	   many local
	   producers of this
		Bianco di Toscana
		 Galestro
		 Moscato di Elba
		 Vernaccia di San
		   Gimignano

Region	Reds	Whites
	wine. There is young Chianti as well as the fuller, more mature Chianti Classico) *Vino Nobile di Montepulciano*	
UMBRIA	*Torgiano*	*Orvieto Abboccato* *Orvieto Secco* *Torgiano*
LATIUM	*Castelli Romani* *Cesanese* *Cori* *Etruria*	*Castelli Romani* *Colli Albani* *Est! Est!! Est!!!* *Etruria* *Marino*
CAMPANIA	*Aglianico* *Lacryma Christi* *Taurasi*	*Capri* *Ischia* *Lacryma Christi*
ABRUZZI	*Montepulciano*	*Trebbiano*
APULIA	*Castel del Monte* *Salentino*	*Castel del Monte*
BASILICATA	*Aglianico del Vulture*	
CALABRIA	*Cafaro* *Cirò*	*Cirò*
SICILY	*Corvo* *Etna* *Segesta*	*Corvo* *Etna* *Segesta*
SARDINIA	*Alghero* *Barbera Sarda* *Cannonau* *Oliena*	*Torgiano* *Vermentino*

* *This is a rose wine.*

** *This is a sparkling wine.*

*** *If you cannot find this particular Lambrusco, do not bother drinking Lambrusco with meals.*

EQUIPMENT FOR MAKING, COOKING, AND EATING PASTA

A large ceramic BOWL for tossing and serving spaghetti, maccheroni, and other pastas.

A CHEESE GRATER *(la grattugia)* is necessary if you are spending good money to buy excellent parmigiano or pecorino. Freshly grated cheese has no rival among all commercially produced grated cheeses.

A COLANDER *(la scolapasta)* is essential for draining cooked pasta quickly. A large metal colander is preferable to one made of plastic.

 A DOUGH SCRAPER *(la spatola di metallo)* is useful for neatly moving excess flour to the side of the working surface while you are kneading the dough.

A FOOD MILL *(il tritatutto)* is very handy for pureeing tomatoes. A particular device used in Italy for this purpose is called *il passapomodoro*.

A good, sharp KNIFE *(il coltello)* is an essential kitchen tool.

A LADLE *(il mestolo)* is useful in cooking tomato sauces. A flatter, slotted ladle or skimmer is ideal for removing gnocchi from boiling water or for pushing *pasta ripiena* back into water.

A LASAGNE PAN: The traditional pans used in Bologna are made of aluminum or stainless steel. They are at least 2 to 3 inches high, and their corners are right-angled, not curved. This allows for even cooking and cutting.

LA MEZZALUNA: This half moon-shaped blade with 2 handles is most useful for chopping onions, peppers, and other ingredients for sauces.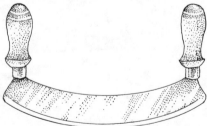

PASTA MACHINE, ELECTRIC *(la impastatrice elettrica)* is a convenient appliance for people in a hurry or for those who do not want to make pasta by hand. Read more about electric pasta machines on page 58.

PASTA MACHINE, MANUAL *(la macchinetta a manovella)* is a handy device for rolling and cutting pasta, though it is by no means essential. Read about manual pasta machines on page 57.

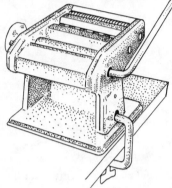

PASTA WHEELS *(rotelline tagliapasta):* There are 2 basic types—straight-edged and fluted. These are sometimes referred to as ravioli wheels. A good knife can usually take the place of a straight-edged wheel, though the latter is easier to use. A fluted wheel is necessary for obtaining the ruffled edge for pastas such as farfalle, pappardelle, and lasagne.

A simple, unglamorous PEPPER MILL *(il macinapepe)* will allow you to cook with freshly ground pepper, an indispensable ingredient in many pasta sauces.

The ideal POT *(la pentola)* for cooking pasta should be broad and deep enough to contain at least 4 quarts of water. I think it should be made of stainless steel, though some Italians use earthenware pots. You might choose to invest in a specially-designed PASTA POT, which features a colander that fits the rim of the pot and can be easily removed, instantly draining the pasta that has boiled in it.

RAVIOLI PRESSES are round or square, small or large, depending upon the size and shape of the agnolotti, ravioli, or anolini you plan to make. Use them according to the directions on page 64.

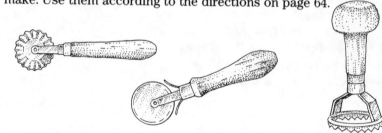

RAVIOLI TRAYS *(le raviolatrici)* are necessary only if you choose to make ravioli according to the instructions on page 68.

It is essential that you have the proper ROLLING PIN *(il matterello)*. Read more about them on page 55.

WORKING SURFACE *(la spianatoia):* Ideally, you should have a board of smooth wood at least 2 feet by 3 feet for kneading and rolling out dough to make fresh pasta. Failing this, formica and plastic are suitable substitutes. Some people use large slabs of marble, which are quite attractive and often very heavy. I like marble, but its coolness tends to chill dough more than necessary, making it more difficult to work with.

WOODEN SPOONS *(i cucchiai di legno)* are ideal for stirring ingredients and sauces.

Sources for Special Foods and Equipment

The following is a brief list of firms that supply foods such as imported pasta, truffles, cheeses, prosciutto, salami, anchovy paste, imported tomatoes and tomato paste, oils, and so forth, and equipment such as pasta machines, lasagne pans, good rolling pins, and so on.

Though most of these merchants are based in New York, many of them also conduct mail order businesses, so these supplies are available to you no matter where you are.

Balducci's
424 Sixth Avenue   Food
New York, NY 10009

Bloomingdale's
1000 Third Avenue   Food and Equipment
New York, NY 10022

Bridge Kitchenware
214 East 52nd Street   Equipment
New York, NY 10022

Dean & Deluca
121 Prince Street   Food and Equipment
New York, NY 10012

Macy's
Herald Square   Food and equipment
New York, NY 10001

Manganaro's
488 Ninth Avenue   Food and equipment
New York, NY 10018

D. G. Molinari and Sons 1401 Yosemite Avenue San Francisco, CA 94124	Salami
Pasta and Cheese 1375 Third Avenue New York, NY 10022 (and other New York locations)	Food
The Professional Kitchen 18 Cooper Square New York, NY 10003	Equipment
Todaro Brothers 555 Second Avenue New York, NY 10016	Food
John Volpi Co. 5256 Daggett Street St. Louis, MO 63110	Prosciutto
Williams-Sonoma Mail Order Dept. P.O. Box 3792 San Francisco, CA 94119	Food and equipment
Zabar's 2245 Broadway New York, NY 10024	Food and equipment

Index

About the Author

Fred Plotkin is the Performance Manager of the Metropolitan Opera. A New York City native, he studied in Italy on a Fulbright scholarship and worked as a tour guide, translator, teacher of English and theater, acting coach for opera singers, and, on occasion, as an actor, film extra, or spear-carrier. Mr. Plotkin learned to make pasta at the elbows of cooks in Bologna and in homes throughout Italy.